The Supabase Handbook

Scalable Backend Solutions for Developers

Robert Johnson

Published by HiTeX Press

For permissions and other inquiries, write to:
P.O. Box 3132, Framingham, MA 01701, USA

Contents

4

7

Introduction

In the rapidly evolving world of software development, building robust and scalable backend solutions has become an imperative for developers seeking to deliver reliable and feature-rich applications. Supabase, an open-source alternative to traditional backend services, offers a comprehensive suite of tools designed to simplify and accelerate the development process while ensuring high performance and security. This book, "The Supabase Handbook: Scalable Backend Solutions for Developers," seeks to provide a detailed exploration of Supabase and its capabilities, catering to developers looking to leverage this powerful platform for their projects.

Supabase has emerged as a prominent choice for developers due to its ability to combine the power of a relational database, real-time capabilities, authentication, and storage in a unified platform. The foundation of Supabase is built on PostgreSQL, a proven and robust relational database system, ensuring that developers can rely on a stable and well-supported backend solution. By combining this with a real-time subscription mechanism and seamless integration with popular frontend frameworks, Supabase effectively enables the creation of modern, interactive web and mobile applications.

The increasing demand for dynamic and data-intensive applications underscores the importance of having a backend system that not only meets performance requirements but also scales with the application's growth. Supabase addresses these needs by providing developers with extensive customization capabilities, real-time data updates, and a straightforward authentication system. This book aims to guide readers through the intricacies of Supabase, presenting structured insights into its setup, features, and application to real-world scenarios.

Throughout this book, readers will embark on a structured learning path, beginning with understanding the architectural fundamentals of Supabase. Following this, readers will gain insights into setting up projects, managing databases, implementing authentication and user management, and leveraging Supabase's real-time functionalities. The latter chapters focus on optimizing performance, integrating with frontend technologies, exploring storage solutions, and examining practical applications through detailed case studies.

In essence, "The Supabase Handbook" aims to equip developers with the knowledge and skills necessary to harness the full potential of Supabase for creating efficient, scalable, and secure applications. Whether readers are new to backend development or seasoned developers looking to explore alternative solutions, this book serves as a valuable resource, presenting clear instructions, practical examples, and best practices to enhance the development experience.

In summary, this introduction sets the stage for a comprehensive engagement with Supabase's powerful features. By diving into each element of Supabase with practical examples and case studies, this book empowers developers to efficiently build and scale their applications, fulfilling today's demands for dynamic and responsive software solutions.

Chapter 1

Introduction to Supabase and Its Core Features

Supabase offers an open-source platform that simplifies backend development by providing robust database management, real-time data capabilities, and flexible authentication. This chapter explores its architectural design, key features, and compares it with traditional backend solutions. Emphasizing its cloud-hosted and open-source nature, the chapter highlights how Supabase leverages community support and flexibility, making it a valuable choice for modern developers seeking scalable and efficient backend solutions.

1.1. Understanding Supabase: An Overview

Supabase is an open-source backend-as-a-service platform engineered to simplify the development of scalable backend solutions. Emerging from the evolving needs of modern web and mobile developers, Supabase was conceived as a streamlined alternative to the traditional complex backend architecture. Initially introduced in early 2020, its development closely followed the increased demand for real-time databases, instant authentication, and overall flexible backend management. Its inception was influenced by the success of services that streamlined frontend development but left developers grappling with setting up and maintaining backend infrastructure. Supabase positions itself to bridge this gap by delivering a robust, integrated platform that reduces development time while ensuring high performance and scalability.

Supabase builds on proven open-source technologies while introducing a modernized stack that emphasizes ease of use without compromising essential backend functionalities. At its core, the platform leverages PostgreSQL as the primary relational database engine, benefiting from its advanced features and stability. This reliance on PostgreSQL not only provides a reliable data storage mechanism but also allows developers to integrate custom SQL queries, stored procedures, and trigger-based workflows without having to learn a proprietary database language. The decision to use a well-regarded and established database system underlies Supabase's commitment to stability and performance.

The platform's architecture is designed with modularity in mind. Its components, including authentication, real-time capabilities, and storage, interact seamlessly to offer a comprehensive backend solution. Developers benefit from a tightly integrated system wherein modifications or extensions to one module minimally affect the behavior of others. By decoupling these concerns internally while presenting a unified interface externally, Supabase achieves a balance between flexibility and ease of maintenance. This integration is critical for projects that require rapid prototyping without sacrificing production-level reliability. As developers integrate Supabase into their projects, they can focus on the unique aspects of their applications rather than reinventing the wheel with redundant backend functionalities.

Supabase is more than just a database as a service. Its authentication module provides developers with built-in support for multiple identity providers. Whether the requirement is to implement OAuth, social logins, or even custom authentication strategies, Supabase offers a cohesive solution to securely manage user identities. This flexibility in managing authentication directly addresses one of the most challenging aspects of application development: securing user data in a scalable manner. Additionally, the platform's real-time data module leverages PostgreSQL's replication features to facilitate live updates to application data. This capability is essential for applications that depend on dynamic user interactions, such as collaborative software, live dashboards, or notification systems.

Given the increasing importance of data-driven applications, Supabase offers comprehensive API capabilities that simplify data retrieval and manipulation. The platform automatically generates RESTful APIs over the underlying PostgreSQL database, reducing the need for manual API coding. This feature not only minimizes development overhead but also enforces a consistent API structure that eases maintenance and debugging. Developers can therefore concentrate more on the application logic rather than managing intricate server configurations and custom endpoints. A typical example of initializing a connection to a Supabase backend in a frontend JavaScript application can be seen in the following code snippet:

```
import { createClient } from '@supabase/supabase-js';
```

13

```
const supabaseUrl = 'https://your-supabase-instance.supabase.co';
const supabaseKey = 'your-anon-key';
const supabase = createClient(supabaseUrl, supabaseKey);

/* Example of fetching data from a table named 'authors' */
async function fetchAuthors() {
    let { data, error } = await supabase
      .from('authors')
      .select('*');
    if (error) {
        ccnsole.error('Error fetching data:', error);
    } else {
        ccnsole.log('Authors data:', data);
    }
}

fetchAuthors();
```

The above snippet illustrates the simplicity of connecting to a Supabase instance and performing database operations. This ease of initial setup is one of the key factors making Supabase an essential tool for developers. It abstracts the complexity of direct database interactions while allowing experienced developers the freedom to execute fine-grained queries when needed.

The rise in popularity of Supabase can be attributed not only to its technical capabilities but also to its vibrant community and continuous open-source development. The platform benefits from a wide network of contributors who continuously improve its features and security protocols. This community-driven model enhances the reliability of the service and ensures that issues are quickly identified and resolved. Open-source contributions provide flexibility, enabling developers to fork the code or integrate customized modifications to better suit their project requirements. The collaborative nature of the platform fosters an environment of innovation and rapid iterations, which is a significant advantage over many traditional proprietary backend systems.

A distinctive aspect of Supabase is its alignment with cloud-native technologies. By hosting backend services in the cloud, Supabase reduces

14

the operational burden on developers. Cloud-hosted backends simplify deployment, scaling, and monitoring of applications, allowing developers to focus on delivering value rather than managing infrastructure. The platform abstracts the complexities of load balancing, redundancy, security patches, and performance tuning. This model is beneficial for startups and small to medium-sized enterprises where development resources are limited and agility is paramount.

Supabase also continuously integrates industry-standard security practices. For example, the use of row-level security policies in PostgreSQL enhances data protection by ensuring that only authorized users can access or modify specific pieces of data. Such security measures help mitigate common risks associated with multi-tenant architectures. The embedded security configurations align with modern compliance standards, making it easier for developers to build applications that are both secure and scalable without extensive security expertise.

Overall, Supabase has redefined the backend development landscape by streamlining core functionalities into a singular, cohesive package. Its history of rapid evolution combined with its robust technical capabilities has cemented its status as an essential tool for developers. The ability to quickly stand up a complete backend, including database management, real-time communication, and secure authentication, dramatically shortens development cycles and simplifies the maintenance of production systems. By integrating these services into a cloud-hosted environment and fostering a strong open-source community, Supabase provides a dependable foundation for both rapid prototyping and high-performance production environments.

A practical illustration of Supabase's integration in a development workflow highlights its versatility. Developers working on a data visualization dashboard, for instance, can rely on Supabase to provide instantaneous data updates using its real-time subscription feature. An example of subscribing to data changes in a table might appear as follows:

```
const subscription = supabase
  .from('metrics')
  .on('INSERT', payload => {
      console.log('New metric recorded:', payload.new);
  })
  .subscribe();
```

An output produced by this subscription in a testing environment could be observed in a terminal as:

```
New metric recorded: { id: 101, value: 342, timestamp: '2023-10-05T12:35:20Z'
}
```

The succinctness of these snippets underscores Supabase's ability to handle complex backend operations with minimal code. Such simplicity is critical for developers, particularly those transitioning from client-side or frontend-centric roles into full-stack development. It provides a low entry barrier without compromising on the sophistication required for modern application architectures.

The evolution of Supabase as a tool reflects broader trends in software development, particularly the shift toward integrating cloud services and open-source solutions within the core of application design. The platform's success underscores the importance of having accessible, modular, and scalable backend solutions that can adapt to rapidly changing technological landscapes. By embracing both the principles of modern cloud computing and the collaborative power of open-source development, Supabase ensures that developers can build secure, efficient, and maintainable applications.

1.2. Exploring Supabase Architecture

Supabase's architecture is designed to deliver a seamless, integrated backend solution by leveraging established open-source technologies

16

and modern cloud-native principles. The core design of Supabase is built around several key components that work in unison to offer comprehensive backend services. The primary components include a PostgreSQL database, authentication services, real-time data handling, storage, and a unified API interface. Each of these components plays a distinct role, yet they are closely integrated to ensure consistency, security, and ease of use.

At the center of the Supabase stack is PostgreSQL, a robust and feature-rich relational database management system. PostgreSQL is renowned for its reliability, extensibility, and support for advanced SQL querying. By using PostgreSQL, Supabase ensures that developers have access to a mature, high-performance database that can handle complex queries, transactional integrity, and sophisticated data management tasks. The choice to use PostgreSQL also means that developers can leverage a host of existing tools and extensions, such as PostGIS for geospatial queries or native JSON support for handling semi-structured data.

Surrounding the PostgreSQL core, Supabase provides an authentication service that is built to handle both traditional password-based logins and a variety of modern authentication methods, including OAuth and social logins. The authentication module is tightly integrated with the database, enabling developers to enforce row-level security (RLS) policies. RLS allows precise control over which users can access or modify data in specific tables, thereby adding an important security layer without requiring additional infrastructure. The integration of authentication with database-level security ensures that access control is inherently part of the data layer rather than an afterthought.

Real-time data processing is another fundamental component of Supabase's architecture. The platform leverages PostgreSQL's built-in replication mechanisms and event triggers to monitor data changes as they occur. Whenever an insert, update, or delete operation is performed, these events are captured and broadcast to connected clients

17

using a subscription-based system. This is particularly valuable for applications that require live updating features, such as interactive dashboards or collaborative editing tools. The real-time engine abstracts the underlying complexity, allowing developers to subscribe to changes in the data with minimal configuration.

The storage component of Supabase further extends its backend capabilities by providing a scalable solution for managing files and media. This module is designed to work hand in hand with the PostgreSQL database and authentication system, ensuring that file access is properly secured and managed. Developers can store, retrieve, and manage files using a standard interface, applying the same security protocols as with other backend data. This unified approach minimizes the need for additional third-party services and simplifies the overall handling of both structured and unstructured data.

Central to Supabase's architecture is the unified API that serves as the gateway for interaction with the various backend components. Upon setting up a Supabase project, developers automatically receive a RESTful API generated from the underlying PostgreSQL schema. This API is capable of handling standard CRUD operations and adheres to a strict, consistent structure that follows modern best practices. The auto-generated API reduces the need for developers to write custom endpoints, simplifying the process of building and maintaining applications that require backend integration.

A practical example demonstrates the ease with which a developer can interact with these architectural elements. Consider a scenario where an application needs to both retrieve data from a database table and listen for real-time updates. The following JavaScript code snippet illustrates how to initialize the Supabase client, fetch initial records from a table called orders, and subscribe to any changes on that table:

```
import { createClient } from '@supabase/supabase-js';

const supabaseUrl = 'https://your-project.supabase.co';
```

```
const supabaseKey = 'your-anon-key';
const supabase = createClient(supabaseUrl, supabaseKey);

// Function to fetch current orders from the database
async function fetchOrders() {
    let { data, error } = await supabase
      .from('orders')
      .select('*');
    if (error) {
        console.error('Error retrieving orders:', error);
    } else {
        console.log('Current orders:', data);
    }
}

// Subscribe to changes in the orders table
const orderSubscription = supabase
  .from('orders')
  .on('INSERT', payload => {
      console.log('New order received:', payload.new);
  })
  .on('UPDATE', payload => {
      console.log('Order updated:', payload.new);
  })
  .subscribe();

fetchOrders();
```

The snippet above exemplifies how Supabase abstracts the complexities of both data retrieval and real-time event handling. The unified interface negates the need for separate implementations for REST and WebSocket communications, streamlining development and reducing boilerplate code.

Another critical aspect of Supabase's architecture is the emphasis on modularity. Each component—whether it is the database, authentication, or storage—operates as an independent module that communicates through well-defined interfaces. This modular design allows for easier updates and maintenance. As each module evolves, changes in one do not necessarily propagate errors into others, thereby ensuring overall system stability. The ability to update components individually without affecting the entire system is a significant advantage for projects that require high uptime and minimal disruptions.

Supabase's reliance on open-source technologies means that the platform is continuously improved by a global community of developers. Contributions from the community play a pivotal role in enhancing features, optimizing performance, and securing the overall system. This collaborative approach not only accelerates the development cycle but also ensures that the platform remains at the forefront of technological advancements. The open-source model also means that developers can inspect the source code, identify potential vulnerabilities, or modify components to better suit their specific needs. This transparency is a distinct advantage over proprietary backend solutions.

The interplay between Supabase's components is further reinforced by the use of modern deployment practices. Supabase is predominantly deployed in cloud-hosted environments where scalability is a primary concern. Cloud deployment allows the platform to automatically manage resource allocation, load balancing, and redundancy. These capabilities are particularly important for handling varying workloads and ensuring that the backend remains responsive under high demand. The cloud-native design complements the modular architecture, making it straightforward to scale individual components—such as the database or authentication service—without affecting the overall performance of the system.

Security is an inherent part of the architectural design. Supabase implements security measures at multiple layers, starting with data encryption at the database level, moving through secure API endpoints, and extending to authentication and access control measures. For example, the use of row-level security (RLS) policies within PostgreSQL significantly limits data exposure by ensuring that users can only interact with data they are permitted to access. This fine-grained security control is directly integrated into the API layer and enforced across all interactions. Additionally, communications between the client and server are encrypted using industry-standard protocols, thereby safe-guarding data in transit.

A further illustration of the architectural interplay between components can be observed in scenarios involving stored procedures and triggers within the PostgreSQL database. These database-level constructs can encapsulate business logic and data transformation operations, which are triggered automatically upon data modification. As a result, application logic can be embedded directly in the database, which in turn simplifies the client-side code. For example, the following SQL snippet creates a trigger that automatically logs any insertions into the transactions table:

```
CREATE OR REPLACE FUNCTION log_transaction()
RETURNS TRIGGER AS $$
BEGIN
    INSERT INTO transactions_log(transaction_id, logged_at)
    VALUES (NEW.id, NOW());
    RETURN NEW;
END;
$$ LANGUAGE plpgsql;

CREATE TRIGGER trigger_log_transaction
AFTER INSERT ON transactions
FOR EACH ROW EXECUTE FUNCTION log_transaction();
```

This example demonstrates how Supabase leverages PostgreSQL features to simplify backend operations, ensuring that processes such as auditing and logging occur consistently without additional code in the application layer.

Supabase also supports additional integrations aimed at extending and personalizing the backend environment. Developers can incorporate custom functions, webhooks, or even integrate third-party services to extend the native capabilities offered. This flexibility allows for highly customizable setups that maintain the standard benefits of Supabase's core architecture while addressing specific business requirements. The planned evolution of Supabase includes deeper integration with edge computing services to further decrease latency and distribute workload closer to the end user, paving the way for highly responsive applications.

The architectural design of Supabase, with its focus on modularity, scalability, and integration of multiple open-source tools, provides developers with a robust framework for rapid application development. It addresses common backend challenges by abstracting difficult-to-manage components behind a cohesive and unified platform, reducing the overall burden on developers. By consolidating essential backend services into a single, managed ecosystem, Supabase maximizes efficiency and streamlines the development process for both small-scale projects and enterprise-level applications.

The architecture of Supabase exemplifies how modern backend solutions can be both powerful and accessible. Its integrated components—database, authentication, real-time processing, storage, and API services—work together to offer a comprehensive solution that addresses data management, security, and scalability. As projects grow in complexity, the clear separation of concerns combined with tight integration ensures that Supabase remains a viable option for developers seeking a balance between rapid development and long-term maintainability.

1.3. Core Features and Capabilities

Supabase consolidates several essential backend features into one integrated platform, delivering a powerful suite of tools that are critical for modern application development. At its core, Supabase offers robust database services, a flexible authentication system, real-time data processing, and automatic API generation. Each element is engineered to work cohesively within the ecosystem, reducing development overhead while ensuring that applications remain scalable, secure, and responsive.

The foundation of Supabase is its PostgreSQL-based database service. PostgreSQL is a proven relational database system known for its reliability and advanced SQL capabilities. Supabase leverages PostgreSQL to provide a fully managed data layer where developers can perform complex queries, enforce schema constraints, and utilize extensions that enhance functionality. With native support for stored procedures, triggers, and advanced indexing techniques, the database service facilitates efficient data operations. Developers are encouraged to take advantage of PostgreSQL's full feature set, including support for JSON data types that permit the manipulation of semi-structured data within a structured schema. For example, a basic insert operation into a table named users can be executed as follows:

```
INSERT INTO users (username, email, created_at)
VALUES ('jdoe', 'jdoe@example.com', NOW());
```

The availability of advanced database features translates directly into improved application performance and smoother handling of data-intensive tasks.

Complementing the database functionality, Supabase provides a versatile authentication mechanism that caters to various modern security requirements. The authentication system supports traditional email and password sign-ups, social logins through third-party OAuth providers, and even multi-factor authentication when necessary. This diverse approach to identity management ensures that applications built on Supabase are not only accessible but also secure by design. Integrated into the core platform, authentication also works seamlessly with PostgreSQL's row-level security (RLS) policies. RLS empowers developers to enforce granular access control dynamically, ensuring that each authenticated user only accesses data for which they have appropriate permissions. A practical example of creating a new user and assigning an authenticated session might be managed through Supabase's JavaScript client as shown below:

```javascript
import { createClient } from '@supabase/supabase-js';

const supabaseUrl = 'https://your-project.supabase.co';
const supabaseKey = 'your-anon-key';
const supabase = createClient(supabaseUrl, supabaseKey);

async function signUpUser(email, password) {
  const { user, session, error } = await supabase.auth.signUp({
    email: email,
    password: password
  });

  if (error) {
    console.error('Error during sign-up:', error);
  } else {
    console.log('User signed up successfully:', user);
  }
}

signUpUser('newuser@example.com', 'strong_password');
```

This code snippet illustrates the simplicity of integrating user registration and authentication into an application, eliminating the need for building and securing a custom authentication system from scratch.

Real-time data capabilities form another critical pillar of Supabase's feature set. Modern applications increasingly rely on real-time feedback, pushing the boundaries of user engagement and responsiveness. Supabase capitalizes on PostgreSQL's logical replication and event triggers to capture changes to data as they occur. These changes are then propagated to subscribed clients using WebSocket connections. The setup for real-time subscriptions is straightforward. Developers can subscribe to insert, update, and delete events on a specified table, enabling functionality such as live dashboards, instant notifications, and real-time collaboration. The following JavaScript example demonstrates how to subscribe to real-time updates for a table called messages:

```javascript
const subscription = supabase
  .from('messages')
```

```
.on('INSERT', payload => {
  console.log('New message received:', payload.new);
})
.on('UPDATE', payload => {
  console.log('Message updated:', payload.new);
})
.subscribe();
```

Real-time subscriptions remove the burden of implementing custom push notification systems, ensuring that applications remain dynamic and highly interactive with minimal additional coding.

Another significant capability offered by Supabase is the automatic generation of APIs directly from the database schema. When a Supabase project is initialized, RESTful endpoints are generated without manual intervention, providing an immediate bridge between the frontend and backend. This feature empowers developers with a reliable interface to perform CRUD operations while maintaining consistency with the underlying data structure. Auto-generated APIs adhere to REST standards, thus simplifying integration with various clients and ensuring that database changes are seamlessly reflected in the API layer. Developers can extend or customize these endpoints using serverless functions or custom logic if their application requires additional processing. This flexibility is particularly useful in scenarios where rapid iterations and prototype deployments are necessary.

In addition to RESTful APIs, the platform supports GraphQL integration, offering further flexibility in how clients query and manipulate data. The support for GraphQL allows front-end developers to request precisely the data they need, reducing over-fetching and improving efficiency in data transfers. While REST provides a straightforward and standardized interface, GraphQL's dynamic querying capabilities make it an attractive option for applications with complex data requirements. By providing both options, Supabase caters to a broad range of development preferences and project specifications.

Storage services in Supabase extend the functionality beyond structured data management. Developers can utilize the storage module to handle media assets, documents, and other file types in a secure manner. The storage system integrates seamlessly with the authentication and database services, ensuring that file access is controlled by the same robust security policies applied to other parts of the system. Files are stored in scalable cloud storage, and links to these assets can be managed alongside database records. The inherent integration simplifies the development of content-heavy applications where both a file system and a relational database are required to function in tandem.

A key aspect of Supabase's core capabilities is the integration of these features into a coherent, unified platform. The decoupled yet interdependent nature of these components enables developers to use only what is necessary, without enforcing a monolithic backend solution. This modularity allows for efficient maintenance and scale as individual components can be updated or replaced with minimal impact on the overall system. For instance, while the auto-generated API interface ensures immediate accessibility to data, developers can later integrate custom business logic by modifying the underlying PostgreSQL functions. Such flexibility enables continuous refinement of application behavior without drastic changes in the architecture.

Security remains a common thread that connects all core features. Supabase integrates best security practices at every layer—from data encryption at rest in PostgreSQL to secure WebSocket connections for real-time data and authentication tokens for API access. Row-level security (RLS) exemplifies the atomic application of security measures directly at the data layer, ensuring that even if the frontend or API logic is compromised, data exposure remains controlled. For authentication-related functionalities, additional measures such as email verifications, password recovery endpoints, and multi-factor authentication ensure that end-user accounts remain secure. The comprehensive approach to security significantly reduces the potential vulnerabilities that are typically encountered in custom-built backends.

The platform's commitment to open-source principles further enhances its core capabilities. Being open-source allows developers full visibility into the infrastructure, enabling independent security audits, custom code extensions, and community-driven enhancements. This transparency not only fosters trust but also encourages collaboration within the developer community. Developers can contribute to bug fixes, new feature development, and performance improvements, ensuring that the platform continually evolves to meet emerging technology demands.

Operational simplicity is another decisive advantage of Supabase's core features. The platform manager provides developers with tooling to monitor performance metrics, manage API usage, and configure settings directly from a unified dashboard. This centralized management eliminates the need for disparate administrative tools, thus reducing operational complexity. Cloud hosting means that scaling resources, managing backups, and handling failovers are automated processes, which enable developers to focus on business logic instead of infrastructure concerns.

Practical considerations in application development demand that these backend tools integrate well with modern development frameworks. Supabase's client libraries and SDKs for various programming languages ensure seamless integration with popular frameworks such as React, Vue, Angular, and even mobile development environments. An example demonstrating the integration in a React application might involve fetching data from a Supabase-backed table and handling real-time updates with React's state management. Such integrations simplify the development workflow and enable rapid prototyping with proven, scalable technologies.

The documentation and community resources provided by Supabase further solidify its position as a tool with extensive core capabilities. Detailed guides, code examples, and community forums allow developers to quickly overcome implementation challenges and explore best practices. The level of community support ensures that even complex integrations or customizations have readily available solutions, which directly translates to reduced development times and improved productivity. The combination of comprehensive documentation with a robust support network provides an environment where both novice and experienced developers can maximize the benefits of the platform.

Supabase is engineered to address both the immediate and long-term needs of application development. Its core features not only provide a quick-start solution for rapid development but also lay a scalable foundation for enterprise-level applications. The inherent flexibility, modularity, and integration capabilities unify what would otherwise be disparate systems. Through features such as managed PostgreSQL services, diverse authentication strategies, real-time data propagation, and auto-generated APIs, Supabase transforms the backend into a configurable, secure, and efficient component of modern web development.

1.4. Supabase vs Traditional Backends

Supabase embodies a modern, integrated backend solution that contrasts sharply with traditional backend architectures typically built from scratch or using monolithic frameworks. Traditional backends often require meticulous configuration and extensive coding to manage components such as database connectivity, authentication, API creation, and real-time data handling. In contrast, Supabase offers these features as a unified, pre-integrated platform, streamlining the development process while reducing the need for separate tools and special-

28

ized expertise.

Traditional backend solutions generally involve setting up and maintaining independent layers to manage different functions. For instance, developers might use a relational database management system, write custom RESTful endpoints using frameworks like Express or Django, implement authentication libraries separately, and integrate WebSocket servers for real-time communication. This dispersed architecture introduces complexity and demands continuous management to ensure that each part operates correctly within the system. Supabase, on the other hand, abstracts these complexities into cohesive modules. Its PostgreSQL-based database service, integrated authentication system, real-time data engine, and auto-generated APIs work in tandem without requiring the developer to manually configure each connection or interaction.

A central distinction lies in the approach to database management. In traditional setups, a developer must establish a database instance, design schemas, configure user access, and build connections between the application and the database using middleware or custom drivers. This process may involve manual tuning, optimization, and writing extensive SQL queries, which can be time-consuming and error-prone. Supabase leverages PostgreSQL's inherent robustness, ensuring that sophisticated querying, indexing, and transactional operations are available from the outset. This means that developers can immediately harness advanced database features, such as JSON support and stored procedures, without additional boilerplate code. The result is a cleaner, more maintainable codebase that focuses on application logic rather than database plumbing.

Authentication services further illustrate the contrast between traditional backends and Supabase. In conventional architectures, incorporating user management typically involves selecting a dedicated authentication library, setting up password management, and integrating third-party OAuth services, each requiring its own configuration. Such implementations can introduce potential security lapses if not managed carefully. Supabase consolidates these functionalities into a single, secure module. Its authentication system supports email and password logins, social OAuth integrations, and even multi-factor authentication out of the box. Coupled with PostgreSQL's row-level security (RLS), the system enforces granular access control automatically. This integration simplifies the process of securing user data as the configuration exists in a unified environment with consistent security policies applied across all data interactions.

Real-time data handling presents another area where Supabase diverges significantly from traditional backends. Custom implementations of real-time features in a conventional stack typically entail setting up additional servers or using third-party services to monitor database changes, translating these changes into event streams, and then integrating these streams into the client-side of the application. In such setups, developers must ensure the consistency, reliability, and scalability of each additional component, which can lead to increased complexity and potential maintenance challenges. Supabase natively accommodates real-time capabilities by leveraging PostgreSQL's replication and trigger functionalities. Changes in the database are automatically detected and communicated to subscribed clients via a WebSocket-based mechanism. This transparent integration reduces development overhead and allows developers to focus on deriving insights from real-time data rather than configuring complex pipelines.

API generation represents a transformational feature that sets Supabase apart. Many traditional backends rely on custom-coding API endpoints to expose data and business logic to frontend and mobile applications. This approach requires explicit definition and thorough testing of each endpoint, maintenance of version control, and rigorous security validations to prevent unauthorized access or data leaks.

30

Supabase automatically generates RESTful APIs directly from the underlying database schema at project initialization. This feature streamlines the development process by eliminating the need for manual endpoint creation, enabling developers to interact with data using standard HTTP methods in a consistent manner. The generated APIs adhere to modern standards and can be extended or customized if necessary, offering both simplicity and extensibility.

A tangible example of a traditional backend implementation using Node.js and Express can further highlight these differences. Consider the following code snippet, which shows how a developer might construct a RESTful API endpoint manually:

```
const express = require('express');
const { Pool } = require('pg');
const app = express();
app.use(express.json());

const pool = new Pool({
  user: 'postgres',
  host: 'localhost',
  database: 'your_database',
  password: 'your_password',
  port: 5432,
});

app.get('/api/items', async (req, res) => {
  try {
    const result = await pool.query('SELECT * FROM items');
    res.json(result.rows);
  } catch (error) {
    console.error('Error executing query', error);
    res.status(500).send('Internal Server Error');
  }
});

app.listen(3000, () => {
  console.log('Server listening on port 3000');
});
```

This example illustrates several challenges inherent in traditional approaches. Developers must explicitly manage database connections, configure error handling, and write queries for each resource. In contrast, Supabase provides an environment where these tasks are handled internally, allowing developers to emphasize application-specific logic rather than infrastructure management.

Beyond the technical implementation, the maintenance and operational aspects of traditional backends can introduce further complications. Systems built using disparate services require constant monitoring for performance, security vulnerabilities, and compatibility issues among various components. Each update to a dependency or library might necessitate corresponding changes across the system. Supabase's integrated architecture reduces these friction points by providing a uniform update and deployment process. The platform is managed in the cloud, ensuring that issues such as load balancing, failover, and security patching are addressed at the service level, thereby reducing the administrative burden on developers.

The economic and time-to-market advantages of using Supabase are considerable. Traditional backend development often involves significant upfront investment in both time and resources. Establishing sound architectural patterns, configuring multiple independent systems, and ensuring security compliance can substantially delay the launch of an application. Supabase lowers these barriers by offering a complete backend infrastructure that is ready to deploy. This rapid setup is particularly beneficial for startups and small teams that need to iterate quickly on their ideas without dedicating excessive resources to backend development.

Despite these advantages, there are situations where traditional backends might offer certain benefits over Supabase. Highly specialized applications requiring extensive customization beyond the standard features may find traditional solutions more adaptable to their specific needs. In scenarios where developers need complete control over every aspect of the backend, reliance on a managed service could potentially introduce limitations in customization and fine-tuning. Additionally, while Supabase emphasizes ease of use and rapid deployment, enterprises with existing legacy systems or unique compliance requirements might opt for a more conventional stack that allows for granular control over security protocols and performance optimization.

Scalability represents another area for careful consideration. Supabase, deployed in a cloud-hosted environment, offers automated scaling and redundancy, which alleviates the immediate need to manage infrastructure during periods of growth. However, while built-in scalability features address many common load concerns, traditional backends can be optimized and customized at a granular level to meet extreme performance requirements. Organizations with vast resources and highly specialized needs may prefer to design and operate their own infrastructure to fine-tune every aspect of performance, while Supabase strives to provide a balanced solution for a "majority use-case" scenario.

Another important consideration is vendor lock-in. Traditional backends developed in-house provide complete control over the technology stack, minimizing dependency on third-party platforms and thereby reducing risks associated with service discontinuation or strategic changes by the provider. Supabase is open source, which mitigates some of these concerns by allowing developers to inspect, modify, and self-host the platform if necessary. However, when opting to use the hosted version, organizations must weigh the benefits of rapid deployment and maintenance convenience against the potential risk of reliance on an external service provider.

The decision between Supabase and traditional backends ultimately depends on the specific project requirements, team expertise, and long-term product goals. For many applications, Supabase provides an elegant balance of simplicity, integrated features, and real-time capabilities, offering a robust backend solution that can quickly adapt to evolving market needs. For others that require highly specialized performance enhancements or granular operational control, a traditional approach might be more appealing despite the higher complexity and longer development time.

By integrating critical backend services into a cohesive platform, Supabase redefines how developers approach backend architecture. Its auto-generated APIs, robust database services, integrated authentication, and real-time data engine reduce redundancy, accelerate development, and lower maintenance costs. Moreover, the system promotes best practices in security and scalability through built-in features like row-level security and cloud-managed environments.

The comparative analysis delineates a clear advantage for developers seeking rapid iteration and integrated service management, where the trade-offs in customization are often outweighed by the benefits of reduced development time and consistent, reliable performance. Traditional backends continue to have value in scenarios requiring fine-grained customization and legacy integration, yet the modern demands of agile development increasingly favor solutions like Supabase that offer turnkey, cloud-native backend infrastructures.

1.5. Cloud-Hosted Backend: Benefits and Challenges

Cloud-hosted backends have transformed the way developers design, deploy, and manage application infrastructures. Supabase exemplifies this paradigm by offering a cloud-native solution that abstracts complex server management tasks. Its cloud-hosted approach integrates database services, authentication, real-time data streaming, and storage into a single platform managed in the cloud. This integration affords developers rapid deployment capabilities, scalability, and operational simplicity. Nevertheless, this model also comes with challenges that require careful evaluation in the context of application requirements and long-term operational strategies.

Cloud-hosted backends eliminate the need for manual server provisioning and maintenance. By managing infrastructure components through a centralized service, Supabase reduces the overhead associated with hardware management, security patching, and software updates. Developers gain immediate access to pre-configured components, such as a PostgreSQL database embedded with advanced features and integrated authentication modules that support various sign-on methods. Cloud hosting further simplifies scalability. As application demands increase, the platform can dynamically allocate resources to maintain performance consistency without manual interventions. This automatic scaling is critical for applications experiencing unpredictable traffic spikes or rapid growth in the user base.

A significant benefit of cloud-hosted backends is the reduction of operational complexity. Traditional setups might require setting up load balancers, configuring firewalls, and implementing monitoring solutions across disparate systems. Supabase's cloud architecture handles these aspects internally while presenting a unified dashboard where developers can monitor system health, performance metrics, and API usage in real time. The cloud environment also assures high availability through redundant systems, ensuring business continuity even in cases of individual component failures. For example, the real-time engine in Supabase uses logical replication from PostgreSQL to deliver a resilient subscription mechanism, where data changes propagate to clients with minimal latency.

The integration of cloud-hosted services into Supabase extends further into security practices. The platform leverages cloud infrastructure to implement robust security measures like data encryption at rest and in transit. Additionally, features such as PostgreSQL row-level security

35

(RLS) are employed to enforce granular access control policies across the cloud-hosted database. This integration is seamless; developers define RLS policies at the database level, and these policies are uniformly applied across all interactions via the auto-generated APIs. This consistent application of security across a distributed system reduces the risk of misconfigurations that often plague self-managed setups.

A practical illustration of accessing a cloud-hosted service with Supabase can be represented by the following code, which demonstrates data retrieval from the cloud-hosted PostgreSQL instance:

```
import { createClient } from '@supabase/supabase-js';

const supabaseUrl = 'https://your-project.supabase.co';
const supabaseKey = 'your-anon-key';
const supabase = createClient(supabaseUrl, supabaseKey);

async function getData() {
    const { data, error } = await supabase
      .from('projects')
      .select('*');
    if (error) {
      console.error('Error fetching data:', error);
    } else {
      console.log('Fetched data:', data);
    }
}

getData();
```

The above snippet underscores the simplicity with which developers can interact with cloud-hosted resources. The abstraction provided by Supabase allows for rapid prototyping and immediate integration without the need to manage low-level networking configurations.

Despite its benefits, the cloud-hosted model brings certain challenges that must be addressed. One primary concern is performance variability. While cloud providers offer dynamic scaling, there exists a trade-off between the abstraction of hardware and fine-tuned control over performance. Developers transitioning from a self-hosted en-

36

vironment might find it challenging to diagnose and resolve performance bottlenecks when they manifest in a shared multi-tenant environment. Although Supabase monitors and optimizes resource allocation, edge cases involving unusually high loads or specific workload patterns might require targeted interventions, sometimes necessitating custom solutions or vendor support.

Another challenge inherent in cloud-hosted solutions is ensuring data security and compliance with jurisdiction-specific regulations. While Supabase implements robust security features, sensitive applications dealing with highly regulated data must carefully consider data residency and compliance factors. Developers may need to ensure that data stored in the cloud adheres to policies such as GDPR, HIPAA, or other regulatory frameworks. This can complicate deployment strategies, as it may require negotiating specific cloud configuration settings or even considering a self-hosted variant of the service if extreme control over data location is required.

Vendor lock-in is an additional risk associated with cloud-hosted backends. When using a managed service like Supabase, developers become reliant on the service provider's infrastructure, support policies, and update cycles. Although Supabase is open source, the hosted version may incorporate proprietary enhancements or integrations that can complicate a switch to a different provider or self-hosted alternatives. This reliance may limit flexibility over time, especially for organizations with long-term, high-scale projects where custom infrastructural modifications become necessary.

Cost management also constitutes a significant challenge in the cloud-hosted model. Although cloud services are known for their scalability and pay-as-you-go models, unexpected costs can accumulate if resource utilization increases unpredictably. Developers must be vigilant about monitoring usage metrics, such as API call frequency, data storage consumption, and the number of active real-time subscriptions. Budget overruns might occur if the application experiences rapid growth or if inefficient code leads to redundant operations. Tools provided by Supabase to monitor resource usage are helpful, but integrating proper cost-optimization practices remains essential for sustainable growth.

Interoperability with existing systems poses an additional challenge. In many development scenarios, legacy systems or complex multi-cloud environments demand integration with various platforms. While Supabase simplifies many backend operations, integrating it with pre-existing systems may require additional middleware or custom connectors. This can complicate infrastructure planning, especially when specific functionalities supported by traditional backends are absent in the cloud-hosted model of Supabase.

Developers must also consider the evolving nature of cloud infrastructure. Cloud platforms continuously update their services, and while these updates typically provide improved security and performance, they may also introduce breaking changes. Keeping up with these changes requires continuous monitoring of release notes, migration guides, and community discussions. In contrast, in-house managed systems, although more resource-intensive, often provide more predictable environments with long-term stability guarantees.

A balanced analysis of these advantages and challenges is necessary to make informed decisions on adopting cloud-hosted backends. The benefits provided by the cloud—ranging from robust scalability and simplified management to integrated security and automatic API generation—often outweigh the challenges for a large proportion of modern web applications. For instance, rapid application development and deployment become significant competitive advantages when entering markets that demand short product cycles and high adaptability.

From an operational perspective, employing a cloud-hosted backend with Supabase allows development teams to focus on application-level functionalities rather than spending substantial time on server administration and infrastructure debugging. The technical abstraction provided by Supabase also fosters a more efficient development environment where engineers can concentrate on business logic and innovation. For educational and prototyping purposes, the quick setup and immediate feedback loops offered by cloud-hosted solutions dramatically reduce the learning curve for new developers transitioning from local to cloud-based development paradigms.

However, projects with unique performance requirements, extensive legacy integrations, or specialized regulatory needs must conduct thorough due diligence when adopting cloud-hosted backends. In some cases, a hybrid model might provide the best of both worlds— leveraging cloud-hosted services for standard operations while maintaining critical components on-premise or within a dedicated managed service. This hybrid approach mitigates some risks while still enjoying the agility and scalability of cloud environments.

In summary, Supabase's cloud-hosted backend model embodies both the forward-thinking advantages and the inherent challenges of modern cloud infrastructure. Its approach offers an integrated, scalable, and secure backend solution that empowers developers to rapidly build and deploy applications. However, as with all cloud services, careful consideration is required to address potential performance, security, compliance, and cost management issues. Through a nuanced understanding of these factors, developers can effectively leverage cloud-hosted backends like Supabase to achieve a balance between operational efficiency and technical control.

1.6. Open Source: Leveraging Community and Flexibility

Supabase's commitment to open-source principles forms a cornerstone of its development philosophy, enabling an environment where transparency, adaptability, and community collaboration drive innovation. By releasing its codebase under open-source licenses, Supabase invites developers to inspect, modify, and contribute to its growing ecosystem. This approach contrasts with proprietary backend solutions by handing control directly to developers, allowing them to extend functionalities beyond the predefined feature set.

Open-source development fosters trust among users, as the transparent codebase enables independent audits and vulnerability assessments. Developers can examine the integration of critical security features, such as PostgreSQL's row-level security (RLS) implementation and authentication mechanisms. This increased visibility not only builds confidence but also allows community members to suggest improvements or identify potential weaknesses. The opportunity for collaborative scrutiny has resulted in rapid iterations, with frequent patches and performance enhancements contributed by a diverse global community.

Flexibility is another intrinsic benefit of the open-source model adopted by Supabase. Unlike closed systems that impose rigid constraints on customization, Supabase's open-source nature allows developers to tailor the platform to suit unique project requirements. Users can fork the repository, implement custom features, or optimize performance in ways that align with their specific use cases. This adaptability is particularly valuable for organizations with specialized needs, as they can integrate proprietary business logic, establish custom workflows, or create extended modules that work seamlessly with the core platform.

Community contributions extend beyond the modification of core code. Developers actively share plugins, tools, and integrations that extend the functionality of Supabase into new realms. For instance, community-developed connectors for various programming languages and frameworks enhance the platform's reach into ecosystems such as Python, Ruby, and even niche mobile development environments. Such contributions provide practical examples that serve as learning resources for newcomers, enriching the overall developer experience and reducing the onboarding time for new projects.

A practical illustration of community contributions can be seen in how developers integrate Supabase client libraries with popular web frameworks. An example demonstrates the extension of the core Supabase functionality within a Vue.js application. The code snippet below shows how a developer might customize a client component to handle specific authentication flows and real-time updates:

```
<template>
  <div>
    <h2>User Dashboard</h2>
    <div v-if="user">
      <p>Welcome, {{ user.email }}</p>
      <ul>
        <li v-for="msg in messages" :key="msg.id">{{ msg.content }}</
    li>
      </ul>
    </div>
    <div v-else>
      <p>Please sign in.</p>
    </div>
  </div>
</template>

<script>
import { createClient } from '@supabase/supabase-js';
export default {
  data() {
    return {
      supabase: null,
      user: null,
      messages: []
    };
```

```
    },
    async created() {
      const supabaseUrl = 'https://your-project.supabase.co';
      const supabaseKey = 'your-anon-key';
      this.supabase = createClient(supabaseUrl, supabaseKey);
      const { data: user } = await this.supabase.auth.getUser();
      this.user = user;
      this.fetchMessages();
      this.setupRealtimeSubscriptions();
    },
    methods: {
      async fetchMessages() {
        const { data, error } = await this.supabase
          .from('messages')
          .select('*');
        if (!error) {
          this.messages = data;
        }
      },
      setupRealtimeSubscriptions() {
        this.supabase
          .from('messages')
          .on('INSERT', payload => {
            this.messages.push(payload.new);
          })
          .subscribe();
      }
    }
};
</script>
```

The code example above not only highlights the ease with which Su-pabase integrates into modern web frameworks, but it also demon-strates how developers can customize data fetching and real-time up-dates to suit their application logic. Community examples and en-hancements like these are widely shared on platforms such as GitHub, Stack Overflow, and dedicated Supabase forums, forming a knowledge base that accelerates learning and problem resolution.

Another layer where open-source offers significant benefits is in fos-tering innovation. Developers are not bound by limited feature sets dictated by vendors. Instead, open initiatives promote experimenta-tion, with contributions that push the boundaries of what the backend platform can achieve. For example, various community projects have extended Supabase with custom analytics modules, advanced monitoring tools, and alternative storage solutions. This collaborative innovation often leads to the development of plugins that can be seamlessly integrated into existing projects, thereby expanding the functionality while keeping the core platform lean and focused.

The integration of automated testing and continuous integration (CI) in open-source projects like Supabase also embodies community-driven quality assurance. Contributions are subjected to rigorous testing protocols before being merged into the main branch, ensuring that new features and enhancements adhere to high standards of reliability and security. This process is facilitated by numerous open-source tools and platforms that provide automated feedback, thereby reducing the risk of regressions and ensuring that enhancements are robust. The transparent nature of these processes also allows developers to understand the rationale behind design decisions, promoting a culture of shared ownership and continual improvement.

While the benefits of a robust community and open-source flexibility are compelling, there are also challenges inherent in this model. One potential issue is the risk of fragmentation. As developers fork the codebase to create custom versions, maintaining compatibility with the main branch can become challenging. It requires disciplined version control practices and clear communication channels within the community to manage divergent development paths. Supabase mitigates this risk by maintaining a well-documented contribution guideline and a clear roadmap that prioritizes compatibility and gradual integration of community contributions.

Moreover, the open-source model demands active participation from both core maintainers and the broader community. Sustaining momentum in community-driven projects necessitates continuous engagement, mentoring, and a dedicated effort to onboard new contributors. In the case of Supabase, the presence of an enthusiastic and growing developer community has been instrumental in not only expanding the platform's capabilities but also in providing support for newcomers through tutorials, public forums, and live coding sessions. This community support network often mitigates challenges by offering first-hand advice, troubleshooting assistance, and peer reviews of custom enhancements.

A clear advantage of leveraging the open-source model is the ability to integrate Supabase into diverse deployment environments. Organizations concerned with vendor lock-in can choose to self-host the platform, allowing them to maintain complete control over their infrastructure. This option provides flexibility in terms of data residency, compliance with local regulations, and integration with existing enterprise systems. By offering a self-hosted solution without compromising on the benefits of the core features, Supabase caters to a wide range of deployment scenarios—from small-scale projects to large-scale enterprise applications requiring stringent customization and security policies.

The dynamic nature of open-source ecosystems also leads to a rapid pace of feature evolution. As newer technologies and paradigms emerge, community-driven projects like Supabase are well-positioned to incorporate innovative approaches more quickly than proprietary solutions. Future integrations, such as enhanced support for edge-computing techniques or increased automation in deployment pipelines, can be evaluated and adopted by leveraging community experimentation and feedback. This adaptability ensures that the platform remains current with emerging trends and technologies, thereby supporting long-term project viability.

Community forums and documentation further enhance the value of Supabase's open-source model. Detailed documentation, frequently updated by both the core team and community members, provides

44

step-by-step guides, troubleshooting tips, and best practices. This repository of knowledge minimizes the learning curve and facilitates quicker integration of new features. In some cases, community-driven tutorials have reached a level of sophistication that rivals official documentation, offering practical, real-world examples that are directly applicable to common development challenges.

In essence, Supabase's open-source framework fosters an ecosystem where collective innovation, adaptability, and transparency converge to create a backend platform that is both robust and flexible. The ability to inspect and modify the codebase ensures that developers are not confined to a black-box solution; rather, they find a platform that evolves with their needs. Whether integrating custom business logic, extending core functionalities, or contributing to community-led enhancements, users of Supabase benefit from a collaborative environment where every participant has the opportunity to influence the platform's trajectory.

As the platform continues to mature, its open-source nature remains a key differentiator that drives user engagement and accelerates innovation. With each community contribution, Supabase becomes more versatile, addressing an ever-widening array of use cases, from rapid prototyping to enterprise-grade applications. This synergy between community and technology is instrumental in shaping an ecosystem that not only meets current demands but is also resilient in the face of evolving development paradigms.

Leveraging the combined strengths of open-source methodology and community engagement, Supabase provides developers with a powerful toolset. It represents a shift towards a more participatory form of software development, where shared contributions lead to collective success, and flexibility is the default state rather than an afterthought.

Chapter 2

Setting Up Your First Supabase Project

This chapter details the initial steps for creating a Supabase project, from account registration to project deployment. It covers navigating the dashboard, configuring databases, and setting up authentication. Emphasizing best practices, the chapter provides guidance on project settings, testing functionality, and ensuring security and scalability. Readers gain a comprehensive understanding of how to efficiently establish a functional Supabase environment for development.

2.1. Creating a Supabase Account

The process of registering a new Supabase account is designed to be straightforward while ensuring security and ease of use. Registration requires providing essential information such as a valid email address and a secure password. The procedure involves several carefully engineered steps that verify the user's identity and protect against unauthorized access. Each step contributes to establishing a robust foundation for subsequent project development and database configuration.

Users begin by visiting the official Supabase website, where a clear call-to-action button labeled Sign Up directs them to the registration form. The interface is clean and emphasizes user experience by highlighting the necessary fields without distraction from extraneous information. In terms of form validation, Supabase implements immediate feedback on input errors such as invalid email formats or weak passwords. This validation mechanism uses client-side scripting to alert users before submission, thereby reducing the likelihood of mistakes that could delay access or compromise security.

After entering the required details, such as the chosen email and password, users submit the form, which then triggers an email verification process. Verification is crucial in the account creation process because it ensures that the email address provided is valid and currently accessible by the user. The Supabase system sends a verification email that contains a unique link. Clicking this link completes the verification step and transitions the tentative account into an active state. This method of verification not only confirms the ownership of the email address but also serves as a preliminary security check against fraudulent registrations.

The email verification process is implemented in a manner that minimizes latency and maximizes reliability. Should the verification email be delayed or misplaced, users have the option to request a new verification email via a dedicated interface prompt. The system is configured to limit the frequency of such requests to avoid potential abuse. In practice, the verification mechanism relies on secure token generation, where each token is time-bound and linked specifically to the initial registration data. This approach ensures that even if a token is intercepted, its usability is limited to a short period.

Following verification, the next step requires logging into the newly created account. The login interface is essentially a mirror of the registration form, reinforcing design consistency. Users input their email and password, and the system employs a series of backend checks to confirm the credentials. In this phase, the account is cross-referenced against the verified records, and only credentials that have successfully passed the email verification process are granted access. The login procedure adheres to modern security protocols, including the use of HTTPS to guarantee encrypted data transmission during the authentication process.

To optimize the login experience, Supabase has integrated several features that enhance usability. For example, the platform supports session persistence which allows users to remain logged in over extended periods, thereby eliminating the need for frequent re-authentication during normal development activities. Additionally, there is an option to use two-factor authentication (2FA) to further secure access. When enabled, 2FA requires users to provide a secondary code generated via an authentication application on their mobile device. The use of 2FA is highly recommended as it significantly reduces the risk of unauthorized access even if login credentials are compromised.

Developers who prefer to interact with Supabase programmatically may also opt to register or manage their account via API calls. An example of invoking the Supabase API for account operations is illustrated below. This command shows how to send a POST request for account creation using a typical HTTP client. The code snippet directs users on integrating such functionality within their development workflow.

```
curl -X POST https://api.supabase.io/auth/v1/signup \
  -H "Content-Type: application/json" \
  -d '{
      "email": "user@example.com",
      "password": "SecurePassword123!"
    }'
```

On execution, the command returns a JSON response containing the status of the registration request and any necessary information such as an activation token or error codes if the process fails. For instance, a successful registration typically returns a status code of 200 along with a message instructing the user to check their email for further instructions. Sample output might appear as follows:

```
{
  "message": "Signup successful. Please check your email to verify your accou
nt.",
  "status": 200
}
```

This direct interaction with the API model not only enhances developer understanding but also promotes practices that integrate automated account creation within broader application ecosystems. Attention to the API documentation is essential, as details regarding endpoints, required headers, and payload formats may evolve over time.

Ensuring secure storage of credentials is a critical consideration during the registration process. Users are advised to generate and maintain passwords that combine uppercase and lowercase letters, numerals, and special characters. Supabase uses robust hashing and salting techniques on the backend to protect stored passwords, ensuring that even if a data breach occurs, the passwords remain inadvertently unrecoverable. The emphasis on strong password policies is reflective of a commitment to security that extends to every layer of the account management process.

During account creation, several customizable settings may be optionally configured, including language preferences, time zone settings, and notification preferences. These options are managed through an intuitive settings panel accessible immediately after login. Each setting is designed to enhance user-specific customization without compromising the overall uniformity of the Supabase environment. The use of cookies and session data facilitates a personalized experience without requiring repeated input during subsequent sessions.

Developers are encouraged to explore the help documentation available on the Supabase website whenever an unexpected behavior or error occurs during registration. The documentation provides troubleshooting steps for common issues such as email delivery failures, password resets, and verification link expirations. In cases where automated solutions are insufficient, the support team is available through a contact form and extensive community forums, providing multiple avenues to resolve difficulties quickly.

Special consideration is given to regulatory compliance and data protection standards throughout the account creation process. Supabase adheres to established protocols for data storage and user privacy, aligning with international data protection regulations. This compliance is enforced by regular audits and security assessments which help maintain the highest levels of data integrity and confidentiality. Understanding these compliance measures reinforces the reliability of Supabase as a backend service provider.

During the registration process, the system logs various events and audit trails for security monitoring. These logs are essential for diagnosing access issues and tracking unauthorized access attempts. Developers with elevated privileges can access these logs to ensure that account activities conform to the expected security policies. The logging system is designed to minimize storage overhead while retaining sufficient detail to reconstruct any security incidents. In practice, access to and navigation of these logs form an integral part of ongoing system maintenance and incident response strategies.

In terms of user interface design, the registration and login screens are optimized for both desktop and mobile environments, ensuring responsiveness and accessibility. The forms use clear labels and inline validation messages, which contributes to an overall reduction of user error. Consistent use of visual cues throughout the screens guides users naturally from one step to the next without the need for supplementary instructions. The aesthetic and functional elements of the user interface are continuously refined based on user feedback, ensuring that they meet the high standards of developers who rely on quick and efficient interactions.

Considerable effort has been invested in creating a frictionless experience for new account holders. This includes a streamlined process that minimizes redundant data entry and leverages social login integrations where applicable. For users who possess existing accounts on platforms that support OAuth, Supabase offers an alternative path that reduces barriers to entry. Although the primary focus remains on email-based registration, these additional methods demonstrate the platform's dedication to versatile user experience.

The fundamental aspects of the account creation process set the stage for all future interactions with Supabase. By ensuring that each user begins with a verified, secure, and personalized account, the platform builds a robust framework that supports more advanced features such as project creation, database configuration, and user authentication management. Each step in the registration process is designed to integrate seamlessly with later functionalities, ensuring consistency and reliability across the board.

By following these detailed steps during registration—entering validated information, verifying the email address, securely logging in, and optionally interacting with the API—users establish a solid foundation from which to develop their Supabase projects. These carefully implemented measures not only expedite account creation but also ensure that the overall security and integrity of the Supabase environment is maintained as development scales.

2.2. Navigating the Supabase Dashboard

The Supabase dashboard serves as the central interface for managing projects, resources, and ultimately the backend infrastructure of applications built upon the platform. It consolidates a broad range of functionalities that were introduced in previous sections, such as account creation and project initialization, into a cohesive environment designed for efficient control and real-time monitoring of services. The dashboard's design is minimalistic yet highly functional, enabling developers to navigate through complex settings with clarity and precision.

At first glance, the dashboard presents a user-friendly menu with clearly demarcated sections. The left-hand sidebar acts as the primary navigation pane and includes options such as `Overview`, `Database`, `Authentication`, `Storage`, and `Settings`. Each menu item represents a distinct functional component, allowing developers to quickly transition from high-level project insights to granular adjustments of specific services. This layout ensures that users do not need to search through cluttered interfaces to find relevant tools, as every function is readily accessible.

The `Overview` section features real-time metrics that provide insights into system performance. Graphical representations of resource consumption, database queries, and authentication events offer an immediate understanding of how the project is operating. These visualizations are updated periodically to reflect real-time statuses, facilitating proactive monitoring. Developers can use the provided filters to view daily, weekly, or monthly performance data, enabling a thorough analysis of trends over time. Understanding these metrics from the outset is essential for capacity planning and ensuring long-term scalability of the project.

Within the `Database` section, the dashboard displays an organized list

53

of schemas, tables, and views that form the backbone of the project's data structure. Users have the ability to perform actions such as running SQL queries, creating new tables, and modifying existing ones. The integrated SQL editor is a central component that supports syntax highlighting and auto-completion, which greatly enhances the efficiency of query writing. An example SQL query can be executed directly within this interface to retrieve a subset of data for review:

```
SELECT id, name, created_at
FROM users
ORDER BY created_at DESC;
```

Upon executing such queries, the dashboard displays results in an organized table format, making it easier for developers to inspect the data and validate changes directly. Functionality such as query history and saved queries further improves workflow efficiency by allowing repeated execution of common commands without retyping them.

The Authentication section focuses on managing user roles, permissions, and login flows. It provides an interface to configure various aspects of the authentication process including multi-factor authentication, social logins, and email verification settings. This section highlights both current configuration statuses and historical logs of authentication events. Developers are able to track failed login attempts or suspicious activities, which is critical for maintaining the security integrity of the project. The dashboard facilitates adjustments to authentication policies through toggle switches and input fields that are clear and self-explanatory.

Another important component within the dashboard is the Storage area. Here, users manage file uploads and data storage resources associated with the project. The interface is designed to support drag-and-drop file management, detailed file statistics, and configurable storage rules. Storage management covers everything from setting file permissions to organizing data in a hierarchical structure. This is particularly beneficial when handling user-generated content or large media files that need efficient retrieval and storage configurations.

A dedicated `Settings` panel aggregates configuration options that affect the project at a global level. This includes project metadata, security settings, API key management, and integrations with third-party services. By centralizing these options, the dashboard ensures that developers can modify essential project parameters without navigating through disparate menus. The API key management area, for instance, provides both display and regeneration functionalities, ensuring that keys remain secure while still being accessible for integration with external tools or services.

The dashboard also incorporates a robust logging system that captures detailed information about user actions and system events. This logging feature is invaluable during debugging sessions or when auditing system performance, as each event is timestamped and linked to a specific user or system process. Developers can filter logs by types, such as error messages or informational logs, ensuring that the pertinent data remains easily accessible. In this context, the logs serve as both a diagnostic tool and a historical record of project evolution.

Another aspect of the dashboard is its adaptability to various screen sizes and device types. The design is fully responsive, ensuring that developers working on mobile devices or tablets can access all functionalities without a degradation in performance or usability. This responsiveness is particularly useful for in-field monitoring or when quick adjustments are necessary without access to a desktop workstation. Despite the broad array of features presented, the dashboard maintains a consistent user experience across all platforms.

Integration with automation tools is another key highlight. The dashboard provides endpoints and webhooks that allow developers to trigger custom scripts or workflows based on specific events, such as new user registrations or database updates. For instance, a webhook can be configured to notify a continuous integration system whenever a new record is inserted into a critical table. An example of configuring a webhook might involve entering the target URL and specifying the events that should trigger the webhook. This feature ensures that the Supabase dashboard is not a static environment but rather a dynamic control center that interacts fluidly with the broader development ecosystem.

Moreover, the dashboard offers detailed documentation and guided walkthroughs embedded within several sections, helping both newcomers and experienced developers align with best practices. These embedded resources act as contextual help, clarifying complex functionalities such as schema migrations or role-based access control settings. The integration of documentation directly within the workspace minimizes context switching and enhances productivity by ensuring that the requisite knowledge is always at hand.

Interactivity is built into the dashboard through modals and dynamic panels that display context-relevant information without requiring full-page reloads. For instance, clicking on a table in the `Database` section may reveal an inline panel with additional details like column types, indexes, and foreign key constraints. This inline display reduces the cognitive load on developers by presenting detailed technical specifications in a manner that is both accessible and easily navigable. The interactivity also extends to the implementation of drag-and-drop functionalities in the `Storage` section, where file management becomes intuitive and direct.

Complex operations such as configuring advanced security features or managing API integrations are further enhanced by visual aids and step-by-step guides available through the dashboard. These instructional overlays are designed using clear and direct language, and they occasionally feature code examples or command-line instructions that

56

can be directly copied into a development environment. For example, if a developer needs to integrate third-party services, the dashboard might display a snippet similar to the following, which can be used to configure the connection via the Supabase API:

```
import { createClient } from '@supabase/supabase-js';

const supabaseUrl = 'https://xyzcompany.supabase.co';
const supabaseKey = 'public-anon-key';
const supabase = createClient(supabaseUrl, supabaseKey);

// Example function to trigger integration for new file uploads
async function handleFileUpload(file) {
  const { data, error } = await supabase.storage.from('uploads').
    upload(file.name, file);
  if (error) console.error('Upload error:', error);
  else console.log('Upload successful:', data);
}
```

Tooltips and contextual menus are strategically integrated across various sections of the dashboard. When a developer hovers over an icon, an explanatory tooltip appears, offering additional insights into the function of that element. This feature reduces the need for external references and supports rapid onboarding for new users. The consistency of these design elements across different sections reinforces a coherent experience that emphasizes ease of use and efficiency.

Real-time notifications within the dashboard alert users to critical events such as failed authentication attempts, system errors, or pending software updates. These notifications are prominently displayed and accompanied by actionable options that enable developers to react promptly to issues. The ability to manage notifications through customizable settings also ensures that users remain focused on the most relevant alerts without being overwhelmed by less critical messages.

The dashboard is constructed with security as a primary concern. Every interactive element, from the SQL editor to the API key management panel, operates within an environment that enforces strict access controls and role-based permissions. This security framework is visible through the careful arrangement of available functionalities and guides users to implement best practices when managing sensitive project data.

Attention to detail is reflected in the use of whitespace, typography, and color coding throughout the dashboard. These visual cues aid developers in distinguishing between different categories of information and in identifying critical actions quickly. The design adheres to principles of clarity and simplicity, ensuring that even complex tasks such as role assignment or policy configuration can be executed with minimal visual clutter.

The Supabase dashboard exemplifies a balance between functionality and simplicity, distributing complex capabilities across an interface that is equally accessible to beginners and scalable to the demands of enterprise-level projects. The range of tools provided—from real-time analytics to advanced code editing—ensures that every aspect of project management is addressed within a unified, coherent framework. This integration facilitates a seamless transition between different stages of project development, from initial setup and configuration to ongoing maintenance and scaling.

Every interactive component of the dashboard is designed with the developer in mind, ensuring that each action is intuitive and that the overall workflow is optimized for efficiency. The cohesive design of the dashboard reinforces the foundational concepts introduced in earlier sections and serves as the operational core from which all Supabase functionalities are orchestrated.

2.3. Starting Your First Project

Creating a new project on Supabase lays the groundwork for building dynamic, data-driven applications. The process involves establishing a project entity, configuring key settings, and integrating your
project with the Supabase ecosystem. The steps involved are designed
to ensure that every project is initialized with secure defaults, a well-
structured database, and the necessary integration points for further
development.

The process begins by accessing the Supabase dashboard after the
successful creation and verification of your account. Within the
dashboard, a clearly labeled button, such as `New Project` or `Create
Project`, is prominently displayed. Clicking this button opens a
setup form where you need to provide a unique project name, select
a region for deployment, and define initial resource allocations. This
information directly influences the performance and connectivity of
your project, as regional settings determine latency and compliance
with local data protection regulations.

The form generally includes fields for specifying a project name, an
optional description, and a dropdown selection for choosing a server
region. The friendly interface provides tooltips that explain the impact
of each choice. For instance, selecting a region closer to your target
audience minimizes latency and contributes to a more responsive application. Once the required fields are completed, clicking the `Create`
button submits your project configuration.

After submission, the backend system initializes your project's environment by provisioning the necessary resources, such as database instances and API endpoints. This process is automated and generally
completes within a few minutes. During this waiting period, the dashboard provides status updates that indicate progress, ensuring users
are informed of each significant milestone. The completion of this pro-

cess confirms that the project setup has been successful and that the foundations for data storage and retrieval are now in place.

At this point, users are directed to the home page of the new project, where initial configuration options are available. The home page serves as a control panel with an overview of project-specific settings and metrics. It displays key information such as the project name, region, and current status of associated services like the database and authentication modules. The design of this page emphasizes clarity, allowing developers to quickly locate critical settings while also providing an overview of system performance.

One of the first actions generally recommended is to configure the project's database. A newly created Supabase project automatically includes a fully functional PostgreSQL database instance. Accessing the database configuration interface, users can define schemas, create tables, and set up roles by utilizing the integrated SQL editor available on the dashboard. An example of creating a simple table is demonstrated in the following SQL snippet:

```
CREATE TABLE profiles (
  id SERIAL PRIMARY KEY,
  username VARCHAR(50) UNIQUE NOT NULL,
  email VARCHAR(100) UNIQUE NOT NULL,
  joined_at TIMESTAMP WITH TIME ZONE DEFAULT CURRENT_TIMESTAMP
);
```

Executing commands such as the one illustrated enables developers to lay out the initial data structures that serve as the backbone of their applications. Beyond the creation of tables, the dashboard facilitates adjustments to database schema settings, indexes, and relationships, ensuring the database is both efficient and scalable. The integration of real-time data monitoring allows developers to observe the impact of configuration changes immediately.

Another critical aspect of initial project configuration is setting up authentication. The project's authentication module is configured with sensible defaults, including support for email and password-based sign-in. Nevertheless, developers can customize these settings to suit their application's security requirements. From the authentication panel, options can be adjusted to enable multi-factor authentication, social login providers, and password complexity requirements. This flexibility ensures that the project's user management capabilities align with the specific security needs of the application.

For developers looking to configure these settings programmatically, Supabase provides a comprehensive API. Below is an example demonstrating how to update authentication configuration using the Supabase client library:

```
import { createClient } from '@supabase/supabase-js';

const supabaseUrl = 'https://xyzcompany.supabase.co';
const supabaseKey = 'your-service-key';
const supabase = createClient(supabaseUrl, supabaseKey);

// Example function to enable multi-factor authentication
async function enableMFA() {
  const { data, error } = await supabase.auth.api.updateSettings({
    mfa: {
      enabled: true,
      provider: 'totp'
    }
  });
  if (error) {
    console.error('Error updating auth settings:', error);
  } else {
    console.log('Authentication settings updated:', data);
  }
}

enableMFA();
```

The above code provides a template for developers aiming to integrate such configurations into their deployment scripts or continuous integration pipelines. The API-driven approach reinforces consistency across different environments and reduces the manual overhead associated with configuration tasks.

61

Following the initial setup, the project dashboard also provides features for monitoring system health and performance. Important metrics, such as the number of active sessions, query execution times, and storage usage, are displayed in real time. These insights are valuable in identifying potential bottlenecks early in the development cycle and allow for dynamic adjustments as the project grows. Monitoring tools built into the dashboard help identify trends and facilitate proactive adjustments to project settings, such as increasing allocated resources or optimizing database queries.

The next configuration step involves securing the endpoints your project exposes. Supabase automates much of the configuration for API security, providing default protections against common vulnerabilities. However, developers have the flexibility to define additional security policies. For example, access control lists can be implemented to restrict data access to specific roles. Policies can be written and managed through the dashboard's SQL editor using the Row-Level Security (RLS) feature provided by PostgreSQL. An example of creating an RLS policy is shown below:

```
ALTER TABLE profiles ENABLE ROW LEVEL SECURITY;

CREATE POLICY select_profiles ON profiles
  FOR SELECT
  USING (auth.uid() = id);
```

Defining such policies ensures that data access is appropriately restricted according to the application's security requirements. The dashboard provides immediate feedback on policy implementation, and logs are maintained for auditability.

Another area of importance in the initial project setup is the configuration of environment variables and API keys. These are essential for integrating third-party services, managing internal secrets, and establishing communication between various project components. The settings pane within the project dashboard includes a designated area for managing environment variables. Developers can add, modify, or remove these variables, and the interface provides contextual help explaining the implications of each variable. Proper management of these variables is essential to maintaining the integrity of the application as it scales across different environments such as development, staging, and production.

Integration with version control systems and deployment pipelines is streamlined through the dashboard. Linking a Git repository allows for automated deployments when changes are pushed to the repository. This feature is highly advantageous for teams that adopt continuous deployment practices. Detailed logs of deployment events are available, and the dashboard indicates the current status of each deployment, including error messages if issues arise during the process.

During the initial configurations, the Supabase project setup also includes the option to inspect and refine logging settings. A robust logging system is integrated into the project, capturing detailed records of API accesses, authentication events, and system errors. This data is accessible through a logging interface that provides both real-time monitoring and historical analysis. The ability to view logs directly within the dashboard assists developers in quick troubleshooting and optimizes the debugging process during early stages of project development.

An important consideration in the early stages of any project is the incorporation of best practices aimed at performance optimization and security. The Supabase platform encourages users to adopt proven methodologies by offering guidelines and checklists during project initialization. These interim prompts ensure that developers address critical areas such as database indexing, query optimization, and secure API practices before progressing to more advanced development tasks.

After all initial configurations and settings have been established, the project dashboard provides an integrated `Getting Started` guide that outlines next steps and further customization opportunities. This guide is particularly useful for newcomers to the platform, highlighting additional features such as real-time subscriptions, automated backups, and advanced analytics. It serves to bridge the gap between a barebones project setup and a fully functional backend solution that can evolve alongside the application's requirements.

The initial project setup forms the cornerstone of building a robust and scalable application. By following these step-by-step instructions, developers not only create a new project but also ensure that it is configured with best practices in mind. The precise configuration of components such as the database schema, authentication methods, security policies, and environment variables establishes a stable environment where future development can proceed with confidence.

Efficient project startup is further enhanced by the continuous feedback mechanisms provided by the dashboard. Every step of the setup process is documented, and interactive prompts guide users through potential pitfalls. These mechanisms are particularly useful when setting up complex environments that require multiple integrations, as they reduce the likelihood of administrative errors that could impact subsequent functionality.

The streamlined approach to project initialization on Supabase leverages modern standards in software engineering, ensuring that developers benefit from both automated processes and customizable options. This blend of automation and flexibility is critical for establishing a project that is resilient, secure, and ready for subsequent layers of application development.

2.4. Configuring Database Settings

Supabase provides a managed PostgreSQL database that serves as the backbone of your application. Configuring the database within Supabase involves establishing schemas, creating tables, defining relationships, and managing connections, all of which are accessible via the dashboard and the integrated SQL editor. This section outlines a systematic approach to configuring your database settings while emphasizing best practices in schema design and resource management.

The first step in configuration is understanding the concept of schemas within PostgreSQL. Schemas act as namespaces, enabling you to organize database objects (such as tables, indexes, and functions) logically. By creating distinct schemas, you can separate areas of functionality within your application, such as segregating user data from administrative or logging data. In Supabase, the default schema is typically `public`; however, additional schemas may be created to enforce boundaries and enhance security. An example of creating a new schema is shown below:

```
CREATE SCHEMA analytics;
```

In this instance, the `analytics` schema serves as a dedicated namespace for storing data related to user behavior and application performance. Separating concerns in this manner can simplify permission management and minimize the risk of accidental data exposure.

Once schemas are established, tables are the next critical component. Tables in Supabase are created using standard SQL commands, and they form the foundation of your data model. The design of tables should reflect the structure of your application domain. This includes careful consideration of columns, data types, indexes, and constraints. For example, creating a table to store user profiles might involve specifying primary keys, unique constraints, and default values, as illus-

65

trated in the following snippet:

```
CREATE TABLE public.profiles (
  id SERIAL PRIMARY KEY,
  username VARCHAR(50) UNIQUE NOT NULL,
  email VARCHAR(100) UNIQUE NOT NULL,
  created_at TIMESTAMPTZ DEFAULT CURRENT_TIMESTAMP
);
```

In this table definition, the id column is automatically incremented, while the username and email columns enforce uniqueness to prevent duplicate entries. The created_at column is automatically populated with the current timestamp during new record insertions, ensuring a consistent audit trail.

For applications requiring more complex data relationships, foreign keys are essential in establishing connections between tables. A foreign key constraint ensures referential integrity by linking a column in one table to the primary key of another. Suppose you want to create an orders table that references a profiles table to associate orders with users. The SQL statement would resemble the following:

```
CREATE TABLE public.orders (
  order_id SERIAL PRIMARY KEY,
  profile_id INT NOT NULL,
  order_date DATE NOT NULL,
  amount DECIMAL(10,2) NOT NULL,
  FOREIGN KEY (profile_id) REFERENCES public.profiles(id)
);
```

By enforcing this constraint, the database guarantees that every order record corresponds to a valid user profile, thereby preserving data consistency across your application.

Beyond table creation, proper indexing significantly enhances database performance, especially when dealing with large datasets. Indexes allow for faster query execution by reducing the amount of data that must be scanned. While primary keys automatically generate indexes, additional indexes may be necessary for columns

66

that are frequently involved in search queries or join operations. For example, if the `email` field in the `profiles` table is often used in query filters, consider creating an index on this column:

```
CREATE INDEX idx_profiles_email ON public.profiles(email);
```

This index optimizes searches by allowing the query planner to quickly locate rows based on the `email` column. It is important to monitor index usage since excessively indexing every column can lead to increased storage requirements and slower write operations.

Another feature to consider is table partitioning, which can considerably improve query performance and manageability as your database grows. Partitioning divides a large table into smaller, more manageable pieces while retaining the logical integrity of the original table. Supabase, by virtue of its PostgreSQL foundation, supports range, list, and hash partitioning strategies. For instance, if you are managing an `orders` table that spans several years, partitioning by date may be an effective approach:

```
CREATE TABLE public.orders (
  order_id SERIAL PRIMARY KEY,
  profile_id INT NOT NULL,
  order_date DATE NOT NULL,
  amount DECIMAL(10,2) NOT NULL
) PARTITION BY RANGE (order_date);

-- Create partitions for specific date ranges
CREATE TABLE public.orders_2021 PARTITION OF public.orders
  FOR VALUES FROM ('2021-01-01') TO ('2022-01-01');

CREATE TABLE public.orders_2022 PARTITION OF public.orders
  FOR VALUES FROM ('2022-01-01') TO ('2023-01-01');
```

By partitioning the table, queries filtering on the `order_date` column run faster since only relevant partitions are scanned, thereby enhancing overall database performance.

In addition to schema and table configurations, establishing secure and efficient connections to the database is a crucial aspect of database management. Supabase provides connection strings required for external applications and server-side integrations. These connection strings include information such as the database host, port, user credentials, and SSL settings necessary for secure communication. Developers can retrieve the connection details from the Supabase dashboard under the project settings or API configuration section. A typical connection string for PostgreSQL might look like the following:

```
postgres://user:password@db.supabase.co:5432/database_name?sslmode=
    require
```

This connection string can be utilized across various programming environments. For instance, connecting to the Supabase database using Python and the psycopg2 library involves the following code snippet:

```
import psycopg2

connection = psycopg2.connect(
    dbname="database_name",
    user="user",
    password="password",
    host="db.supabase.co",
    port="5432",
    sslmode="require"
)
cursor = connection.cursor()
cursor.execute("SELECT version();")
print(cursor.fetchone())
connection.close()
```

This example demonstrates how to establish a secure connection to the database, execute a basic query, and then gracefully close the connection, ensuring resource cleanup.

Managing database connections efficiently is fundamental in preventing resource exhaustion. Supabase offers connection pooling options that enable the reuse of established connections to minimize overhead. Connection pools are particularly beneficial for applications that execute numerous short-lived transactions. Configuring connection pooling parameters may involve adjustments on both the client side and

68

within the Supabase settings, ensuring optimal resource allocation and performance.

Another critical aspect of configuring database settings is the management of roles and permissions. PostgreSQL's robust role-based access control (RBAC) system allows for precise specification of user privileges, ensuring that each user only has access to the necessary resources. In Supabase, roles can be configured directly through SQL commands. As an example, creating a read-only role for analytics purposes might involve the following commands:

```
CREATE ROLE readonly_user NOINHERIT;
GRANT CONNECT ON DATABASE database_name TO readonly_user;
GRANT USAGE ON SCHEMA public TO readonly_user;
GRANT SELECT ON ALL TABLES IN SCHEMA public TO readonly_user;

-- Ensure future tables also grant the same privileges
ALTER DEFAULT PRIVILEGES IN SCHEMA public
  GRANT SELECT ON TABLES TO readonly_user;
```

These commands provide fine-grained control over database access, thereby reducing the risk of unauthorized data modifications while allowing external systems to query data as needed.

Moreover, Supabase supports advanced PostgreSQL features, such as triggers and stored procedures, which can automate routine tasks and enforce business rules directly within the database layer. Triggers can automatically invoke functions in response to events like data insertion, update, or deletion. For example, a trigger can be implemented to log every time a new user profile is created:

```
CREATE OR REPLACE FUNCTION audit_profile_creation() RETURNS trigger
    AS $$
BEGIN
  INSERT INTO public.audit_logs (profile_id, action, action_time)
  VALUES (NEW.id, 'INSERT', CURRENT_TIMESTAMP);
  RETURN NEW;
END;
$$ LANGUAGE plpgsql;

CREATE TRIGGER profile_insert_audit
```

69

```
AFTER INSERT ON public.profiles
FOR EACH ROW EXECUTE FUNCTION audit_profile_creation();
```

By leveraging such built-in functionalities, developers can streamline operations and maintain data integrity through automated processes.

Supabase's integrated SQL editor provides a powerful tool for executing administrative tasks and testing configurations. The editor supports syntax highlighting, auto-completion, and integrated error checking, allowing developers to experiment with queries and modifications in a controlled environment. This feature is particularly useful during the initial setup phase as it enables developers to validate changes before implementing them in production.

Finally, configuring database settings is an ongoing process rather than a one-time event. Monitoring database performance metrics through Supabase's dashboard helps to identify bottlenecks and optimize queries. Routine reviews of index usage, query execution plans, and system logs contribute to the long-term health and scalability of the application. Adjustments based on these insights ensure that the database remains responsive under varying loads and continues supporting the evolving needs of the project.

Every configuration decision—from schema organization to connection management—plays an integral role in building a secure, efficient, and scalable database environment. The strategies discussed here emphasize precision and clarity in designing database systems that are not only functional but also robust enough to accommodate future enhancements.

70

2.5. Setting Up Authentication

Enabling and customizing user authentication is a critical step in establishing a secure backend for your Supabase project. Supabase offers a comprehensive authentication module that supports various methods such as email/password sign-up, social logins, and multifactor authentication. The authentication system integrates seamlessly with other components, including the client libraries and database permissions, to enforce role-based access controls.

The authentication setup begins within the Supabase dashboard under the `Authentication` panel. This interface provides a centralized view for managing authentication settings, including configuration of external OAuth providers, adjustment of password policies, and enabling optional security layers. Users can toggle between different authentication methods for their project, depending on the security requirements and user base. The dashboard usually displays toggles and input fields that allow developers to enable features like email confirmations, OAuth integrations (e.g., Google, GitHub, Twitter), and session management configurations.

A common task during setup is enabling email/password authentication. Initially, default settings are applied to new projects, but customization is often necessary. For example, refining password strength requirements ensures users select secure credentials. This can be done by modifying the authentication settings in the dashboard or by using the Supabase API. An example API call to update password policies is demonstrated below:

```
import { createClient } from '@supabase/supabase-js';

const supabaseUrl = 'https://your-project.supabase.co';
const supabaseKey = 'your-service-role-key';
const supabase = createClient(supabaseUrl, supabaseKey);

async function updatePasswordPolicy() {
```

71

```
const { data, error } = await supabase.auth.api.updateSettings({
  password_policy: {
    min_length: 8,
    require_uppercase: true,
    require_numbers: true,
    require_special_characters: true
  }
});
if (error) {
  console.error('Error updating password policy:', error);
} else {
  console.log('Password policy updated:', data);
}
}

updatePasswordPolicy();
```

The code snippet above sets a minimum password length and enforces requirements for uppercase letters, numbers, and special characters. Implementing such policies ensures that user accounts maintain a high level of security. This API-driven approach allows integration into automated deployment scripts or continuous integration pipelines, ensuring that security policies are consistent across environments.

Social logins provide an alternative to traditional email/password combinations and can simplify the registration process for users. By integrating popular OAuth providers, developers allow users to authenticate using existing accounts from platforms like Google or GitHub. The Supabase dashboard offers an area dedicated to configuring OAuth credentials. When configuring a social provider, developers need to supply client IDs, secrets, and the correct redirect URLs. This process is divided into two stages: configuring the provider settings on the third-party platform and then entering those values in the Supabase settings.

Integration of OAuth providers is facilitated by the Supabase API as well. A code example of initializing social authentication using the Supabase client is shown below:

```
import { createClient } from '@supabase/supabase-js';
```

```
const supabaseUrl = 'https://your-project.supabase.co';
const supabaseKey = 'your-anon-key';
const supabase = createClient(supabaseUrl, supabaseKey);

// Redirect the user to the social provider's login page
async function signInWithGoogle() {
  const { user, session, error } = await supabase.auth.signIn({
    provider: 'google'
  });
  if (error) {
    console.error('Google sign-in error:', error);
  } else {
    console.log('User signed in:', user);
  }
}

signInWithGoogle();
```

This example demonstrates how to trigger an OAuth login flow. Upon successful authentication, the user is redirected back to the application, and the session is established. Detailed error handling ensures that authentication failures are logged for further analysis.

Another advanced feature is the implementation of multi-factor authentication (MFA). MFA adds an additional security layer by requiring users to provide a second form of verification (e.g., a time-based one-time password from an authenticator app) during sign-in. This feature can be toggled on within the dashboard, and the associated UI components for MFA enrollment are available to end users. Developers can encourage the adoption of MFA by presenting users with enrollment prompts during initial sign-up or profile updates.

Programmatic customization for MFA can also be achieved. An example function to enable MFA using the Supabase API is provided below:

```
import { createClient } from '@supabase/supabase-js';

const supabaseUrl = 'https://your-project.supabase.co';
const supabaseKey = 'your-service-role-key';
const supabase = createClient(supabaseUrl, supabaseKey);

async function enableMFAForUser(userId) {
```

```
const { data, error } = await supabase.auth.api.updateUser(userId,
  {
  mfa_enabled: true,
  mfa_provider: 'totp'
});
if (error) {
  console.error('Error enabling MFA:', error);
} else {
  console.log('MFA enabled for user:', data);
}
}

enableMFAForUser('user-unique-id');
```

In this example, a user's account is updated to include MFA with a TOTP (time-based one-time password) provider. Implementing MFA enhances security and protects sensitive resources by ensuring that a compromised password does not grant complete access.

Session management is yet another key area within authentication configuration. By default, Supabase handles session storage and expiration automatically. However, developers have the option to control session lifetimes and persistence strategies through the dashboard or via API calls. Considerations such as idle timeouts and token renewal policies can have significant impacts on both user experience and security posture. Configuring session expiry times is typically a matter of adjusting settings that dictate the duration of valid tokens. This configuration ensures that even if tokens are intercepted, they become unusable after a set period.

The Supabase platform further supports customizable authentication redirects. These redirects allow developers to control the post-authentication experience, such as navigating to a user dashboard or displaying a welcome screen. Redirect URLs are managed within the authentication settings and must be registered with the project to prevent redirection attacks. The proper configuration of these URLs is critical for maintaining secure sessions. For example, during an

74

OAuth flow, the redirect URL confirms the legitimacy of the request, reducing the risk of open redirect vulnerabilities.

Behavioral analytics concerning authentication are made available through integrated logging and monitoring features. Every sign-in attempt, including successes, failures, and MFA interactions, is logged. Developers can use this information to identify potential security breaches, analyze user behavior, and refine authentication workflows. The dashboard's reporting tools facilitate the extraction of these logs, enabling further analytics and audit trails.

Another layer of customization is the ability to implement custom authentication flows using Supabase's serverless functions or webhooks. Developers may choose to enact additional business logic upon user sign-ups, such as initiating onboarding sequences, sending custom notifications, or interfacing with external identity providers. This flexibility is particularly useful in complex application environments where the default authentication process might require augmentation. An example webhook might capture user registration events and perform immediate post-processing, as shown below:

```
const express = require('express');
const app = express();

app.use(express.json());

app.post('/webhook/user-registered', (req, res) => {
  const { user } = req.body;
  // Custom processing logic for new users
  console.log('New user registered:', user);
  res.sendStatus(200);
});

app.listen(3000, () => {
  console.log('Webhook server running on port 3000');
});
```

This example sets up a basic Express server that listens for incoming registration events from Supabase. Integrating such functionality can help automate and streamline user onboarding processes by triggering additional workflows as soon as a new user account is created.

Customization of authentication extends to error handling and user feedback. Detailed error messages can be used to guide users through the correction of mistakes during sign-in or sign-up processes. While security considerations demand that errors do not reveal sensitive information, the balance between usability and security is carefully managed. For instance, generic error messages such as "Invalid credentials" maintain security, whereas analytics can capture detailed failure reasons on the backend for diagnostic purposes.

Advanced role management is also tied closely to authentication. Supabase enables developers to associate authenticated users with specific roles, thereby controlling access to various parts of the application. This mapping is typically configured using policies within the PostgreSQL database. Developers define policies that grant or restrict access based on user roles, ensuring that only authorized users can interact with sensitive data. An example SQL policy to limit data access might be:

```
ALTER TABLE public.user_data ENABLE ROW LEVEL SECURITY;

CREATE POLICY select_user_data ON public.user_data
  FOR SELECT
  USING (auth.uid() = user_id);
```

This policy restricts access to records in the user_data table so that only the user who owns the data can perform select operations. The integration of such policies with the authentication module provides a robust, secure method for managing data access throughout the application.

Every configuration step within the authentication setup is designed to promote both security and usability. The Supabase authentication framework offers a range of customization options from enforcing strong password policies to integrating multi-factor authentication and OAuth. These capabilities, combined with detailed logging, session management, and custom flow integration, ensure that projects can tailor the authentication experience to meet specific application requirements. This level of configurability empowers developers to build secure, scalable, and user-friendly applications while maintaining full control over authentication processes throughout the project lifecycle.

2.6. Deploying and Testing the Project

Deploying your project on Supabase involves transitioning from a development environment to a production-ready state while ensuring that fundamental functionalities are tested and verified. The deployment process is a structured workflow that integrates configuration adjustments, resource provisioning, and connectivity validation to guarantee that the project performs as intended. The initial step involves confirming that all components, including authentication, database configurations, and API integrations, have been accurately set up as required by previous stages. Once these baseline configurations are in place, developers move towards deploying and testing the project to identify any discrepancies early in the release cycle.

Deployment begins by ensuring that all environment-specific configurations, such as connection strings, API keys, and environment variables, are correctly set up. The Supabase dashboard provides a dedicated section in the project settings where these variables can be managed. It is essential to confirm that the connection string for the PostgreSQL database, for instance, reflects the production credentials and that SSL configurations are enabled to secure data transmission. A sample connection string configured for production might resemble the following:

```
postgres://prod_user:prod_password@db.supabase.co:5432/prod_database?
```

```
sslmode=require
```

After confirming configuration details, developers typically utilize version control systems and continuous deployment pipelines that integrate with the Supabase environment. By linking a Git repository to the Supabase project, automated deployments can be triggered on each commit or on push to a particular branch. This integration minimizes human error and ensures consistency across development stages. The Supabase dashboard often provides a streamlined interface for deploying changes, verifying that the latest commits are correctly pushed to the production instance.

Once deployment is initiated, monitoring tools integrated within the dashboard become pivotal. Real-time analytics display metrics such as query execution times, authentication session counts, and resource utilization, allowing developers to evaluate the performance of their deployed services. These metrics not only reveal the current health of the project but also serve as baselines for ongoing performance tuning. Regular review of these indicators helps in identifying bottlenecks, analyzing unusual traffic patterns, and preemptively resolving potential downtime issues.

Testing the deployed project is an integral component of the release process. It is necessary to verify that all functionalities, including database transactions, authentication flows, and API requests, work as expected. One common method for testing is the use of automated scripts that simulate user interactions with the application. Such scripts can be implemented using frameworks like Jest, Mocha, or Supertest for API testing. Below is an example of testing an API endpoint using the Supertest library in a Node.js environment:

```
const request = require('supertest');
const app = require('./app'); // Your Express application

describe('GET /profiles', () => {
  it('should return all user profiles', async () => {
```

78

```
    const res = await request(app).get('/profiles').expect(200);
    expect(Array.isArray(res.body)).toBeTruthy();
  });
});
```

The above snippet demonstrates how to verify that a GET request to the /profiles endpoint returns an array of user profile objects and a 200 HTTP status code. Implementing such tests across all critical endpoints helps ensure that any changes introduced during deployment do not break existing functionalities.

Manual testing is also recommended, particularly for verifying user interface interactions and authentication flows. This involves logging into the application using different user roles, verifying that the login process functions correctly, and ensuring that session management operates as expected. For example, test scenarios should include signing in with both valid and invalid credentials, testing account lockout mechanisms, and verifying multi-factor authentication (MFA) prompts if enabled. Environment-specific behavior such as redirection to secure pages and proper handling of error messages should be closely monitored.

Furthermore, testing should extend to database operations. Developers must verify that data insertion, updates, and deletions behave consistently with defined constraints and policies. An effective approach to test database interactions is to run a series of SQL queries after deployment to check the integrity of data and the correctness of foreign key relationships. An example SQL query to test data retrieval from the profiles table is as follows:

```
SELECT id, username, email, created_at FROM public.profiles ORDER BY
    created_at DESC;
```

Executing this query through the Supabase SQL editor or via a connected client (e.g., psycopg2 in Python) should return the expected records. Consistent logging of such operations during testing is essential, as it provides an audit trail and helps in diagnosing issues if the data retrieval does not match expectations.

In addition to functional tests, load testing is crucial to assess the performance of the deployed project under real-world conditions. Load testing involves simulating multiple concurrent users and transactions to evaluate how the backend responds to high traffic volumes. Tools such as Apache JMeter and Locust can be employed to generate test traffic and monitor response times, database locking issues, and system resource exhaustion. Proper load testing ensures that the project will remain responsive and behave predictably under peak usage periods.

Security testing is another critical area in the deployment phase. This includes verifying that all API endpoints enforce authentication and that unauthorized access is appropriately prevented. Role-based access controls configured in previous sections should be rigorously tested. An effective practice is to attempt access using credentials or tokens with insufficient privileges and ensure that the system responds with appropriate error messages, typically an HTTP 401 or 403 status code. For example, an attempt to access a protected resource using a user without the required role might be tested as follows:

```
const request = require('supertest');
const app = require('./app');

describe('Unauthorized access check', () => {
  it('should return 403 for access to protected resource', async ()
     => {
    const res = await request(app)
      .get( /admin')
      .set( Authorization', 'Bearer invalid_or_insufficient_token')
      .expect(403);
    expect(res.body.error).toMatch(/forbidden/i);
  });
});
```

On the security front, deploying additional monitoring and alerting mechanisms is recommended. Automated alerts configured within the Supabase dashboard can notify developers immediately upon detecting anomalies such as a surge in failed login attempts, unusual query patterns, or database connection errors. These alerts facilitate prompt responses to security incidents and minimize potential breaches.

Continuous integration (CI) practices enhance both deployment and testing. Integrating automated tests into deployment pipelines ensures that every code change undergoes stringent checks before being merged into production. CI systems like Travis CI, CircleCI, or GitHub Actions can be configured to run the test suites automatically. A typical CI configuration in a YAML file might include stages for linting, unit testing, and integration testing, ensuring that all aspects of the deployment are verified:

```
name: CI Pipeline

on: [push]

jobs:
  build:
    runs-on: ubuntu-latest

    steps:
    - uses: actions/checkout@v2
    - name: Install Dependencies
      run: npm install
    - name: Run Lint
      run: npm run lint
    - name: Run Tests
      run: npm test
```

This automation prevents regressions and maintains high-quality standards by ensuring that deployments are only executed when all tests pass successfully.

Beyond technical validations, comprehensive documentation of the deployment process and testing procedures facilitates collaboration among development and operations teams. Documenting the configuration settings, test plans, and rollback procedures ensures that all stakeholders are aware of the deployment state and can react appropriately to any issues post-deployment. A well-maintained changelog or deployment log can further assist in tracking modifications and resolving discrepancies that may emerge over time.

Post-deployment debugging is an area where integrated logging plays a pivotal role. Debug logs, error logs, and access logs can be compiled and reviewed to verify that every component of the project operates according to plan. In situations where discrepancies arise, these logs provide critical insights into the sequence of events that led to the failure. For instance, a misconfiguration in the database connection might manifest as repeated timeout errors in the logs, prompting developers to revisit their connection settings.

Testing mobile responsiveness and cross-browser compatibility is another layer of verification, especially for projects with a front-end interface. Ensuring that the user interface loads correctly, handles interactive elements appropriately, and performs consistently across various devices is crucial. Tools such as BrowserStack or Selenium can be utilized to automate these tests and capture screen recordings or snapshots for review.

Finally, once deployment has been confirmed as successful and the initial round of testing has validated the setup, it is advisable to conduct a limited rollout or beta testing phase. This strategy allows a subset of users to interact with the deployed project in a controlled environment, providing real-world feedback that can highlight issues not encountered during laboratory testing. Feedback from this beta phase can be invaluable in implementing final adjustments before a full-scale launch.

By following this comprehensive approach—starting from configuration validation, through automated and manual testing, load and se-

curity evaluations, and finally a controlled release—developers can ensure that every aspect of the project is functioning as intended. This
rigorous process not only reduces the risk of post-deployment issues
but also instills confidence in both the development team and end users
regarding the stability and security of the deployed Supabase project.

2.7. Best Practices for Project Setup

Efficient project setup on Supabase requires a thoughtful approach
that balances security, scalability, and maintainability with streamlined workflows and robust troubleshooting mechanisms. The integration of best practices in initial configuration has long-term benefits by
reducing technical debt and minimizing operational issues. A methodical approach involves careful planning of project architecture, thorough adherence to security protocols, proactive scalability planning,
and establishing solid monitoring and debugging frameworks.

One of the primary considerations is security. When setting up a Supabase project, enforce a strong security posture starting with account
creation and extending through every subsequent configuration. Begin
by ensuring that user authentication is configured with strict password
policies, multi-factor authentication (MFA), and OAuth integrations
when possible. As illustrated in previous sections, the use of enforced
password policies via API calls ensures that users create secure credentials. For example, the snippet below demonstrates how password policies can be updated programmatically:

```
import { createClient } from '@supabase/supabase-js';

const supabaseUrl = 'https://your-project.supabase.co';
const supabaseKey = 'your-service-role-key';
const supabase = createClient(supabaseUrl, supabaseKey);

async function updatePasswordPolicy() {
  const { data, error } = await supabase.auth.api.updateSettings({
    password_policy: {
```

83

```
      min_length: 8,
      require_uppercase: true,
      require_numbers: true,
      require_special_characters: true
    }
  });
  if (error) {
    console.error('Error updating password policy:', error);
  } else {
    console.log('Password policy updated:', data);
  }
}

updatePasswordPolicy();
```

This practice minimizes the risk of weak passwords and constrains access in the event of credential breaches. Moreover, employing Role-Based Access Control (RBAC) in the database through PostgreSQL security policies is crucial. Establish rules that limit data access to authorized users, such as enforcing row-level security on sensitive tables. For instance, a policy that restricts table access per individual user can be defined as follows:

```
ALTER TABLE public.user_data ENABLE ROW LEVEL SECURITY;

CREATE POLICY select_user_data ON public.user_data
  FOR SELECT
  USING (auth.uid() = user_id);
```

This policy ensures that users only access their own data, thus reducing the surface area for potential data breaches.

Scalability is another core concern. At the outset, plan your database architecture to accommodate growth. Structure your database using normalized schemas but be open to denormalization where performance demands it. The use of indices and proper partitioning strategies are fundamental techniques for enhancing query performance and managing large datasets. For example, partitioning a large table based on date ranges, as shown below, can significantly reduce query times:

```
CREATE TABLE public.orders (
```

84

```
order_id SERIAL PRIMARY KEY,
profile_id INT NOT NULL,
order_date DATE NOT NULL,
amount DECIMAL(10,2) NOT NULL
) PARTITION BY RANGE (order_date);

CREATE TABLE public.orders_2021 PARTITION OF public.orders
  FOR VALUES FROM ('2021-01-01') TO ('2022-01-01');

CREATE TABLE public.orders_2022 PARTITION OF public.orders
  FOR VALUES FROM ('2022-01-01') TO ('2023-01-01');
```

Evaluating resource allocation from the beginning is also essential. Choose the appropriate server region based on your user base location to reduce latency, and monitor resource usage continuously with Supabase's integrated analytics. Employ connection pooling strategies to handle simultaneous requests efficiently without overwhelming the database server. Review and revise connection parameters periodically as usage patterns change.

An efficient project setup also involves establishing comprehensive testing frameworks. Automated testing for API endpoints, database transactions, and user authentication flows should be integrated into your continuous integration (CI) pipeline. For instance, using a tool like Supertest with Node.js can help verify that API endpoints return the expected responses, as demonstrated below:

```
const request = require('supertest');
const app = require('./app'); // Express application

describe('GET /profiles', () => {
  it('should return all user profiles', async () => {
    const res = await request(app).get('/profiles').expect(200);
    expect(Array.isArray(res.body)).toBeTruthy();
  });
});
```

Integrating these tests into your CI/CD workflow via platforms like GitHub Actions or Travis CI ensures that your deployments maintain their integrity, and any regressions are quickly identified and ad-

85

dressed before merging changes into production.

Troubleshooting common issues is part of best practices that help maintain system robustness. One effective strategy is to enable and regularly review detailed logging. Supabase provides integrated log management features that capture critical data, including API calls, authentication attempts, and database transactions. Setting up alerts for unusual activity, such as repeated failed login attempts or unexpected spikes in database errors, can provide early warnings of systemic issues. Configuring these alerts directly within the Supabase dashboard enables proactive issue resolution.

For further diagnostic measures, ensure that error messages are sufficiently descriptive for developers while maintaining operational security by avoiding disclosure of sensitive system details. Use logging middleware in your APIs to capture errors and user actions, which can be analyzed periodically. In a Node.js environment, logging can be implemented as follows:

```
const express = require('express');
const app = express();

app.use((err, req, res, next) => {
  console.error('Error occurred:', err);
  res.status(500).send({ error: 'An unexpected error occurred.' });
});

app.listen(3000, () => {
  console.log('Server is running on port 3000');
});
```

This middleware captures errors that occur during API requests and logs them, enabling developers to troubleshoot issues based on comprehensive error logs.

Another best practice is to maintain consistency between environments. Ensure that development, staging, and production environments are as similar as possible in terms of configuration and perfor-

mance characteristics. Utilizing environment variables and standardized configuration scripts allows for reproducible deployments. This
consistency minimizes the risk of environment-specific issues, making
the debugging process more straightforward. An example of a scripting
approach to load environment variables in a Node.js project is provided
below:

```
require('dotenv').config();
const dbConnectionString = process.env.DATABASE_URL;
```

Good documentation is a critical component of best practices.
Document every configuration step, API endpoint behavior, and
deployment process clearly. Such documentation should be part
of the version-controlled codebase so that it is updated alongside
code changes and remains accessible to all team members during
troubleshooting and onboarding new developers.

It is also advisable to adopt a modular approach in project architecture. Keep project components loosely coupled so that changes in one
component do not propagate unintended side effects to others. For
example, separating business logic from database access layers makes
it easier to isolate issues and scale parts of the system independently.
Using service-oriented architecture (SOA) principles can further delin-
eate responsibilities and improve overall system robustness.

Regularly reviewing and updating dependencies is another essential
best practice. Supabase and other integrated libraries are subject
to frequent updates that address security vulnerabilities and performance improvements. Establishing a routine process for reviewing update logs and performing dependency audits can prevent exposure to
known vulnerabilities due to outdated libraries.

Furthermore, implement backup and recovery strategies from the on-
set. A robust backup system minimizes data loss and reduces downtime in the event of database corruption or accidental deletion. Su-

pabase offers automated backup solutions and point-in-time recovery options which should be configured according to your project's requirements. Regularly test these backup procedures to ensure that restoration processes are effective and timely.

Scalability also hinges on effective database indexing and query optimization. Continuous monitoring of query performance and periodic evaluation of index usage are essential. As data volume increases, query performance might degrade if indexes are not maintained appropriately. In this regard, use available monitoring tools to review query execution times and adapt indexes based on query patterns. Regular maintenance tasks, such as vacuuming the database and rebuilding indexes, can prevent performance degradation over time.

Error handling across all layers should not be an afterthought. Instead, establish a comprehensive error-handling strategy that categorizes errors into transient, critical, and user-related issues. Transient errors should trigger automatic retries, while critical errors must alert the operations team immediately. A structured error-handling policy ensures that operational disruptions are minimized and that error resolution follows a standardized process. This approach streamlines troubleshooting and aids in faster recovery in case of unexpected issues.

Finally, culture plays an important role in best practices. Encourage regular peer code reviews, team knowledge-sharing sessions, and retrospectives after each major deployment. Sharing insights about encountered issues and solutions contributes to a culture of continuous improvement, ensuring that the project setup remains robust and that lessons from past experiences are integrated into future deployments.

Adhering to these best practices—enforcing stringent security measures, planning for scalability from the early stages, implementing robust testing and logging, ensuring consistency across environments, maintaining documentation, and promoting proactive team collaboration—forms an indispensable foundation for a Supabase project. These practices not only streamline the setup process but also enable rapid troubleshooting and long-term sustainability, ensuring that the project remains secure, efficient, and capable of adapting to future growth and evolving technological demands.

Chapter 3

Database Management with Supabase

This chapter provides an in-depth guide to managing databases with Supabase, focusing on PostgreSQL. It covers table creation, data insertion and retrieval, and managing relationships with foreign keys. Topics include data validation, backup and recovery strategies, and query optimization techniques. Readers are equipped with essential skills to maintain data integrity, enhance database performance, and effectively utilize Supabase's robust database management capabilities.

3.1. Understanding Supabase's PostgreSQL Database

PostgreSQL serves as the foundation of Supabase's database management, providing a robust and feature-rich relational database system.

Its adherence to SQL standards, combined with extensibility and high performance, makes PostgreSQL an excellent choice for developers seeking scalability and reliability. Through Supabase, PostgreSQL is seamlessly integrated with modern development workflows, offering a layered abstraction that simplifies complex database interactions while still granting direct control over SQL.

PostgreSQL's mature ecosystem encompasses a range of advanced features such as support for JSON data types, full-text search, custom data types, and procedural languages. This spectrum of capabilities enables developers to design sophisticated data architectures and execute complex queries. When integrated with Supabase, these functionalities are further enhanced by real-time subscriptions, instant RESTful APIs, and a comprehensive suite of tools to manage authentication, storage, and functions—all built upon the underlying robustness of PostgreSQL.

At its core, PostgreSQL in Supabase promotes a strong emphasis on data integrity and consistency. With built-in support for ACID (Atomicity, Consistency, Isolation, Durability) properties, the database guarantees that transaction processing remains reliable even in high-concurrency scenarios. This is critical for applications where precision and correctness are paramount. The use of transactions further allows developers to execute grouped operations, ensuring that either all operations succeed or none do, preventing partial updates that could introduce data anomalies.

Developers benefit significantly from PostgreSQL's powerful indexing mechanisms and query optimization capabilities. These features enable rapid retrieval of data even as datasets scale. Supabase leverages PostgreSQL's sophisticated planner and optimizer to ensure that queries are executed in an efficient manner, reducing latency and resource consumption. This is particularly valuable for applications handling large volumes of data or requiring real-time reporting.

The integration of PostgreSQL within Supabase abstracts many complexities of database management. For instance, the automated generation of RESTful endpoints for each table simplifies data access. This approach removes the traditional barrier of having to manually configure API endpoints. A concise example of interacting with a table in Supabase is illustrated below:

```
SELECT * FROM users WHERE active = true ORDER BY created_at DESC;
```

This query takes advantage of PostgreSQL's SQL syntax and can be directly executed through the Supabase dashboard or via its API. The ability to seamlessly switch between direct SQL commands and high-level API calls exemplifies the flexible nature of the platform, allowing developers to adopt the approach that best fits their use-case.

A distinctive aspect of PostgreSQL as utilized by Supabase is its support for advanced data types and operators. JSONB is one such data type that has seen widespread adoption. It allows storing semi-structured data within a relational framework, enabling hybrid data models that combine traditional relational integrity with the flexibility of document storage. This is particularly useful when dealing with data that does not adhere strictly to a fixed schema. Developers can store and query JSONB data efficiently, mixing relational and document-oriented paradigms in a single system.

```
INSERT INTO orders (order_id, customer_details)
VALUES (101, '{"name": "Alice", "address": "123 Main St", "
    order_total": 49.99}'::jsonb);
```

The above example showcases how JSONB data can be inserted into a table, allowing for a blend of rigid structural integrity with flexible, nested data storage. As application requirements evolve, this blend is invaluable in absorbing schema changes and accommodating semi-structured data without significant reengineering.

Supabase's implementation also facilitates the use of real-time capabilities. PostgreSQL's logical replication and change data capture mechanisms are harnessed to provide a live feed of data modifications. This enables developers to build reactive applications where changes in the database immediately propagate to client interfaces. By combining PostgreSQL's reliability with Supabase's subscription-based APIs, developers can implement dashboards, monitoring solutions, and collaborative systems that remain updated without manual refreshes.

Performance tuning and query optimization in PostgreSQL are further bolstered by extensive tooling and administrative functions. The inclusion of EXPLAIN and EXPLAIN ANALYZE commands allows developers to inspect query plans and identify potential bottlenecks. Supabase integrates these capabilities into its monitoring tools, providing a layer of analysis that can guide performance improvements. For example, a developer troubleshooting a slow query might use:

```
EXPLAIN ANALYZE SELECT * FROM orders WHERE order_total > 100 ORDER BY
    created_at DESC;
```

Such diagnostics help in understanding the execution flow and resource utilization, ensuring that database operations are optimized for efficiency. This granular level of control is crucial for high-performance applications that must sustain large scales of operation.

Beyond performance and data integrity, PostgreSQL's extensibility accommodates custom functions and procedural languages such as PL/pgSQL. Supabase provides an accessible interface for managing these functions, allowing developers to encapsulate business logic within the database itself. This modular approach fosters maintainability and can reduce round-trip latency by processing data server-side. Custom functions are defined once and can be invoked repeatedly by various application components. An illustrative snippet is shown below:

```
CREATE OR REPLACE FUNCTION calculate_discount(total numeric)
```

94

```
RETURNS numeric AS $$
BEGIN
    RETURN total * 0.90;
END;
$$ LANGUAGE plpgsql;
```

This function encapsulates a simple discount calculation, promoting code reuse and ensuring that business rules remain consistent across different parts of an application. The capacity to integrate such procedural logic directly into the database environment exemplifies the deeper level of integration Supabase offers to developers.

Security remains a central concern in modern application design, and PostgreSQL's role within Supabase addresses this through fine-grained access control and robust authentication mechanisms. Role-based access control (RBAC) is implemented at the database level, ensuring that only authorized users or applications can perform specific operations. Supabase enhances this with additional security layers provided by its authentication services, which integrate seamlessly with PostgreSQL user management. The ability to define precise permission sets allows developers to enforce the principle of least privilege, mitigating potential security vulnerabilities.

Data integrity constraints such as primary keys, unique constraints, and foreign keys are native to PostgreSQL and are utilized extensively in Supabase. These constraints ensure consistency and prevent the introduction of invalid data across related tables. The enforcement of these rules at the database level eliminates much of the error handling that would otherwise be required at the application layer. For example, defining a foreign key constraint can be accomplished as follows:

```
ALTER TABLE orders
ADD CONSTRAINT fk_customer
FOREIGN KEY (customer_id) REFERENCES customers(id);
```

Such constraints ensure that relationships between tables remain valid, thereby supporting the integrity of complex data models. Efficient enforcement of these rules is vital in applications that require consistent transactional behavior across large datasets.

The synergy between PostgreSQL and Supabase is evident in the way it abstracts database complexities while exposing powerful features to developers. The platform's user-friendly dashboard, comprehensive documentation, and active community further extend the accessibility of advanced database management concepts. As developers gain proficiency in direct SQL operations, they can effortlessly transition to utilizing Supabase's high-level APIs to streamline development workflows.

Enhancing the developer experience is another demonstrable benefit of this integration. The reduction in boilerplate code and the abstraction of repetitive tasks accelerate productivity, allowing developers to focus on application-specific logic rather than on the intricacies of database management. Through a blend of automated API generation and direct SQL capabilities, Supabase ensures that both novice and experienced developers can harness the full potential of PostgreSQL without significant overhead.

The utilization of PostgreSQL's features within Supabase promotes a balanced development paradigm: one that leverages traditional relational databases' structured nature while incorporating modern development practices such as real-time data synchronization, API-first interactions, and scalable cloud deployments. This balance is particularly important for developers building cloud-native applications who require the reliability of established database systems together with the flexibility of modern development environments.

The deliberate integration of PostgreSQL into the Supabase stack allows developers to scale their applications horizontally while maintaining consistency and performance. By offloading heavy transactional operations to a robust database management system and concurrently utilizing Supabase's supportive ecosystem, developers can achieve optimal application performance. This approach minimizes downtime and resource contention, even as user demand increases and data volumes grow.

The comprehensive capabilities of PostgreSQL as implemented by Supabase also pave the way for future advancements. With the continuous evolution of both the PostgreSQL engine and Supabase's platform, developers can expect an expanding feature set, improved performance metrics, and enhanced security measures. This forward compatibility ensures that systems built today remain robust and scalable in the long term, even as requirements evolve.

The combination of PostgreSQL's reliability, scalability, and extensibility with Supabase's comprehensive toolset supports a wide range of application scenarios, from rapid prototyping to enterprise-level deployments. Developers are equipped with a foundation that not only meets current needs but is also prepared for future growth, ensuring sustained application performance and data integrity over time.

3.2. Creating and Managing Tables

In Supabase, table management is fundamental to structuring data effectively. Utilizing PostgreSQL as its underlying engine, Supabase enables developers to create, modify, and delete tables with a comprehensive set of SQL commands while automatically generating APIs to facilitate seamless data interactions. The process of managing tables starts with thoughtful schema design, ensuring that tables are constructed to support application requirements, maintain data integrity, and allow for future scalability.

The first step in table creation is to define the table structure using the `CREATE TABLE` statement. A well-designed table typically includes a unique identifier, concise column names, appropriate data types, and constraints that enforce business rules. For example, a simple table for storing user information might include a primary key, names, and timestamps for record management. The example below illustrates the creation of a basic table in Supabase:

```
CREATE TABLE users (
  id SERIAL PRIMARY KEY,
  username VARCHAR(50) NOT NULL UNIQUE,
  email VARCHAR(100) NOT NULL UNIQUE,
  active BOOLEAN DEFAULT true,
  created_at TIMESTAMP WITH TIME ZONE DEFAULT CURRENT_TIMESTAMP
);
```

This command establishes basic parameters such as the primary key id, unique constraints on username and email, and default values for the active and created_at fields. The careful selection of data types—such as SERIAL for auto-incrementing identifiers and VARCHAR for string-based content—provides the necessary balance between performance and flexibility.

Schema design principles are critical when managing tables. One principle is normalization, which involves structuring tables to minimize redundancy and dependency. By organizing data into discrete, related tables, developers can improve data integrity and reduce anomalies during data operations. For instance, separating user credentials from profile information or preferences can lead to a more maintainable schema in larger applications.

In addition to initial creation, modifications to table schemas are often required as application requirements evolve. Alterations can encompass adding new columns, modifying existing column types, and updating constraints. PostgreSQL provides the ALTER TABLE statement to manage these changes without disrupting active applications. For example, to add a new column for storing a user's biography, the following command is used:

```
ALTER TABLE users
ADD COLUMN bio TEXT;
```

This command adds a `bio` column of type `TEXT`, providing flexibility for storing longer form content. Schema modifications must be approached cautiously, particularly in live systems, to prevent data corruption or downtime. It is essential to consider the performance implications of altering large tables, and using transaction blocks can help ensure atomicity during schema changes.

Deleting tables is another aspect of table management. While the `DROP TABLE` statement can remove tables from the database, it should be executed with caution. Dropping a table eradicates all associated data and constraints, which can have significant consequences if performed accidentally. A controlled approach to table deletion might involve creating backup snapshots or validating that the table is no longer in use. An example command is shown below:

```
DROP TABLE IF EXISTS obsolete_data;
```

Utilizing the conditional clause `IF EXISTS` prevents errors if the table does not exist, assuring a smoother execution flow. In environments where multiple instances of the database are maintained, such as development and production, careful version control and review processes are necessary to synchronize schema changes across systems.

Effective table management also involves restructuring tables to optimize performance and data retrieval. Indexing is a powerful tool for enhancing query performance, particularly on columns frequently used in `WHERE` clauses or joins. PostgreSQL offers various index types including B-tree, hash, and GIN indexes. In Supabase, indexes can be created with SQL commands to significantly reduce response times. For example, indexing the `username` column in the users table can be performed as follows:

```
CREATE INDEX idx_username ON users(username);
```

Indexes can also be composite, spanning multiple columns, which is advantageous when combining search criteria. However, it is important to balance the performance benefit of indexes against the overhead during insert and update operations, as excessive indexing can slow down these processes.

Another critical aspect of managing tables is handling relationships between them. In relational databases, establishing foreign keys ensures referential integrity, meaning that relationships between tables are maintained correctly. When designing a schema, it is common to decompose data into related tables that can reference one another. For instance, consider a scenario where user activity logs are stored in a separate table linked to the users table. The following example demonstrates creating a table with a foreign key constraint:

```
CREATE TABLE activity_logs (
   log_id SERIAL PRIMARY KEY,
   user_id INT NOT NULL,
   activity TEXT NOT NULL,
   log_timestamp TIMESTAMP WITH TIME ZONE DEFAULT CURRENT_TIMESTAMP,
   CONSTRAINT fk_user FOREIGN KEY (user_id) REFERENCES users(id)
);
```

The foreign key constraint fk_user ensures that each log entry corresponds to a valid user, thereby maintaining the integrity of the relationship between the two tables. Such relational designs help in enforcing data consistency and facilitate complex queries that join data from multiple tables.

When managing tables, it is also pertinent to plan for future migrations and schema evolution. Tools that integrate with Supabase can assist in version-controlling schema changes, adopting practices such as incremental migrations. This method organizes modifications in a coherent sequence, ensuring that database versions remain consistent across different deployment environments. Developers often script these migrations to standardize updates and reduce manual errors. Automated migration frameworks not only allow smooth transitions but also provide rollback capabilities in case of issues, a vital capability in maintaining system stability.

In addition to creating, modifying, and deleting tables, developers must consider table maintenance operations. Routine tasks such as vacuuming, reindexing, and analyzing tables are essential for optimal performance, particularly as data volume grows. PostgreSQL's maintenance commands improve the health of the database by reclaiming storage and updating statistical information used by the query planner. Within Supabase, these operations may be scheduled automatically or executed manually as part of routine administration. For example, a manual vacuum command may be executed as follows:

```
VACUUM ANALYZE users;
```

This command reclaims disk space and optimizes the execution planning by refreshing data statistics. Regular maintenance is crucial for sustaining peak performance and ensuring that the database remains responsive under high load conditions.

Effective table management extends into considerations of security and access control. Supabase leverages PostgreSQL's role-based access control (RBAC) mechanisms to assign permissions to different users or applications. When tables hold sensitive or critical information, defining robust access controls prevents unauthorized modifications. This involves granting specific privileges, such as SELECT, INSERT, UPDATE, and DELETE, to roles. An example command to grant read access might be:

```
GRANT SELECT ON users TO readonly_user;
```

Such granular control fosters a secure environment by ensuring that each user or service only has the necessary privileges to perform its tasks. Coupled with Supabase's authentication and API management features, this approach significantly reduces the risk of unauthorized data access.

The integration of SQL command line operations with Supabase's intuitive dashboard further bridges the gap between traditional database administration and modern web applications. While direct SQL provides full control over table management processes, the graphical interface offers visualization of schema configurations, automated backup management, and monitoring tools. This duality supports both novice developers who may rely on intuitive interfaces and experienced professionals seeking direct command-line control.

Overall, the process of creating and managing tables in Supabase emphasizes sound schema design, the disciplined application of data integrity rules, and the judicious use of PostgreSQL's advanced features. These practices collectively ensure that the database layer remains robust, scalable, and secure. By combining rigorous schema planning with modern administrative tools, developers can create dynamic and high-performing backends that meet contemporary demands while remaining flexible for future growth.

Developers must continuously refine their approach to table management as both application requirements and database technologies evolve. Building a flexible, secure, and efficient schema forms the cornerstone of sustainable backend solutions. This understanding of table creation, modification, and deletion within Supabase lays a critical foundation for advanced data operations, ensuring consistency and reliability throughout the lifecycle of database applications.

3.3. Data Insertion and Retrieval

In Supabase, the processes of inserting and retrieving data are critical for interacting with the PostgreSQL backend. Developers can choose between executing direct SQL commands and leveraging Supabase's auto-generated RESTful APIs, both of which offer flexibility based on the application's requirements. Effective data manipulation is dependent on a proper understanding of the underlying SQL syntax, as well as the supplementary tools provided by Supabase, resulting in efficient, scalable, and secure operations.

Data insertion begins with constructing well-formed SQL INSERT statements. Traditionally, the INSERT statement is used to add one or more records to a table. The syntax allows developers to specify values explicitly, enforce constraints, and utilize default parameters. An archetypal example for inserting a new user into the users table is provided below:

```
INSERT INTO users (username, email, active)
VALUES ('jdoe', 'jdoe@example.com', true);
```

In this command, default values for columns such as created_at are automatically resolved by PostgreSQL. Developers must ensure that field values align with the data types defined in the schema, and that unique constraints or other validations are satisfied during insertion. Batched insertions can improve performance when processing large volumes of data, thereby reducing the overhead of multiple round-trip communications to the database server.

Several key considerations enhance reliable data insertion. Error handling, for example, is crucial when inserting data into tables that enforce constraints like unique keys or foreign keys. PostgreSQL provides mechanisms to catch exceptions during insertion, and Supabase's API layer further supports error reporting. In more refined use cases, the INSERT ... ON CONFLICT clause enables developers to handle duplicate key errors gracefully. The following example demonstrates how duplicate entries can be managed:

```
INSERT INTO users (username, email, active)
VALUES ('jdoe', 'jdoe@example.com', true)
ON CONFLICT (email)
DO UPDATE SET active = EXCLUDED.active;
```

This statement ensures that on encountering a duplicate email, the existing record is updated rather than generating an error, thus maintaining data consistency. Such conflict resolution strategies are essential in multi-user applications where concurrent data insertions may occur.

Supabase's API layer serves as an abstraction over these SQL commands. It allows developers to communicate with the PostgreSQL database using HTTP requests. The API exposes endpoints corresponding to database tables, enabling operations like data insertion without necessitating direct SQL command inputs. A common workflow involves sending a POST request to an endpoint to add new records. An illustrative example using JavaScript is given by:

```
const { data, error } = await supabase
  .from('users')
  .insert([
    { username: 'jdoe', email: 'jdoe@example.com', active: true }
  ]);
```

In the above snippet, the Supabase client library abstracts HTTP requests, returning the inserted data or an error object. This method significantly reduces the barrier for integrating database operations into web applications and mobile platforms, allowing developers to focus on front-end functionality while ensuring that backend operations remain secure and efficient.

Data retrieval in Supabase leverages both SQL queries and the RESTful API. Standard SQL SELECT statements remain a powerful and flexible method for querying data. These queries can be simple or elaborate, depending on application needs. For instance, retrieving all active users sorted by their creation timestamp can be achieved with the following command:

```
SELECT * FROM users
WHERE active = true
ORDER BY created_at DESC;
```

This query filters records based on the active status and orders the results, ensuring that the latest data is retrieved first. The ability to join tables, apply aggregation functions, and incorporate subqueries makes SQL a robust language for data retrieval even in complex database schemas. In scenarios where relationships are defined using foreign keys, developers can construct JOIN operations to consolidate data from multiple tables. For example, combining user details with their corresponding activity logs might be expressed as:

```
SELECT u.username, l.activity, l.log_timestamp
FROM users u
JOIN activity_logs l ON u.id = l.user_id
WHERE u.active = true
ORDER BY l.log_timestamp DESC;
```

Such queries form an integral part of building dynamic application functionalities, including dashboards, reporting tools, and real-time data displays.

The Supabase API also simplifies data retrieval by abstracting SQL query syntax into intuitive HTTP request parameters. Utilizing the API endpoint, the same data retrieval operation mentioned in the previous SQL command can be performed with structured GET requests. An example using JavaScript is illustrated below:

```
const { data, error } = await supabase
  .from('users')
  .select('*')
  .eq('active', true)
  .order('created_at', { ascending: false });
```

In this example, the select method specifies the columns to retrieve, while the eq and order methods filter and sort the data, respectively. The API syntax is closely aligned with the underlying SQL semantics, permitting developers to quickly translate their SQL-based knowledge into API calls without extensive retraining.

Advanced data retrieval techniques involve pagination, filtering, and conditional queries. When dealing with large datasets, pagination is essential to manage the volume of data returned by queries. Supabase's API supports methods to specify ranges of rows. For example, retrieving a specific range of rows might involve:

```
const { data, error } = await supabase
  .from('users')
  .select('*')
  .range(0, 9);  // Retrieves the first 10 rows
```

This method is particularly beneficial in web applications where user interfaces display data across multiple pages. Similarly, the API allows for sophisticated filtering using comparators such as gt (greater than) and lt (less than), empowering developers to construct nuanced queries without directly managing SQL syntax.

Ensuring that data insertion and retrieval operations are optimized for performance is another key aspect of database management. Performance considerations include the efficient use of indexes, query planning, and minimizing network latency. When inserting data, bulk operations are preferential over multiple single-row inserts as they reduce the number of round-trips to the database. In addition, retrieving only the necessary columns rather than using SELECT * can dramatically improve query performance by reducing the amount of data transmitted over the network.

Transaction management is also crucial when performing multiple related data operations. Transactions allow multiple commands to be executed as a single unit, ensuring that either all operations succeed or none do. This is particularly important when data consistency is paramount. The following example demonstrates a transaction block that ensures atomic operations for multiple insertions:

```
BEGIN;

INSERT INTO orders (order_id, customer_id, total)
VALUES (101, 1, 250.00);

INSERT INTO order_items (order_id, product_id, quantity)
```

```
VALUES (101, 5, 2);

COMMIT;
```

This transaction guarantees that either both the order and its corresponding items are inserted or, in the event of an error, neither operation is carried out. Supabase's integration of PostgreSQL allows developers to leverage such transaction controls, ensuring the integrity of complex, multi-step operations.

Developers also need to consider error handlings, such as handling exceptions in both direct SQL operations and API calls. In SQL, error handling can be implemented using EXCEPTION clauses within procedural languages like PL/pgSQL. For API operations in Supabase, error messages and status codes provide guidance for debugging and correcting issues. Incorporating rigorous error checking and logging mechanisms into both data insertion and retrieval routines is critical for building robust applications.

Furthermore, the combination of direct SQL and the Supabase API encourages developers to adopt a versatile approach. Advanced applications might use SQL procedures and functions for intensive data transformations, then expose these routines via endpoints in the API. This combination allows for the heavy lifting to be performed server-side, streamlining the client-side logic. The dual approach ensures that developers can optimize performance while maintaining clarity in the architecture.

Integrating data insertion and retrieval processes within a secure framework is also paramount. Supabase offers role-based access control (RBAC) and integrates authentication mechanisms to ensure that only authorized users can perform these operations. Appropriate permission levels must be granted for insertion, modification, and querying of data to provide a secure and stable environment for database interactions. For instance, a simple command to grant a restricted user access to retrieval operations without write privileges is illustrated by:

```
GRANT SELECT ON users TO readonly_user;
```

The grant command reinforces a security ethos by ensuring that only users with the proper credentials can execute specific operations, a critical detail in maintaining database integrity and reliability.

The strategic choice between native SQL commands and the API provided by Supabase can often be determined by the specific needs of an application. Direct SQL is ideal for developers well-versed with complex query operations and concerned with fine-tuning performance at a granular level. On the other hand, the Supabase API is tailored for rapid development by abstracting many complexities associated with data manipulation. This versatility allows projects of various scales to benefit from PostgreSQL's robust foundation while enjoying the streamlined development workflow that Supabase promotes.

By employing a systematic approach to data insertion and retrieval, developers can ensure that their application remains responsive even as data volume grows. Whether through direct SQL or the API, robust practices such as transaction management, efficient error handling, and appropriate indexing will sustain the performance and reliability of the backend. The interplay between carefully crafted queries and the conveniences provided by Supabase is a cornerstone of modern database management, enabling developers to build applications that are both highly functional and inherently secure.

This integrated approach to working with data, combining the precision of SQL with the abstraction of modern APIs, forms the basis of a scalable and maintainable backend architecture. The techniques and examples highlighted above provide a foundation upon which developers can construct powerful data-driven applications, ensuring that data flows reliably between the database and application components while maintaining optimal performance throughout the lifecycle of the project.

3.4. Using Relationships and Foreign Keys

Relational databases rely on relationships between tables to organize data in a structured and interconnected manner. In PostgreSQL, as implemented by Supabase, foreign keys serve as the primary mechanism to enforce referential integrity between different tables. They ensure that data remains consistent and that relationships are maintained accurately even as records are inserted, updated, or deleted. Establishing these relationships is a critical aspect of database design, and it is achieved through a careful definition of foreign key constraints, proper indexing, and the use of cascading rules.

Defining a foreign key involves specifying a column in one table that references the primary key (or a unique column) of another table. For example, when constructing a one-to-many relationship between a users table and an orders table, each order can be associated with a specific user by including a user_id column in the orders table that references the id column in the users table. The following SQL snippet demonstrates the creation of these tables with a foreign key relationship:

```
CREATE TABLE users (
  id SERIAL PRIMARY KEY,
  username VARCHAR(50) NOT NULL UNIQUE,
  email VARCHAR(100) NOT NULL UNIQUE,
  created_at TIMESTAMP WITH TIME ZONE DEFAULT CURRENT_TIMESTAMP
);

CREATE TABLE orders (
  order_id SERIAL PRIMARY KEY,
  user_id INT NOT NULL,
  total_amount NUMERIC(10,2) NOT NULL,
  order_date TIMESTAMP WITH TIME ZONE DEFAULT CURRENT_TIMESTAMP,
  CONSTRAINT fk_user
    FOREIGN KEY (user_id)
    REFERENCES users(id)
```

```
    ON DELETE CASCADE
    ON UPDATE CASCADE
);
```

In this example, the foreign key constraint fk_user in the orders table ensures that every order refers to a valid user from the users table. The use of ON DELETE CASCADE and ON UPDATE CASCADE facilitates the automatic propagation of deletions or updates from the parent table to the child table, thereby maintaining data consistency without requiring additional application logic.

Understanding the implications of cascading rules is essential. With ON DELETE CASCADE, when a record in the users table is removed, all corresponding records in the orders table are automatically deleted. This prevents orphan records from persisting in the database. Similarly, ON UPDATE CASCADE ensures that any change in the primary key value of a user is automatically reflected in the orders table. Such constraints not only simplify application development but also reduce the potential for human error when managing data relationships.

Foreign keys can also be applied in more complex scenarios, such as many-to-many relationships. In these cases, an additional junction table is introduced to effectively model the relationship. Consider a scenario where a system needs to track which users belong to multiple groups. A junction table, for instance, user_groups, can be constructed as follows:

```
CREATE TABLE groups (
  group_id SERIAL PRIMARY KEY,
  group_name VARCHAR(100) NOT NULL UNIQUE
);

CREATE TABLE user_groups (
  user_id INT NOT NULL,
  group_id INT NOT NULL,
  PRIMARY KEY (user_id, group_id),
  CONSTRAINT fk_user
    FOREIGN KEY (user_id)
    REFERENCES users(id)
```

```
    ON DELETE CASCADE,
  CONSTRAINT fk_group
    FOREIGN KEY (group_id)
    REFERENCES groups(group_id)
    ON DELETE CASCADE
);
```

Here, the user_groups table uses a composite primary key made up of the user_id and group_id columns. It contains two foreign key constraints, each ensuring that the entries correspond to valid records in the users and groups tables respectively. This pattern is common in relational designs for modeling many-to-many relationships and is particularly effective in preserving data integrity across interconnected entities.

Implementing self-referencing foreign keys can be useful in scenarios where table records have hierarchical relationships. For instance, consider a table that maintains a list of categories where each category may have a parent category. The SQL below demonstrates the creation of such a table:

```
CREATE TABLE categories (
  category_id SERIAL PRIMARY KEY,
  category_name VARCHAR(100) NOT NULL,
  parent_id INT,
  CONSTRAINT fk_parent
    FOREIGN KEY (parent_id)
    REFERENCES categories(category_id)
    ON DELETE SET NULL
);
```

The parent_id here is a foreign key that references category_id within the same table. The clause ON DELETE SET NULL ensures that if a parent category is deleted, the child categories are not deleted automatically; instead, the parent_id is set to NULL, thereby preserving the child records without a dangling reference.

Aside from establishing foreign key constraints during table creation, it is possible to add them later on using the ALTER TABLE command.

111

This flexibility is vital when modifying legacy databases or when relationships need to be defined after initial table creation. An illustrative
example of adding a foreign key to an existing table is:

```
ALTER TABLE orders
ADD CONSTRAINT fk_user
  FOREIGN KEY (user_id)
  REFERENCES users(id)
  ON DELETE CASCADE
  ON UPDATE CASCADE;
```

This command appends the foreign key constraint to the `orders` table,
ensuring that all future operations adhere to the established referential
integrity rules. Graphical interfaces provided by Supabase can also be
used to define and modify these constraints, thereby accommodating
developers who prefer visual tools over command-line operations.

The careful design of foreign key relationships is intertwined with
database normalization. Proper normalization eliminates data redundancy and ensures that each table represents a distinct entity. By de-
composing data into multiple related tables and linking them with foreign keys, developers can create a more flexible schema that supports
advanced queries while maintaining consistency. For example, storing customer data and order details in separate tables, then linking
them through a foreign key, avoids duplicative data entry and simplifies maintenance tasks.

Query optimization is another significant benefit derived from properly defined relationships. When tables are interconnected via indexed
foreign keys, the database query planner can execute join operations
more efficiently. A typical join query combining data from the `users`
and `orders` tables may appear as follows:

```
SELECT u.username, o.order_id, o.total_amount
FROM users u
JOIN orders o ON u.id = o.user_id
ORDER BY o.order_date DESC;
```

This query utilizes the foreign key relationship defined in the `orders` table to quickly correlate user data with their corresponding orders. Proper use of indexing on foreign key columns further accelerates such queries, making them suitable for high-traffic applications where performance is critical.

As application requirements evolve, it is essential to consider the impact of schema changes on existing relationships. When modifying a foreign key relationship, particularly in production environments, adopting incremental changes and performing thorough testing is crucial. Supabase provides migration tools that allow developers to version-control schema changes, ensuring that modifications to foreign key definitions do not disrupt ongoing operations. Incremental migrations facilitate the addition of new relationships or the alteration of cascading rules without risking data integrity.

It is also important to implement error handling and logging mechanisms when dealing with relational constraints. When inserting or updating records, violations of foreign key constraints can lead to errors that need to be captured and resolved gracefully. Supabase's monitoring tools and PostgreSQL logs can provide detailed insights into constraint violations, empowering developers to diagnose issues quickly. By proactively addressing these errors, engineers can design systems that maintain robust data integrity even in the face of complex transactional operations.

In scenarios involving high concurrency, the enforcement of foreign key constraints becomes critical. These constraints guarantee that simultaneous operations do not lead to data anomalies, thereby preventing potential conflicts that might otherwise arise from concurrent transactions. The consistency ensured by these constraints is indispensable for applications that process a large number of transactions, such as e-commerce platforms and social media applications.

Furthermore, it is common practice to periodically review and optimize foreign key constraints as part of routine database maintenance. Over time, as tables grow and usage patterns shift, reevaluating the need for cascading rules or updating indexes can lead to significant performance improvements. Routine analysis of query execution plans and database profiling can assist in identifying any inefficiencies related to foreign key constraints, allowing developers to take corrective actions as needed.

The combination of clear schema design, stringent enforcement of foreign keys, and the use of cascading options forms the backbone of a resilient relational database. Supabase, by integrating PostgreSQL's advanced constraint capabilities with a user-friendly interface, simplifies the task of managing complex relationships between data tables. The ability to define, modify, and optimize foreign key relationships ensures that applications built on this platform are both scalable and maintainable, safeguarding data consistency over time.

By leveraging these principles, developers can design databases that not only handle intricate relationships between data entities but also support robust query execution and high concurrency. The judicious use of foreign keys, as illustrated by the examples provided, enables the creation of interrelated tables that preserve data integrity, minimize redundancy, and allow for efficient retrieval of related data. Such a carefully constructed relational model ultimately leads to backend systems that respond reliably to both operational demands and future growth.

3.5. Implementing Data Validation and Constraints

Ensuring data quality and consistency is a foundational element of robust database design. In Supabase, which leverages PostgreSQL as its underlying database engine, a variety of constraints and validation mechanisms are available. These mechanisms enforce business rules at the database level, ensuring that only valid data is stored and that relationships between data remain intact. Using constraints—such as NOT NULL, UNIQUE, CHECK, and primary/foreign keys—in conjunction with custom validation rules, developers can drastically reduce erroneous inserts and updates, thereby safeguarding the integrity of the application data.

One of the simplest and most common constraints is the NOT NULL constraint. This constraint ensures that a column always contains a valid value and prevents the insertion of NULL where an actual value is required. For instance, when creating a table of user profiles, it may be essential that fields such as username and email are never left empty. The following SQL statement illustrates a practical implementation of such restrictions:

```
CREATE TABLE user_profiles (
  id SERIAL PRIMARY KEY,
  username VARCHAR(50) NOT NULL,
  email VARCHAR(100) NOT NULL,
  bio TEXT,
  created_at TIMESTAMP WITH TIME ZONE DEFAULT CURRENT_TIMESTAMP
);
```

The use of the NOT NULL constraint here ensures that every record in the user_profiles table will include a username and an email, reflecting a basic level of data validation at the schema level.

Beyond simple NOT NULL constraints, unique constraints are critical for enforcing data uniqueness across rows. They prevent duplication of values in columns that should remain distinct, such as email addresses or usernames. When these constraints are applied, the database automatically rejects any attempt to insert a duplicate value. The following example extends the previous table by adding a UNIQUE constraint on both the email and username columns:

```
CREATE TABLE user_profiles (
    id SERIAL PRIMARY KEY,
    username VARCHAR(50) NOT NULL UNIQUE,
    email VARCHAR(100) NOT NULL UNIQUE,
    bio TEXT,
    created_at TIMESTAMP WITH TIME ZONE DEFAULT CURRENT_TIMESTAMP
);
```

A further level of data validation is achieved through CHECK constraints. These allow developers to specify arbitrary logical conditions that stored data must satisfy. For example, a table storing product information might include a price field that must always be non-negative. This can be enforced as follows:

```
CREATE TABLE products (
    product_id SERIAL PRIMARY KEY,
    product_name VARCHAR(100) NOT NULL,
    price NUMERIC(10,2) NOT NULL,
    CONSTRAINT positive_price CHECK (price >= 0)
);
```

By incorporating a CHECK constraint, efforts to insert a negative price are blocked at the time of data entry, ensuring that the product data remains logically consistent.

In many cases, data validation requirements extend beyond what basic constraints can enforce. For instance, validating a specific format for an email address or ensuring that a date field adheres to a business rule may require more complex logic. PostgreSQL enables the creation of custom functions and triggers to handle such cases. A trigger can call a user-defined function to perform detailed validations before data is inserted or updated. The example below demonstrates the process of creating a trigger to enforce a specific email format using a regular

116

expression:

```
CREATE OR REPLACE FUNCTION validate_email_format()
RETURNS TRIGGER AS $$
BEGIN
  IF NEW.email NOT SIMILAR TO '%_(at)_%' THEN
    RAISE EXCEPTION 'Invalid email format: %', NEW.email;
  END IF;
  RETURN NEW;
END;
$$ LANGUAGE plpgsql;

CREATE TRIGGER email_format_trigger
BEFORE INSERT OR UPDATE ON user_profiles
FOR EACH ROW EXECUTE PROCEDURE validate_email_format();
```

In this example, the trigger `email_format_trigger` is invoked before any insertion or update on the `user_profiles` table. The associated function, `validate_email_format`, uses the SIMILAR TO operator to verify if the new email adheres to a simple pattern. Although this pattern is rudimentary, it exemplifies how custom validations can extend the capabilities of standard constraints.

Foreign key constraints also play a crucial role in data validation by maintaining referential integrity between related tables. These constraints ensure that relationships between data remain consistent, such as ensuring that every foreign key value in a child table corresponds to a primary key in a parent table. For example, suppose there is a table of orders linked to a table of customers. A foreign key constraint in the orders table ensures that each order references a valid customer:

```
CREATE TABLE customers (
  customer_id SERIAL PRIMARY KEY,
  customer_name VARCHAR(100) NOT NULL,
  email VARCHAR(100) NOT NULL UNIQUE
);

CREATE TABLE orders (
  order_id SERIAL PRIMARY KEY,
  customer_id INT NOT NULL,
  order_total NUMERIC(10,2) NOT NULL,
```

117

```
    order_date TIMESTAMP WITH TIME ZONE DEFAULT CURRENT_TIMESTAMP,
    CONSTRAINT fk_customer
      FOREIGN KEY (customer_id)
      REFERENCES customers(customer_id)
      ON DELETE CASCADE
);
```

In this schema, the fk_customer constraint guarantees that each record in the orders table is associated with an existing customer, thereby preventing the possibility of orphaned records.

Validation can also be implemented at the column level with default values. Defaults provide a fallback when no value is provided during the insertion of a record. This mechanism can be coupled with constraints to ensure that even automatically applied values meet the business rules. For example, a creation timestamp that defaults to the current time ensures that every record has a valid timestamp:

```
CREATE TABLE transactions (
    transaction_id SERIAL PRIMARY KEY,
    amount NUMERIC(10,2) NOT NULL CHECK (amount > 0),
    transaction_date TIMESTAMP WITH TIME ZONE DEFAULT CURRENT_TIMESTAMP
);
```

This statement enforces two validations: the CHECK constraint ensures a positive transaction amount, and the default value provides a consistent way to record time-related data without requiring explicit input.

In addition to the built-in constraint types, PostgreSQL supports complex data validations through domain definitions. Domains allow developers to create user-defined data types with inherent constraints. This approach centralizes validation logic that can be reused across multiple tables. For example, suppose a system requires that phone numbers adhere to a specific numeric pattern. A domain can be created to encapsulate this requirement:

```
CREATE DOMAIN phone_number AS VARCHAR(15)
    CONSTRAINT valid_phone CHECK (VALUE ~ '^\+?[0-9]{10,15}$');

CREATE TABLE contacts (
```

118

```
contact_id SERIAL PRIMARY KEY,
name VARCHAR(100) NOT NULL,
phone phone_number NOT NULL
);
```

Using a domain in this manner not only enforces validation but also promotes consistency across tables that require similar formats.

Another advanced validation technique involves the use of triggers to perform cross-field validations or enforce business logic that spans multiple columns. For example, suppose a table records discount information where the discount value must not exceed the order total. A trigger can verify this condition before data manipulation:

```
CREATE OR REPLACE FUNCTION check_discount()
RETURNS TRIGGER AS $$
BEGIN
  IF NEW.discount > NEW.order_total THEN
    RAISE EXCEPTION 'Discount cannot exceed the order total';
  END IF;
  RETURN NEW;
END;
$$ LANGUAGE plpgsql;

CREATE TRIGGER discount_check_trigger
BEFORE INSERT OR UPDATE ON orders
FOR EACH ROW EXECUTE PROCEDURE check_discount();
```

In this scenario, the function check_discount ensures that the discount applied in an order does not surpass the total value of the order. Employing such triggers offloads complex validations from the application layer to the database, thereby consolidating logic and reducing potential points of failure.

Implementing data validation and constraints not only enhances data quality but also aids in performance optimization. By filtering out invalid data at the time of insertion, subsequent queries run on the assumption that data adheres to the defined business rules, thereby simplifying query logic and reducing runtime errors. Moreover, constraints enable faster error detection during data operations, allowing

119

developers to address inconsistencies immediately rather than encountering issues further downstream in the application.

It is important to note that while constraints and validations significantly contribute to data integrity, they must be carefully designed and tested during the development phase. Changes to constraints, such as modifying a CHECK condition or altering a default value, should be approached through version-controlled migrations to ensure that such modifications do not inadvertently affect existing data or impact performance negatively.

Supabase's platform, with its integration of PostgreSQL's robust constraint system, enables a comprehensive approach to data governance. Developers benefit from a range of built-in validations that can be extended via custom functions and triggers, ensuring that both simple field-level validations and complex business rules are enforced uniformly at the database level. As applications scale and evolve, maintaining a rigorous validation framework becomes even more critical, as it provides assurance that the data repository remains consistent, reliable, and resistant to anomalies.

By integrating a broad spectrum of data validations—from basic NOT NULL and UNIQUE constraints to sophisticated triggers and domain-specific checks—database designers can create systems that not only ensure high data quality but also facilitate easier maintenance and improved performance. These techniques form an integral part of any scalable backend architecture, underlining the importance of embedding data integrity measures within the database system itself.

3.6. Database Backup and Recovery

Ensuring the availability and integrity of data is critical for any application, and a comprehensive backup and recovery strategy is essential for mitigating the risks of data loss. In Supabase, which employs PostgreSQL as its underlying database engine, several methods are available for creating consistent backups and restoring data when necessary. This section outlines strategies for backing up your Supabase database and discusses methodologies for recovering data in the event of failure, drawing from both native PostgreSQL tools and the features provided by Supabase.

A primary approach to database backup in PostgreSQL is the use of pg_dump and pg_restore utilities. The pg_dump tool creates a logical backup by exporting SQL commands that can be executed to recreate the database schema and data. This method is especially useful for continuous integration environments and development scenarios where portability is a key concern. For example, a command to back up a database using pg_dump might be executed from the command line as follows:

```
pg_dump -h your_host -U your_username -d your_database -F c -b -v -f
    "backup_file.backup"
```

In this command, the option -F c designates the custom archive format, which allows for compression and increased flexibility during restoration. The -b flag indicates that large objects will be included, while -v produces verbose output, offering insights into the backup process. This approach produces a backup file that can later be restored using pg_restore, as illustrated below:

```
pg_restore -h your_host -U your_username -d your_database -v "
    backup_file.backup"
```

In production environments, regular backups are vital. Administrators often employ automated scripts and cron jobs to schedule backups during periods of low activity. Supabase usually manages such backup tasks automatically on the infrastructure side; however, understanding these native tools is beneficial for cases where custom backup routines or additional safeguard measures are required.

For situations where a rapid recovery is necessary, point-in-time recovery (PITR) offers the capability to restore the database state to a specific moment. PostgreSQL supports PITR through a combination of base backups and continuous archiving of the write-ahead log (WAL). By archiving WAL files, it is possible to replay transactions following a base backup to reach a desired state. The setup typically involves configuring the `archive_mode` and `archive_command` parameters in the PostgreSQL configuration file. An example configuration might include:

```
archive_mode = on
archive_command = 'cp %p /path_to_wal_archive/%f'
```

Using such configurations, database administrators can execute a recovery that replays archived WAL files starting from the time of the base backup. Although Supabase abstracts much of the low-level configuration, having an understanding of these techniques is critical for designing systems that require minimal downtime during disaster recovery.

In addition to native PostgreSQL utilities, Supabase provides a user-friendly dashboard that simplifies many backup operations. The dashboard may offer scheduled and on-demand backups, allowing developers to export the entire database or specific schemas in an automated fashion. This feature is particularly useful for teams that prefer a graphical interface over command-line interactions. Data migration tools integrated into Supabase also support backup and restore workflows, ensuring that backup policies adhere to best practices.

Backup strategies should also account for incremental backups, which capture only the changes made since the last full backup. Incremental backups reduce the volume of data transferred and stored, providing efficiency and cost-effectiveness, especially in environments with large datasets. While PostgreSQL does not explicitly support incremental logical backups via `pg_dump`, physical backups performed via file system-level tools or replication setups can achieve similar goals. In scenarios where incremental backups are essential, administrators might employ third-party tools that integrate with PostgreSQL's physical backup capabilities.

High availability and disaster recovery architectures can further benefit from replication setups. Supabase leverages PostgreSQL's streaming replication to maintain standby databases that can serve read-only queries and, if necessary, be promoted to primary in the event of a failure. Replication ensures that a recent copy of the data is available across different regions or servers, offering protection against catastrophic failures. Configuring replication typically involves setting up a primary server and one or more standby replicas. The configuration on the primary server might include parameters such as:

```
wal_level = replica
max_wal_senders = 5
hot_standby = on
```

Standby servers connect to the primary and continuously apply changes from the WAL. In the event that the primary server becomes unavailable, a standby can assume its role through a controlled failover process. This strategy not only minimizes downtime but also ensures that backup and recovery processes do not interrupt user operations.

When recovering from a failure, in addition to restoring data from a recent backup or switching to a standby replica, it is crucial to verify the integrity of the restored data. Validation steps, such as running consistency checks or using checksums, can confirm that the backup restoration was successful and that no corruption occurred during the backup process. PostgreSQL provides several internal tools to validate database integrity, and these can be supplemented by application-level tests to ensure that business logic remains intact.

It is advisable to maintain backup logs and metadata that record the time of backup, backup size, and any errors encountered during the process. Such metadata facilitates troubleshooting in cases where restoration issues arise and helps in auditing data recovery practices. Database administrators should also consider retention policies for backup files. Storing backups indefinitely is impractical due to storage constraints and the increased risk of data breaches. Instead, a rolling backup strategy that retains backups for a predetermined period ensures that restoration points are available while managing storage costs.

Another essential aspect of backup and recovery is testing the restoration process periodically. Regularly scheduled recovery drills allow teams to verify that backup files are intact and that restoration procedures can be executed within acceptable recovery time objectives (RTOs). These tests should simulate various failure scenarios, including partial data loss and corruption, to ensure that the recovery process is robust and that personnel are familiar with their roles during an actual disaster.

In scenarios involving large-scale data migrations or structural changes to the database, performing a full backup before initiating changes is critical. This precautionary measure enables the rollback of the entire system to a known good state if the migration fails or introduces unforeseen complications. Automated migration tools often incorporate pre-migration backup capabilities, creating snapshots that serve as checkpoints throughout the development cycle.

Security considerations are also paramount in backup and recovery strategies. Backup files contain sensitive information and must be protected from unauthorized access. Encrypting backup files both in transit and at rest is a recommended practice. PostgreSQL supports encryption at various levels, and external tools or cloud services can be employed to ensure that backup data remains secure. Access control should be enforced on backup storage endpoints, and audit trails should be maintained to monitor any access to these files.

Moreover, integrating backup strategies with cloud storage solutions can offer additional layers of redundancy. Many cloud providers offer specialized services for automated backups and geographically distributed storage, reducing the risk of data loss due to localized failures. Supabase, operating in a cloud-centric environment, benefits from such distributed backup strategies by ensuring that even in the event of regional outages, data remains safe and recoverable.

Investment in comprehensive backup and recovery strategies ultimately pays dividends in the form of enhanced system resilience and data reliability. The blending of native PostgreSQL tools with the streamlined processes available through Supabase allows developers to establish an environment where data loss is minimized, and recovery times are within acceptable limits. The combination of scheduled backups, replication, point-in-time recovery, and rigorous testing forms a layered defense against data loss incidents.

Developers and database administrators must collaborate to tailor backup and recovery policies to the specific needs of their applications, balancing operational overhead against acceptable risk levels. Detailed documentation of processes, regular review of backup logs, and continuous improvement initiatives are integral to maintaining a resilient database environment. As data volumes grow and application architectures become more complex, evolving backup strategies will remain a cornerstone of system reliability and business continuity.

3.7. Efficient Query Optimization

Query performance is a critical factor in ensuring that applications built on Supabase remain responsive and scalable. Optimizing SQL queries involves a multifaceted approach that touches on database schema design, indexing strategies, query rewriting, and the use of analytical tools provided by PostgreSQL. Fine-tuning queries not only reduces response times, but it also minimizes resource consumption and enhances overall system throughput.

At the foundation of query optimization is the proper design of the database schema. Normalization reduces data redundancy and ensures that each piece of information is stored only once. However, over-normalization can lead to complex joins that might slow down query performance. A balanced approach, often supported by denormalization in high-read scenarios, can reduce join complexity and improve query response times. Schema design should also consider the types of queries most frequently executed. For tables subjected to heavy read operations, implementing appropriate indexes on frequently filtered columns can significantly speed up data retrieval.

Indexes are perhaps the most powerful tool in the arsenal of query optimization. PostgreSQL supports various index types, including B-tree, hash, GIN, and GiST indexes, each suited to different query patterns. For instance, B-tree indexes are effective for range queries and equality searches, while GiST indexes are useful for spatial data and full-text search. Creating an index is straightforward; below is an example of creating a B-tree index on a column often used in filters:

```
CREATE INDEX idx_users_email ON users(email);
```

While indexes can dramatically improve read performance, they also incur overhead for write operations such as inserts, updates, and deletes. The design of an indexing strategy should take into account the read-write balance. Often, composite indexes (covering multiple columns) are beneficial when queries filter using multiple criteria. It is important to periodically review and adjust indexes based on query patterns and execution plans.

Analyzing and understanding the query execution plan is crucial for identifying bottlenecks. PostgreSQL provides the EXPLAIN and EXPLAIN ANALYZE commands for this purpose. These commands output the query plan detailing how the database planner intends to execute a query, including join methods, index usage, and estimated cost. For example, the following command provides insights into a complex join query:

```
EXPLAIN ANALYZE
SELECT u.username, o.order_id, o.total_amount
FROM users u
JOIN orders o ON u.id = o.user_id
WHERE u.active = true
ORDER BY o.order_date DESC;
```

Reviewing the output from EXPLAIN ANALYZE can reveal if indexes are being utilized effectively, or if sequential scans and nested loops are introducing inefficiencies. Rewriting queries based on these insights can often result in substantial performance gains. For instance, if the query planner chooses a sequential scan because of missing indexes, adding the appropriate index may change the plan to utilize an index scan, thus reducing latency.

Query rewriting is an essential technique in optimization. Often, the performance of a query can be improved by reordering join operations, replacing subqueries with joins, and limiting the amount of data processed by using more selective WHERE clauses. Consider a scenario where an application needs to retrieve details for active users, but the initial query employs an inefficient subquery. Transforming the subquery into a join, as demonstrated below, can lead to performance improvements:

```
-- Inefficient query using a subquery
SELECT u.username, u.email
FROM users u
WHERE u.id IN (
    SELECT user_id FROM orders WHERE total_amount > 100
);
```

127

```
-- Optimized query using a join
SELECT DISTINCT u.username, u.email
FROM users u
JOIN orders o ON u.id = o.user_id
WHERE o.total_amount > 100;
```

In this example, converting the subquery into a join not only simplifies the query structure but also allows PostgreSQL to leverage indexing on the join columns, thereby enhancing query execution speed.

Another technique for optimizing queries is to limit the amount of data returned by the query. This can be achieved through the use of the LIMIT clause, selecting only necessary columns rather than using SELECT *, and applying more restrictive filters. For instance, if an application displays only a subset of columns to end users, specifying only those columns in the select statement reduces the overhead of data transfer and processing:

```
SELECT username, email
FROM users
WHERE active = true
LIMIT 50;
```

Restricting the number of rows processed in the query plan is particularly important in large datasets. Pagination, implemented with the LIMIT and OFFSET clauses, allows efficient loading of data in manageable chunks rather than overwhelming the system with large result sets.

Advanced techniques include the use of materialized views to improve query performance for complex and frequently executed queries. A materialized view stores the result of a query physically and can be refreshed periodically. This is beneficial when the underlying data is mostly static or when immediate data consistency is not critical. An example of creating a materialized view is as follows:

```
CREATE MATERIALIZED VIEW active_users_summary AS
SELECT u.id, u.username, COUNT(o.order_id) AS order_count
FROM users u
```

```
JOIN orders o ON u.id = o.user_id
WHERE u.active = true
GROUP BY u.id, u.username;
```

Materialized views reduce the computational load on the database during peak times by serving precomputed results, though they require a refresh mechanism to ensure that data remains current with underlying tables.

Query optimization also involves judicious use of caching mechanisms. PostgreSQL benefits from an internal cache that stores frequently accessed data pages, but application-level caching can further reduce the frequency of database hits. Supabase's API layer sometimes incorporates cache controls that can be tailored to application needs. Implementing caching strategies at the application layer, such as using Redis or in-memory caches, is especially useful in scenarios where the underlying data does not change frequently.

Additionally, database parameter tuning should not be overlooked. Configuration parameters such as `work_mem`, `shared_buffers`, and `effective_cache_size` influence the performance of query execution plans. Adjusting these parameters based on workload characteristics can offer improvements in join operations, sorting, and other in-memory operations. For instance, increasing `work_mem` allows larger sorts to happen in memory rather than spilling to disk, which can reduce query execution times for complex operations.

It is also beneficial to regularly monitor system performance and query execution metrics. Tools integrated within Supabase and external monitoring solutions can provide real-time insights into query performance. Regular analysis of slow queries, log files, and system health metrics can help preempt performance degradation. By identifying trends and recurring bottlenecks, developers can proactively refine queries and adjust database configurations before they impact the end-user experience.

Optimizing queries is an iterative process that benefits from a constant review of workload changes and evolving data patterns. As user bases grow and new features are deployed, existing queries might need to be recalibrated to maintain performance. Employing a robust version control system for schema and query changes, coupled with automated testing for performance benchmarks, helps ensure that optimizations remain effective over time.

In complex systems where multiple factors contribute to query performance, it is essential to combine several optimization strategies. This holistic approach may involve reconfiguring indexes, rewriting queries, adjusting system parameters, and implementing caching, all while monitoring performance with detailed metrics. The nuanced understanding of query plans provided by PostgreSQL's diagnostic tools empowers developers to make data-driven decisions on optimization measures, resulting in a system that responds quickly under varying loads.

Efficient query optimization in Supabase is achieved through a combination of sound database design, strategic indexing, careful query rewriting, and proactive system monitoring. By leveraging tools such as EXPLAIN ANALYZE, constructing materialized views, and tuning system parameters, developers can significantly reduce response times and enhance the performance of their applications. A proactive, iterative approach to optimization allows for continuous improvement, ensuring that the database remains capable of handling high volumes of data with minimal latency. This dedication to performance not only benefits the application in terms of speed and scalability but also contributes to a smoother and more reliable user experience over time.

Chapter 4

Authentication and User Management

This chapter explores the setup and management of user authentication using Supabase, detailing account management, password recovery, and third-party integrations. It covers implementing role-based access control and securing data transmission. By emphasizing best practices, readers gain insights into effectively managing user profiles and ensuring secure and efficient user interactions within their applications, leveraging Supabase's comprehensive authentication features.

4.1. Authentication Concepts in Supabase

Supabase leverages a robust authentication system that integrates tightly with PostgreSQL to provide secure and scalable user verification mechanisms. The system is designed to establish trust between the client application and the backend through proven industry standards such as JWT (JSON Web Tokens), secure session management, and fine-grained access control policies. In this section, we explore the conceptual underpinnings of Supabase's authentication model and how these enhance overall security in modern application development.

At the core of Supabase's authentication system is the use of JWTs, which encapsulate user identity and claims in a cryptographically signed token. This approach allows client-side applications to authenticate by presenting tokens that the backend server validates without necessitating stateful session management on the server side. The use of tokens reduces latency and simplifies horizontal scaling. On the server side, token validation is performed by verifying the signature against a known secret or public key, ensuring that tokens have not been tampered with. This design supports distributed systems in which each service can independently verify the authenticity of the token. The following code snippet demonstrates how one might validate a JWT in a server-side script:

```
const jwt = require('jsonwebtoken');
const secret = process.env.JWT_SECRET;

function verifyToken(token) {
    try {
        const decoded = jwt.verify(token, secret);
        return decoded;
    } catch (error) {
        console.error('Invalid JWT:', error);
        return null;
    }
}
// Example token usage
const userData = verifyToken(receivedToken);
```

Supabase's user management system extends this basic token mechanism by incorporating additional layers of security such as secure password storage and the use of multi-factor authentication (MFA). Passwords are stored using adaptive, slow-hashing algorithms which are designed to withstand brute-force attacks. The system typically uses bcrypt, argon2, or a similarly resilient algorithm to hash passwords along with a unique salt for each user, drastically reducing the risk of password reuse attacks. In addition, Supabase supports the option to enable MFA, which adds an extra verification step beyond the standard username and password combination. This additional step forces an attacker to overcome another barrier even if the primary credentials are compromised.

Another important aspect of Supabase's authentication model is its reliance on Role-Level Security (RLS) policies within PostgreSQL. By integrating RLS, developers can define and enforce policies that restrict data access based directly on the authenticated user's attributes. These policies are created in SQL and leverage JWT claims to match the user's identity against database records. This integration ensures that even if a malicious request bypasses application-level checks, the underlying database enforces security constraints. The following example illustrates how a policy might be defined to restrict access to a user's own data:

```
CREATE POLICY "Users can access their own profiles"
ON user_profiles
FOR SELECT
USING (id = auth.uid());
```

Incorporating RLS policies reduces the potential attack surface by ensuring that the database itself becomes a primary gatekeeper for access control. This approach minimizes the reliance on application logic for enforcing security policies, thereby creating an additional layer of defense. RLS is particularly effective in environments where multiple users interact with the same set of data, as it provides a consistent and enforceable security model across complex relationship structures.

Supabase also supports external authentication providers as part of its broader authentication concept, enabling developers to offer multiple methods of identity verification. Integration with third-party providers such as Google, Facebook, GitHub, and others is facilitated through OAuth 2.0 protocols, which standardize the process for authorization across varied platforms. These integrations allow users to authenticate using credentials from an already secure and established identity provider, thereby leveraging the robust security mechanisms of those providers. This reduces friction for users and improves overall security by delegating a portion of the authentication process to specialists in identity management.

When integrating third-party authentication, the system typically issues a JWT that contains claims populated by the external provider. The claims may include user identifiers, roles, and permissions that are then used throughout the application. The integration process involves careful configuration to ensure that the data received is trusted and that tokens are correctly validated. The following code example, demonstrated using a Node.js framework, illustrates a basic approach to exchange OAuth tokens for a local JWT:

```
const axios = require('axios');
const jwt = require('jsonwebtoken');

async function exchangeOAuthToken(oauthToken) {
    // Validate and get user info from the external provider
    const response = await axios.get('https://provider.com/userinfo',
      {
        headers: { 'Authorization': `Bearer ${oauthToken}` }
    });
    const userInfo = response.data;

    // Create a local JWT with retrieved user info
    const localToken = jwt.sign({
        id: userInfo.id,
        email: userInfo.email,
        role: 'user'
    }, process.env.JWT_SECRET, { expiresIn: '1h' });

    return localToken;
}
```

The design of Supabase's authentication services emphasizes modularity and resilience. By decoupling the authentication logic from the application code, the Supabase framework allows developers to focus on business logic with the confidence that security controls are managed consistently across all access points. In addition, asynchronous verification and renewal of tokens ensure that sessions remain active only for the duration necessary, with minimal delay in response times when tokens are refreshed or invalidated.

Securing data transmission is another critical component of the authentication process. Supabase enforces SSL/TLS protocols for all client-server communications, thereby protecting login credentials and sensitive user information from interception and man-in-the-middle attacks. The framework encourages developers to adopt secure coding practices such as parameterized queries and proper error handling to mitigate vulnerabilities like SQL injection or cross-site scripting (XSS). Implementing these practices alongside the built-in authentication mechanisms creates a comprehensive security posture.

The emphasis on secure session management also intersects with considerations of token revocation and expiration. Tokens are designed with an expiration time that limits the duration of an authenticated session, reducing the window of opportunity for potential attackers. Developers are encouraged to implement token refresh mechanisms and to store tokens securely on the client side. Moreover, the ability to revoke tokens remotely allows administrators to immediately disable user access if a breach is detected, thereby containing potential damage swiftly.

Supabase supports a seamless developer experience by offering comprehensive configuration options via both the web-based dashboard and command-line interfaces. Developers can quickly enable or disable various authentication features and inspect logs to determine if unusual activity is occurring. These capabilities are complemented by extensive documentation and integration with development frameworks, which further simplifies the adoption of best practices in application security. The following example illustrates the configuration settings for setting a token expiry limit in a Supabase project:

```
ALTER SYSTEM SET auth.jwt_expiry = '3600'; -- Set token expiry to 1
    hour
SELECT pg_reload_conf();
```

This structured approach to configuration ensures that developers can adjust security parameters to align with the specific requirements of their applications. A critical aspect of the authentication mechanisms is also the logging and monitoring capabilities provided by Supabase. Detailed audit logs help track authentication attempts, token issuance, and password recovery events. This record-keeping facilitates quick identification and remediation of anomalous activities, which is essential for maintaining compliance with regulatory standards and internal security policies.

The integration of diverse authentication concepts in Supabase not only reinforces user data protection but also aids in delineating the boundaries between various components in a microservices architecture. By relying on well-defined JWT claims and database-level security policies, applications gain an inherent ability to partition access based on the principle of least privilege. This segmentation becomes pivotal in environments where services require isolation to prevent lateral movement in case of a breach.

The conceptual coherence of Supabase's authentication model rests on a balance between flexibility and security. The system is designed to accommodate varying authentication workflows ranging from traditional email and password verification to federated identity solutions. Such flexibility ensures that applications can evolve without compromising on security, whether deploying new authentication methods or integrating additional identity providers as user requirements change. The inherent adaptability of the model furthers its utility in dynamic, real-world scenarios where security must be both proactive and responsive to emerging threats.

Overall, the design choices employed by Supabase's authentication implementation underscore a commitment to secure-by-design principles. The utilization of cryptographic tokens, adaptive hashing, role-based access control, and encrypted data exchanges collectively form a robust solution that addresses the multifaceted challenges of modern authentication. This architecture serves as a key building block in the broader ecosystem of scalable backend solutions, ensuring that user interactions remain both efficient and secure.

4.2. Setting Up User Authentication

Setting up user authentication in Supabase is a structured process that involves configuring the Supabase project, adjusting settings in the Supabase dashboard, and integrating client-side code with the backend. The process begins by creating and initializing a project in the Supabase dashboard. Once the project is created, developers have access to a suite of authentication tools that include pre-configured parameters for JWT tokens, secure password handling, and options for third-party provider integrations. Each step of this guide details the configuration of authentication and illustrates how to integrate the authentication flow into an application.

The initial step is to create a Supabase project, which is performed via the Supabase dashboard. Upon project creation, Supabase automatically configures an authentication container that includes several key components such as API keys, token expiry settings, and callback URLs. Within the dashboard, the authentication settings panel gives developers the ability to enable or disable various authentication op-

137

tions including email and password authentication, magic links, and OAuth-based sign-in. In many cases, the default settings are adequate for development, but customization may be required for production-level applications to enforce stricter security policies. The dashboard also provides a logging section which tracks authentication events, aiding in debugging and monitoring.

Following project initialization, it is essential to configure environment variables in the client-side application. These variables, such as the Supabase URL and PUBLIC API key, are necessary for secure communication between the client and the backend. For example, in a JavaScript application, the configuration is established by importing the Supabase client library and initializing it with the project credentials as shown in the following snippet:

```
import { createClient } from '@supabase/supabase-js';

const supabaseUrl = process.env.SUPABASE_URL;
const supabaseKey = process.env.SUPABASE_ANON_KEY;
const supabase = createClient(supabaseUrl, supabaseKey);
```

Once the client library is properly initialized, developers can proceed to implement sign-up and sign-in functionalities. The Supabase API provides a straightforward interface for user management. For instance, to create a new user with email and password authentication, a simple call to the provided function is sufficient. The following example demonstrates how to register a new user:

```
async function signUpUser(email, password) {
    const { user, error } = await supabase.auth.signUp({ email,
    password });
    if (error) {
        console.error("Registration error:", error.message);
    } else {
        console.log("User registered successfully:", user);
    }
}
```

Similarly, for signing in an existing user, the authentication API ac-

138

cepts email and password credentials and returns a session object upon
successful validation:

```
async function signInUser(email, password) {
    const { user, error } = await supabase.auth.signIn({ email,
    password });
    if (error) {
        console.error("Sign-in error:", error.message);
    } else {
        console.log("User signed in:", user);
    }
}
```

Beyond basic sign-in and registration, Supabase also supports advanced features such as magic links, social logins, and multi-factor authentication. Developer requirements may dictate the need to enable
one or more of these methods. For instance, enabling magic links facilitates passwordless sign-ins, a technique that enhances security by limiting the use of static passwords. The selected authentication method
is configured by toggling the appropriate options in the Supabase dashboard. Once enabled, the API adapts to support the chosen method; for
example, initiating a magic link sign-in flow is as simple as invoking the
corresponding function with the user's email address.

During configuration, it is crucial to manage additional settings that
affect token validity and session management. The authentication
tokens—generally implemented as JWTs—include parameters such as
expiration time. This time limit determines how long a session remains
valid before the user must reauthenticate. Adjusting token expiry settings is accomplished through direct queries to the Supabase database
configuration as demonstrated below:

```
ALTER SYSTEM SET auth.jwt_expiry = '3600'; -- Set token expiry to 1
    hour
SELECT pg_reload_conf();
```

Developers should also consider configuring callback URLs for successful sign-ins or special events such as password resets. Callback

URLs are registered in the project settings on the Supabase dashboard and ensure that users are redirected appropriately after authentication events. Such configuration is particularly useful in single-page applications where state preservation across routes is necessary.

An integral aspect of setting up authentication involves testing the configuration in both development and staging environments. Utilizing logging directly from Supabase's authentication system provides insights into token issuance, expiration events, and potential error messages. The audit logs available in the Supabase dashboard facilitate the identification of vulnerabilities or misconfigurations by recording every authentication attempt. Developers can simulate sign-up and sign-in events locally and check the logs to validate that the process is secure and performing optimally.

Integration with modern development workflows often requires connecting the Supabase authentication system with front-end frameworks. In a React application, for example, the use of hooks may simplify handling authentication state. The state management logic encapsulates whether a user is logged in, and updates are triggered on token renewal or user sign-out. The following code snippet illustrates the use of a custom React hook to manage authentication state:

```
import { useState, useEffect } from 'react';
import { supabase } from './supabaseClient';

function useAuth() {
    const [user, setUser] = useState(null);

    useEffect(() => {
        const session = supabase.auth.session();
        setUser(session ? session.user : null);

        const { data: listener } = supabase.auth.onAuthStateChange((
        event, session) => {
            setUser(session ? session.user : null);
        });

        return () => {
            listener.unsubscribe();
```

```
        };
    }, []);

    return { user };
}

export default useAuth;
```

Enhancing the user experience further, error handling should be integrated throughout the authentication process. By capturing specific error codes returned from the Supabase API, developers can prompt users with precise feedback. Better error handling not only improves usability but also contributes to enhanced security by discouraging brute-force and credential stuffing attacks through the application of rate limiting or temporary lock-out mechanisms.

In addition to implementing the basic authentication methods, configuring security-related middleware can add another layer of protection. Developers are encouraged to implement interceptors that verify the authenticity of a user session before sensitive API calls are executed. This can be accomplished by setting up endpoint guards, which ensure that only requests containing a valid JWT are processed. The following pseudo-code depicts the logic of an endpoint guard in a middleware function:

```
async function endpointGuard(request, response, next) {
    const token = request.headers.authorization?.split(' ')[1];
    if (!token) {
        return response.status(401).send('Unauthorized');
    }
    try {
        const decoded = jwt.verify(token, process.env.JWT_SECRET);
        request.user = decoded;
        next();
    } catch (error) {
        return response.status(401).send('Invalid token');
    }
}
```

When deploying the application, close attention must be paid to securing environment variables, especially those related to the Supabase project. It is critical to limit access to the project's API keys, particularly the private keys, and ensure that they are stored securely using environment variable managers or secret vaults. Tools such as Docker and Kubernetes often come with built-in secrets management, further ensuring that sensitive information remains protected.

A comprehensive approach to setting up user authentication in Supabase also includes regular monitoring and updating configurations based on evolving security standards. Developers should periodically review the Supabase documentation for changes in recommended practices or new features that can be integrated into the project. Automated tests that mimic authentication flows add an extra layer of assurance that updates do not introduce regressions or vulnerabilities.

While configuring authentication, developers might encounter integration challenges, especially when combining multiple authentication methods. Thorough documentation provided by Supabase, combined with robust community support, generally mitigates these challenges. In scenarios where conflicts arise between different authentication flows, a systematic debugging approach—starting from validating API keys in the dashboard, checking environment variable consistency, and then verifying the authentication logs—can prove highly effective.

The iterative nature of establishing secure authentication in a Supabase project necessitates collaboration between developers and security auditors. Regular security audits, including penetration tests, help identify potential weak points that may not be evident during initial integration. This practice ensures that user data remains secure and that the authentication flows adhere to industry best practices. Supabase's integrated logging system simplifies the audit process by providing comprehensive traces of all authentication events.

The detailed configuration steps outlined here form the basis of establishing a secure authentication module in a Supabase project. By following the procedures to initialize a project, adjust authentication settings, embed client-side authentication flows, and configure security middleware, developers can ensure that the user authentication system is both robust and scalable. Properly set up authentication is fundamental to protecting user data and building a secure backend architecture, serving as the cornerstone for further enhancements such as role-based access control and secure data transmission.

4.3. Managing User Accounts and Profiles

Managing user accounts and profiles within the Supabase platform is a critical component for establishing personalized and secure user experiences. The platform provides a comprehensive API and a suite of tools that facilitate the creation, modification, and deletion of user data. This section details procedures and best practices for the complete lifecycle management of user accounts and profiles, building on previously discussed authentication concepts and setup procedures.

The Supabase authentication API integrates user account management with row-level security (RLS) policies in PostgreSQL, enabling developers to safely store and retrieve profile data. Upon registration, a user is automatically associated with a unique identifier. This primary key is employed across multiple tables to establish relationships between the authentication data and user-specific information stored in custom tables such as user_profiles. Establishing this relationship is fundamental for ensuring that operations on profile data are secure and aligned with the principle of least privilege.

A common approach is to enforce that each user can only access and modify their own profile information. This is accomplished by defining security policies using SQL commands. For example, creating a policy that allows users to update only their own profile may take the form demonstrated below:

```
CREATE POLICY "Update own profile"
ON user_profiles
FOR UPDATE
USING (id = auth.uid());
```

By leveraging such RLS policies, Supabase enforces the rules at the database level, preventing unauthorized access even if application-level security is bypassed. This integration between the application and its underlying data store provides a robust mechanism for managing user profiles.

The process of creating a user profile typically occurs immediately after the user is authenticated. Since the authentication process returns essential user details, the next step is to create an associated profile record. Using Supabase's JavaScript client library, developers can insert the necessary profile information into a dedicated table. The following code snippet demonstrates how a new user profile is created upon successful registration:

```
async function createUserProfile(userId, additionalData) {
    // additionalData may include fields such as 'first_name', '
    last_name', or 'avatar_url'
    const { data, error } = await supabase
        .from('user_profiles')
        .insert([{ id: userId, ...additionalData }]);
    if (error) {
        console.error('Error creating profile:', error.message);
        return null;
    }
    return data;
}

// Example usage after sign-up:
const { user } = await supabase.auth.signUp({ email, password });
if (user) {
    await createUserProfile(user.id, { first_name: 'John', last_name:
        'Doe' });
}
```

Updating user profile information is similarly supported through Su-

144

pabase's query builder. Developers can use the update method to modify attributes within the user profile table. Along with employing RLS to restrict modifications to the current user, the update operation can be invoked securely as depicted in the following example:

```
async function updateUserProfile(userId, updatedData) {
    const { data, error } = await supabase
        .from('user_profiles')
        .update(updatedData)
        .eq('id', userId);
    if (error) {
        console.error('Update error:', error.message);
        return null;
    }
    return data;
}

// Example usage: updating the avatar URL for the authenticated user
const currentUser = supabase.auth.user();
if (currentUser) {
    const updatedProfile = await updateUserProfile(currentUser.id, {
    avatar_url: 'https://example.com/avatar.png' });
    console.log('Profile updated:', updatedProfile);
}
```

Supabase also supports querying user profile information with filtering, sorting, and pagination capabilities. This is particularly useful in administrative interfaces or applications where users are allowed to view lists of profiles—for instance, in social networking apps or content management systems. Developers can perform queries to retrieve either a single record or multiple entries that satisfy certain conditions. The following example shows how to retrieve a user's profile based on the unique identifier:

```
async function getUserProfile(userId) {
    const { data, error } = await supabase
        .from('user_profiles')
        .select('*')
        .eq('id', userId)
        .single();
    if (error) {
        console.error('Fetch error:', error.message);
        return null;
    }
```

```
    return data;
}

// Example usage: fetching the profile for the logged-in user
const profile = await getUserProfile(supabase.auth.user().id);
console.log('User profile:', profile);
```

A critical aspect of managing user profiles is ensuring data consistency and security. Supabase encourages developers to separate authentication data from profile data. Sensitive authentication details are stored in secure, system-managed tables while public or semi-public user profile data is stored in custom tables that can be controlled via RLS policies. This separation minimizes the risk of inadvertent exposure of sensitive information. Detailed logging and audit trails provided by Supabase further help in monitoring changes to user accounts and profiles, thereby assisting in early detection of suspicious activities.

Handling the deletion of user accounts is another important task in the user management lifecycle. Supabase provides an API function to delete a user from the authentication system. However, the deletion of the associated profile data must be managed explicitly. A common pattern is to use database triggers or cascade delete rules in PostgreSQL to ensure that when an account is removed, the corresponding profile record is also deleted, maintaining consistency and reducing orphaned data. An example of a cascade delete rule is shown below:

```
ALTER TABLE user_profiles
ADD CONSTRAINT fk_user
FOREIGN KEY (id) REFERENCES auth.users (id)
ON DELETE CASCADE;
```

In cases where a user opts to temporarily deactivate their account rather than permanently deleting it, developers can implement a soft delete mechanism. This approach involves adding a flag in the user profile table (e.g., `is_active`) that indicates whether the account is active. The application logic then conditionally excludes profiles marked as inactive from queries. The following example illustrates how to update the status of an account to inactive:

```
UPDATE user_profiles
SET is_active = false
WHERE id = 'user-id';
```

Restoring a soft-deleted account entails toggling the flag back to true and performing any additional reactivation steps necessary. Such mechanisms allow for reversible account deactivation, which can be crucial in scenarios requiring temporary suspension due to security concerns or policy violations.

Managing user accounts also involves routine maintenance tasks such as verifying email addresses and updating passwords. Supabase supports functionalities for sending verification emails and securing password reset pages. Developers can invoke these functions via the client library. For example, initiating a password recovery flow is as simple as calling the appropriate function, which sends a password reset email to the user:

```
async function requestPasswordReset(email) {
    const { data, error } = await supabase.auth.api.
    resetPasswordForEmail(email);
    if (error) {
        console.error('Password reset error:', error.message);
        return null;
    }
    return data;
}

// Example usage: requesting password reset for a user
requestPasswordReset('user@example.com');
```

Likewise, developers can prompt users to verify their email addresses by triggering the verification step upon registration. Email verification adds another layer of security and provides a means to confirm that a user owns the claimed email address. This step is often integrated with the sign-up process and may be enforced using middleware that checks for an email verified flag in the user's metadata. Ensuring that email

147

addresses are verified before granting access to sensitive features can prevent many common security risks.

The Supabase platform also provides mechanisms for bulk managing user accounts, which can be invaluable in administrative contexts. For instance, performing batch updates of user profiles can be achieved by constructing queries that target multiple records based on specific criteria. This feature is especially useful when applying policy changes across a user base or when migrating data during system upgrades. Here is an example of a batch update command:

```
UPDATE user_profiles
SET status = 'active'
WHERE last_login > NOW() - INTERVAL '30 days';
```

Throughout the process of creating, updating, and managing user accounts and profiles, it is essential to incorporate thorough validation both on the client side and at the database level. Client-side validations provide immediate feedback to users, while database constraints and triggers ensure data consistency and protect against attempts to bypass the client validation. For example, utilizing check constraints in the database can prevent invalid data from being stored inadvertently:

```
ALTER TABLE user_profiles
ADD CONSTRAINT valid_email
CHECK (email ~* '^[A-Za-z0-9._%+-]+@[A-Za-z0-9.-]+\.[A-Za-z]{2,}$');
```

The interplay between client-side operations and server-side validations lies at the heart of secure user management. Developers must ensure that their application logic, API calls, and database design are aligned with security best practices to provide a seamless experience while mitigating risks.

Incorporating detailed error handling, logging, and audit trails within the user management flow is crucial. By leveraging Supabase audit logs, developers can monitor events such as profile updates, password resets, and account deletions, ensuring traceability in cases of unexpected behavior or security discrepancies. This systematic logging, when combined with robust error handling in the application code, aids in maintaining the integrity of the user management system and facilitates prompt remediation efforts if anomalies are detected.

Integrating these management procedures within a broader application infrastructure also involves the implementation of state management solutions. Framework-specific solutions, such as custom hooks for React or Vuex modules for Vue.js, help maintain synchronization between the user's profile data and the application state. This synchronization is particularly important in real-time applications where user data may change frequently. Maintaining consistency between the frontend display and the backend data is achieved by consistently querying the Supabase API and updating the client state accordingly.

The administration of user accounts and profiles in Supabase is a scalable process designed to accommodate diverse application architectures. Whether the need is for simple user management in small-scale applications or for complex relational mappings in enterprise-level solutions, the Supabase platform provides flexible and secure mechanisms to handle account data. The synergy between secure authentication, database-level policies, and API-driven interactions results in a reliable system that can adapt to evolving requirements and security paradigms.

4.4. Password Management and Recovery

Secure password management and an efficient password recovery process are essential components of a robust authentication system. Supabase integrates advanced security methodologies such as adaptive hashing, token-based recovery mechanisms, and configurable expiry parameters. This section details the practices for secure password management along with the implementation of password recovery options, building on previous discussions related to authentication and account management.

Central to secure password management is the use of cryptographic hashing algorithms, which convert plain-text passwords into non-reversible hashed values. Supabase leverages resilient algorithms such as bcrypt or argon2 that incorporate work factors or memory hardness to resist brute-force attacks. This approach minimizes the risk of password compromise by ensuring that even if the hashed values are exposed, the computational effort required to revert them to plain-text is prohibitive. In addition, incorporating a unique salt for each password further prevents attackers from using precomputed lookup tables, such as rainbow tables. The following SQL snippet illustrates the importance of using a secure hashing function when storing a password in a user management system:

```
-- Example using PostgreSQL's cryptographic functions
INSERT INTO auth.users (email, password_hash)
VALUES (
    'user@example.com',
    crypt('plain_password', gen_salt('bf'))
);
```

In this example, the crypt() function in combination with gen_salt() automatically generates a salt and computes the hash using bcrypt. Regularly updating the work factor or algorithm configuration ensures that password storage remains resilient against evolving computational capabilities of attackers.

Beyond the initial storage of passwords, robust password recovery processes are crucial to maintain a balance between user convenience and security. The password recovery process typically involves verifying the user's identity without exposing sensitive data. In Supabase, this is achieved by using a token-based recovery mechanism, where a unique, time-limited token is generated and sent to the user's registered email address to authorize a password reset. This process relies on secure channels, typically enforced by SSL/TLS, to prevent interception of the token.

The first step in the password recovery workflow is request initiation. The application triggers a function to send an email containing a secure link. This link embeds a recovery token, which is created using a secure random generator and stored temporarily on the backend. The token is associated with a short expiration time, commonly one hour, which limits the window during which an attacker could execute a potential misuse. The following JavaScript example demonstrates a simple password recovery request using Supabase's client library:

```javascript
async function requestPasswordReset(email) {
    // This function sends a password reset email to the user's
    registered address
    const { data, error } = await supabase.auth.api.
    resetPasswordForEmail(email, {
        redirectTo: 'https://your-app.com/reset-password'
    });
    if (error) {
        console.error('Password reset request error:', error.message)
        ;
        return null;
    }
    console.log('Password reset email sent:', data);
    return data;
}

// Example usage
requestPasswordReset('user@example.com');
```

The recovery email typically contains a link pointing to a secure password reset page in the client application. Upon clicking the link, the application extracts the embedded token and prompts the user to provide a new password. At this stage, it is critical to validate the token on the server side to ensure that it is both valid and unexpired. Token verification is performed using cryptographic checks to ensure that the token has not been tampered with. The subsequent step is to update the user's stored password with the new, securely hashed value. The following code snippet illustrates the process of updating a password after a password reset:

```
async function updatePassword(newPassword, recoveryToken) {
    // Update the user's password using the recovery token provided
    const { user, error } = await supabase.auth.api.updateUser(
    recoveryToken, { password: newPassword });
    if (error) {
        console.error('Password update error:', error.message);
        return null;
    }
    console.log('Password updated successfully for user:', user);
    return user;
}

// Example usage after token verification
updatePassword('new_secure_password', 'recovery-token-from-email');
```

Throughout the password recovery process, additional security measures can be applied. One best practice is to enforce strong password policies where the new password must meet certain complexity requirements (e.g., minimum length, a combination of letters, numbers, and special characters). This is particularly important during a reset operation where users might opt for simpler credentials. Enforcing these policies both on the client side and via server-side validations ensures consistency and protection against weak passwords.

Moreover, the system should monitor and rate-limit password recovery attempts. Tracking each request and limiting the number of recovery emails sent to a single account within a specific time frame diminishes the risk of denial-of-service or automated exploitation. Logging these recovery requests also provides an audit trail that is valuable for security reviews and incident investigations.

The token used for password recovery must be stored securely, often in a designated table that maps tokens to user identifiers alongside a timestamp for expiry. After a successful password reset, these tokens should be explicitly invalidated to prevent reuse. The following SQL snippet outlines a simple method for token invalidation post-reset:

```
UPDATE auth.password_reset_tokens
```

```
SET is_valid = false
WHERE token = 'recovery-token-from-email';
```

Integrating token invalidation into the recovery workflow not only preserves the one-time nature of tokens but also reinforces the overall security model by ensuring that stale tokens cannot be exploited.

Regular audits and security updates form a critical part of maintaining a secure password management lifecycle. Developers should periodically assess the parameters of password hashing functions and the expiration times of recovery tokens. As new vulnerabilities are discovered in cryptographic libraries or algorithms, prompt updates and migrations become necessary. Automated scripts and scheduled jobs can monitor and enforce these updates, ensuring that the system remains protected against advanced threats.

Another aspect of password management is handling password changes initiated by the user while they are authenticated, as opposed to the recovery process. In authenticated sessions, users may desire to change their password to maintain ongoing account security. Supabase provides endpoints to facilitate a secure password change, where users must supply their current password along with the new credentials. This additional step validates that the request is legitimate. The following example outlines a typical flow for changing a password during an active session:

```
async function changePassword(currentPassword, newPassword) {
    // Reauthenticate user with current password before updating to
    new password
    const { data: signInData, error: signInError } = await supabase.
    auth.signIn({
        email: supabase.auth.user().email,
        password: currentPassword
    });
    if (signInError) {
        console.error('Reauthentication error:', signInError.message)
        ;
        return null;
    }
```

```
const { user, error } = await supabase.auth.update({ password:
 newPassword });
if (error) {
    console.error('Password change error:', error.message);
    return null;
}
console.log('Password changed successfully:', user);
return user;
}
```

The process of changing a password requires exact validation, ensuring that the current credentials match the stored secure hash before the transition to a new password is permitted. This validation step acts as a safeguard against session hijacking and unauthorized changes in the event of compromised sessions.

From a developer's perspective, implementing secure password recovery workflows requires attention to both usability and security. The design of the recovery process should minimize the exposure of sensitive user data while providing a seamless user experience. Keeping error messages generic during recovery processes prevents leakage of information regarding account details. For instance, a message like "If an account exists for this email, a reset link has been sent" maintains security without confirming whether the email is registered.

Encouraging users to frequently update their passwords and pairing these practices with biometric or multi-factor authentication (MFA) can help elevate the overall security standard. The combination of these techniques ensures that even if one layer of defense is compromised, additional safeguards remain in place.

Implementing client-side checks using modern frameworks further locks down the process. Front-end validations that enforce password complexity rules reduce the need for users to submit weak passwords. Real-time feedback via user interfaces facilitates immediate correction before hitting server-side constraints, reducing unnecessary rounds of server communication and minimizing potential attack vectors.

Finally, monitoring and logging all operations related to password changes and recovery is a best practice that enhances visibility into the authentication system. Detailed logs, integrated with Supabase's auditing system, enable administrators to track suspicious activities or repeated recovery attempts that may indicate broader security concerns. These logs can be configured to integrate with security information and event management (SIEM) solutions, thereby elevating the overall security posture of the system.

The strategies discussed here form a holistic approach to secure password management and recovery. By incorporating state-of-the-art hashing techniques, token-based recovery mechanisms, strict frontend and backend validations, and robust logging practices, Supabase ensures that password operations are resistant to common attack vectors. This multi-layered security framework addresses the critical aspects of both managing and recovering passwords without compromising on user experience or system performance.

4.5. Third-Party Authentication Providers

Integrating third-party authentication providers into a Supabase project expands the authentication landscape by allowing users to leverage existing accounts from trusted identity providers such as Google, Facebook, GitHub, and others. Supabase supports OAuth 2.0 protocols, enabling developers to seamlessly incorporate these external services into their authentication workflows. This section details the configuration, implementation, and considerations for third-party authentication, building on the previously discussed topics of user authentication setup and account management.

The integration process begins in the Supabase dashboard, where providers can be enabled by configuring relevant OAuth settings. Each provider requires specific credentials, such as a client ID and a client secret, which must be obtained through the provider's developer portal. In the dashboard, input fields corresponding to these credentials allow Supabase to securely store them for use during the authentication process. Additionally, callback or redirect URLs must be defined to ensure that, following authentication on the provider's platform, users are redirected back to the appropriate location in the application.

Once these settings are established, Supabase automatically handles most of the OAuth flow. The flow typically involves the following steps: the user is redirected to the third-party authentication provider's login page, the user enters their credentials, and, upon successful authentication, the provider redirects the user back with an authorization code. Supabase exchanges this code for an access token and, in many cases, a JWT token that encapsulates user details. These tokens are then used for establishing a session in the Supabase client. The following JavaScript snippet illustrates how to initiate third-party sign-in using the Supabase client library:

```
async function signInWithProvider(provider) {
    // provider can be 'google', 'facebook', 'github', etc.
    const { user, session, error } = await supabase.auth.signIn(
        { provider: provider },
        { redirectTo: 'https://your-app.com/auth/callback' }
    );
    if (error) {
        console.error(`Error during ${provider} authentication:`,
     error.message);
    } else {
        console.log(`${provider} authentication successful:`, user);
    }
}
```

In this example, the `signInWithProvider` function initiates the sign-in process by specifying the provider name. The `redirectTo` option directs users back to a preconfigured callback URL after successful authentication. The use of this mechanism significantly reduces the overhead of manually handling OAuth flows, with Supabase abstracting much of the complexity associated with token exchanges and session validation.

In parallel to the client-side process, robust backend configuration is essential. Supabase's role-level security (RLS) policies can be adapted to incorporate tokens issued by third-party providers. When a JWT includes claims from providers such as Google or Facebook, these claims can be used to map the user's external identity to the application's internal user record. For example, if a Google account is used, an RLS policy might enforce that the unique identifier passed in the JWT is linked to a corresponding record in the user profiles table. A SQL snippet to enforce such a policy might resemble the following:

```
CREATE POLICY "Third-Party Users Can Access Own Profile"
ON user_profiles
FOR SELECT
USING (
    id = auth.uid() OR
    google_id = current_setting('jwt.claims.google_id')
);
```

In this example, the policy uses a JWT claim often provided by external providers (google_id) to grant access to parts of the profile data. This approach demonstrates how integrating third-party sign-ins does not compromise security, as proper checks ensure that only authorized profiles are accessible.

The user management flow must also accommodate account linking. Users who initially sign up using one authentication method, such as email and password, might wish to link their account to a third-party provider. Linking accounts enhances user experience and provides flexibility, as users can choose their preferred sign-in method. Supabase supports this by allowing developers to merge external provider details with existing user profiles. An example API call for linking an account is similar to updating the user record with the third-party identifier after authentication:

```
async function linkAccountToProvider(provider, accessToken) {
    // This function links a third-party account to an existing user
```

157

```
    session
const { user, error } = await supabase.auth.update({
    provider: provider,
    access_token: accessToken
});
if (error) {
    console.error(`Error linking ${provider} account:`, error.
 message);
} else {
    console.log(`${provider} account linked successfully:`, user)
 ;
}
}
```

In practice, linking accounts requires server-side logic to detect potential conflicts, such as when a third-party email already exists in the system. Careful handling ensures that linking does not inadvertently overwrite or duplicate a user's data. For instance, the application might prompt the user to confirm the linking operation if an account with the same email is found.

Security practices specific to third-party integrations require emphasizing token revocation and session management. Third-party access tokens generally come with a limited lifespan, and it is crucial for the system to handle token expiration seamlessly. Developers should design the authentication logic to refresh tokens where necessary or prompt users to reauthenticate when a token expires. The following pseudocode outlines typical token refresh logic within a middleware function:

```
async function refreshTokenMiddleware(request, response, next) {
    const token = request.headers.authorization?.split(' ')[1];
    if (!token) {
        return response.status(401).send('Unauthorized');
    }
    const decoded = jwt.decode(token);
    if (decoded.exp < Date.now() / 1000) {
        // Token expired, trigger refresh process
        const refreshResponse = await supabase.auth.api.
 refreshAccessToken(token);
        if (refreshResponse.error) {
            return response.status(401).send('Token refresh failed');
```

```
        }
        // Replace token in header and continue
        request.headers.authorization = `Bearer ${refreshResponse.
    data.access_token}`;
    }
    next();
}
```

This example demonstrates a basic token refresh strategy, highlighting the importance of gracefully handling token expiry without degrading the user experience. Robust error handling and logging within these middleware functions can further enhance security and provide developers with insights into potential operational issues.

In addition to directly integrating sign-in flows, third-party providers enable the application to offer additional user data, such as profile images, contact information, and verified email statuses. Once a user is authenticated via a provider, the returned JWT may contain claims that can be utilized to prepopulate user profiles or adjust access policies. For instance, if a user signs in via Facebook, the application might automatically store the user's profile picture and friends list, enhancing the personalization of the application experience. The following example illustrates how additional data from a third-party provider might be used to update a user profile:

```
async function updateProfileWithProviderData(providerData) {
    const { user } = supabase.auth.session();
    if (!user) {
        console.error('No authenticated user found');
        return;
    }
    const profileData = {
        avatar_url: providerData.picture || null,
        full_name: providerData.name || null,
        provider_email: providerData.email || null
    };
    const { data, error } = await supabase.from('user_profiles')
        .update(profileData)
        .eq('id', user.id);
    if (error) {
        console.error('Error updating profile with provider data:',
```

159

```
    error.message);
  } else {
      console.log('User profile updated with provider data:', data)
  ;
  }
}
```

When handling data returned from external providers, it is critical to validate and sanitize all inputs to prevent potential security vulnerabilities. Sensitive information received from a provider should be stored in accordance with privacy and data protection standards. In many cases, developers might choose to only store essential claims and request additional permissions only when necessary.

Environmental configuration plays an important role in managing third-party authentication. API keys and client secrets must be securely stored and accessed via environment variables or secret management systems. Exposing these credentials in the codebase can lead to significant security risks. Developers should ensure that their deployment pipelines follow best practices for secrets management. An example of securely loading environment variables in a Node.js application might look like the following:

```
require('dotenv').config();  // Ensure that .env is not committed to
    version control
const googleClientId = process.env.GOOGLE_CLIENT_ID;
const googleClientSecret = process.env.GOOGLE_CLIENT_SECRET;
```

A similar pattern should be applied to all third-party provider credentials, ensuring that sensitive data is handled correctly across different environments, such as development, staging, and production.

Monitoring and auditing also play a vital role when integrating third-party authentication. Supabase's logging functionality captures a record of authentication events, including successful and failed attempts from external providers. Regular review of these logs assists in early detection of potential abuse or misconfigured provider settings. Developers can integrate these logs with external monitoring systems to create alerts and track unusual patterns, ensuring the application maintains compliance with security standards.

Advanced configurations may include multi-provider sign-in flows where a user is allowed to choose among several external authentication options. Managing such flows requires clear user interface cues and a consistent back-end logic to handle the variety of possible authentication responses. The user experience should be designed to provide clarity on which provider is connected and allow for easy switching or linking between different accounts.

The ability to integrate multiple providers also enhances the redundancy of the authentication system. If one provider experiences downtime or service degradation, users can opt to authenticate via an alternate channel, thereby reducing the likelihood of a complete outage affecting user access. This redundancy is particularly beneficial in applications with a diverse global user base where regional preferences for specific providers may vary.

Finally, documentation and community support contribute significantly to the success of third-party integrations. Supabase offers detailed documentation that covers the configuration steps, potential error messages, and best practices for integrating external authentication services. Developers are encouraged to leverage community forums and official tutorials to stay updated on new integrations or changes in provider requirements. Continuous education and iterative development ensure that applications remain secure, feature-rich, and responsive to the evolving landscape of identity management.

Implementing third-party authentication providers not only streamlines the sign-in process but also improves user engagement by reducing friction during account creation. By following the detailed configuration steps, leveraging robust code examples, and adopting best practices for secure token management and logging, developers can create a reliable authentication experience that seamlessly integrates external user identities with the Supabase backend.

4.6. Implementing Role-Based Access Control

Role-based access control (RBAC) is a fundamental security mechanism that ensures users have appropriate permissions to interact with system resources. In Supabase, RBAC is implemented through a combination of PostgreSQL role definitions, row-level security (RLS) policies, and the inclusion of claims within JSON Web Tokens (JWT). This section outlines the steps and reasoning required to set up RBAC in a Supabase project, providing detailed configuration instructions, code examples, and best practices for managing permissions.

The first step in implementing RBAC is to define the roles within the system. Roles are designed to encapsulate a set of permissions that determine what domain actions a user can perform. Common examples include roles such as `admin`, `editor`, and `viewer`. In Supabase, roles can be managed both at the database level and embedded within the authentication tokens. Assigning roles during the user sign-up process or linking them to actions performed in the application ensures that each user is granted a suitable permission set. When a user logs in, their JWT can contain a claim that denotes their specific role. The following SQL snippet demonstrates how to update a user record with a role claim:

```
UPDATE auth.users
SET raw_user_meta_data = jsonb_set(raw_user_meta_data, '{role}', '"
    editor"')
WHERE id = 'user-id';
```

Once roles are defined, the next crucial step is to enforce these roles at the database level using PostgreSQL's row-level security. RLS policies

162

enable fine-grained control over which rows in a table can be accessed or manipulated based on the role of the authenticated user. In a typical implementation, tables such as user_profiles or business-specific tables are secured so that only users with the appropriate role can perform certain operations. Consider the following example policy that restricts the update operations on a sensitive table to users with the role admin:

```
CREATE POLICY "Admins can update records"
ON sensitive_data
FOR UPDATE
USING (
    current_setting('jwt.claims.role') = 'admin'
);
```

In this policy, the current_setting function is used to extract the role claim from the JWT. This ensures that only users whose role claim matches the allowed role can update records in the sensitive_data table. Similar policies can be tailored for different operations such as SELECT, INSERT, or DELETE, and for various roles as required by the application's security model.

For applications that have more complex authorization requirements, it is common to implement multiple RLS policies targeting various roles. For example, an editor might be allowed to modify content only if they are the owner of that content. The policy can then check for both the role and a matching identifier for ownership:

```
CREATE POLICY "Editors can update own content"
ON content
FOR UPDATE
USING (
    current_setting('jwt.claims.role') = 'editor'
    AND author_id = auth.uid()
);
```

This policy demonstrates a compound condition that not only verifies the user's role but also ensures that the record being modified belongs to the authenticated user. Such granular control is essential in multi-user systems where permissions must be carefully partitioned to prevent unauthorized access.

Implementing RBAC in the client-side application involves ensuring that the JWT sent by the client contains the necessary role information. This can be achieved by configuring the authentication flow to include custom claims. During the token generation process in Supabase, custom claims can be defined so that each token carries the role of the user. When using providers such as Supabase Auth, the administration console or configuration scripts can be used to adjust the JWT payload. Here is an example of how a developer might inspect the token to verify the inclusion of the role claim in a client-side JavaScript application:

```
import jwt_decode from 'jwt-decode';

function getUserRole() {
    const session = supabase.auth.session();
    if (!session) {
        return null;
    }
    const decodedToken = jwt_decode(session.access_token);
    return decodedToken.role || null;
}

const role = getUserRole();
console.log('User role:', role);
```

In this sample code, the jwt-decode library is used to extract and log the role claim from the access token. This verification step is critical during development and debugging, as it ensures that the authentication system is correctly propagating role information throughout the application.

Managing roles also requires provisioning and deprovisioning mechanisms when users' permissions change. For instance, when an employee is promoted or their department changes, their role must be updated accordingly in both the authentication system and the database. Administrators can design user management interfaces that allow for role modifications, and the changes are then reflected in the system via secure update operations similar to the SQL example provided earlier. Maintaining an audit log of role changes is a recommended practice, offering traceability and assisting in compliance with organizational policies and regulatory requirements.

An important best practice in implementing RBAC is to always enforce default-deny policies. This means that if no explicit permission is granted to a particular role for a specific operation, access is automatically denied. When writing RLS policies, developers should avoid overly permissive conditions by default. Policies should be written to specifically allow access for known roles rather than attempting to deny access to all others. By following this principle, applications reduce the risk of accidental exposure of sensitive data.

For applications with the need to support multiple types of roles, consider building a role hierarchy where certain roles inherit permissions from others. Although PostgreSQL RLS policies do not explicitly support role inheritance, this can be simulated by carefully designing policies with combined conditions. For example, if an admin should have all the permissions of an editor, the policy for updating content might include an OR condition that allows both roles:

```
CREATE POLICY "Editors and Admins can update content"
ON content
FOR UPDATE
USING (
    (current_setting('jwt.claims.role') = 'editor' AND author_id =
    auth.uid())
    OR current_setting('jwt.claims.role') = 'admin'
);
```

This approach verifies if the user is either an editor updating their own content or an admin, who is granted permissions regardless of ownership. The design of such policies should be guided by the business logic and operational security requirements of the specific application.

Another consideration when implementing RBAC is the performance impact of RLS policies. While RLS provides powerful security features, complex policies with multiple conditions can lead to increased query execution time. Developers should strive to optimize policies and indexing strategies to mitigate this issue, especially in high-load environments. Detailed logging and performance monitoring are recommended to identify any operations that might be impacted by intensive policy checks. Regular database tuning and query optimization best practices should be applied to ensure the system remains responsive.

Integrating external systems is another common requirement when implementing RBAC. Modern applications often interface with various microservices or partner systems that need access to protected resources. In such cases, tokens with role claims can be passed along with API requests to assert the permissions of the caller. The receiving service should validate these tokens and enforce its own access control policies based on the role information provided. Utilizing standardized protocols, such as OAuth 2.0 and OpenID Connect, can streamline this process and ensure interoperability between different services.

Implementing role-based access control in Supabase requires a combination of secure client-side configurations, meticulous database policy definitions, and a robust operational strategy. The integration of these components provides a scalable and maintainable security model that adapts to evolving application requirements. Developers are encouraged to document their RBAC configurations, test various role scenarios meticulously, and periodically review and update policies as business needs change.

Finally, testing is a critical phase when implementing RBAC. Automated tests that simulate different user roles and attempt to perform restricted actions help ensure that policies are correctly enforced. Unit tests and integration tests should be written to cover edge cases, and security audits should be conducted to confirm that no unintended ac-

cess is permitted. The following pseudocode illustrates an integrated
test case scenario:

```
describe('RBAC Tests', () => {
    it('should allow admin to update any record', async () => {
        // Simulate an admin user
        const adminSession = createTestSession({ role: 'admin', id: '
        admin-id' });
        const result = await attemptUpdateRecord(adminSession,
        someRecordId, newData);
        expect(result.success).toBe(true);
    });

    it('should prevent editor from updating record not owned', async
    () => {
        // Simulate an editor user
        const editorSession = createTestSession({ role: 'editor', id:
        'editor-id' });
        const result = await attemptUpdateRecord(editorSession,
        differentRecordOwnerId, newData);
        expect(result.success).toBe(false);
    });
});
```

These tests validate that role-based restrictions are effectively preventing unauthorized updates while ensuring legitimate operations succeed. Comprehensive testing not only reinforces confidence in the security model but also streamlines the troubleshooting process when
policy changes are introduced.

By following the detailed procedures laid out in this section, developers can implement a robust role-based access control system in their
Supabase projects. Such a system offers granular control over permissions, limits exposure to unauthorized data manipulation, and supports the evolving security needs of modern applications.

4.7. Ensuring Secure Data Transmission

Securing data transmission during authentication and user management processes is essential to protect sensitive information such as passwords, tokens, and user data from interception and tampering. Supabase relies on industry-standard protocols and best practices to ensure that data exchanged between clients and servers is encrypted, authenticated, and resistant to man-in-the-middle attacks. This section examines the methods and configurations required to secure data transmission across both client-side and server-side components, building upon earlier discussions of authentication, RBAC, and account management.

The foundation of secure data transmission rests on Transport Layer Security (TLS), which is used to encrypt HTTP traffic between the client and server. Supabase enforces TLS for all communications, ensuring that sensitive data such as JWTs, credentials, and user information remain confidential during transit. It is critical that developers verify the proper installation and configuration of TLS certificates on their servers. In a typical deployment scenario, a reverse proxy or load balancer is configured to manage TLS termination. For instance, when using Nginx as a reverse proxy, a secure configuration may be implemented as shown below:

```
server {
    listen 443 ssl;
    server_name your-app.com;

    ssl_certificate /etc/ssl/certs/your-cert.pem;
    ssl_certificate_key /etc/ssl/private/your-key.pem;
    ssl_protocols TLSv1.2 TLSv1.3;
    ssl_ciphers HIGH:!aNULL:!MD5;

    location / {
        proxy_pass http://localhost:8000;
        proxy_set_header Host $host;
        proxy_set_header X-Forwarded-For $proxy_add_x_forwarded_for;
    }
```

168

```
}
```

This configuration ensures that all communications to your-app.com are encrypted using strong protocols and ciphers, and that the server only accepts connections via TLS version 1.2 or higher. In cloud deployments, similar security configurations are often managed through built-in security groups and load balancer settings.

In addition to TLS, proper certificate management plays a crucial role in preventing man-in-the-middle attacks. Certificates should be obtained from reputable Certificate Authorities (CAs) and regularly rotated to avoid the use of expired or compromised credentials. Automated certificate renewal via tools such as Let's Encrypt can help maintain continuous security without introducing administrative overhead. On the client side, developers should ensure that applications validate server certificates rigorously. Many modern libraries perform this check by default, but custom configurations or non-standard environments may require explicit validation. For instance, in a Node.js environment, developers can enforce certificate verification when making HTTPS requests:

```
const https = require('https');

const options = {
    hostname: 'your-app.com',
    port: 443,
    path: '/api/secure-endpoint',
    method: 'GET',
    rejectUnauthorized: true  // Ensures that only valid certificates
      are accepted
};

const req = https.request(options, (res) => {
    res.on('data', (d) => {
        process.stdout.write(d);
    });
});

req.on('error', (e) => {
    console.error(e);
```

```
});

req.end();
```

The use of `rejectUnauthorized: true` instructs the HTTPS client to refuse any connection if the server's certificate is invalid or does not match the expected domain, thereby mitigating potential security risks.

Beyond the transport layer, encrypted transmission of sensitive tokens and credentials is critical. Supabase utilizes JWTs for maintaining sessions and transferring claims. Ensuring that these tokens are sent only over secure channels is a best practice that minimizes exposure. Developers should configure client libraries to automatically enforce secure connections. For example, when initializing the Supabase client in a JavaScript application, environment variables such as `SUPABASE_URL` should always reference `https://` endpoints:

```
import { createClient } from '@supabase/supabase-js';

const supabaseUrl = process.env.SUPABASE_URL; // Should be 'https://
    your-app.supabase.co'
const supabaseKey = process.env.SUPABASE_ANON_KEY;
const supabase = createClient(supabaseUrl, supabaseKey);
```

Securing data transmission also involves proper handling of API keys and tokens on the client side. These policies recommend that sensitive keys are never hard-coded into the client application. Instead, they should be injected through secure environment variables during the build process or runtime configuration. Furthermore, headers containing tokens, such as authorization headers, must be set only through secure, server-validated libraries to prevent exposure through client-side vulnerabilities.

Another aspect of ensuring secure data transmission is data integrity. Cryptographic hashing and digital signatures can be used to verify that data is not altered during transit. While TLS inherently provides in-

170

tegrity checks, additional layers such as HMAC (Hash-based Message Authentication Code) can augment security, particularly when integrating multiple services or external APIs. For example, when sending critical data between services, a signature may be computed as follows:

```javascript
const crypto = require('crypto');

function generateHmacSignature(message, secret) {
    return crypto.createHmac('sha256', secret).update(message).digest
        ('hex');
}

const message = JSON.stringify({ data: 'secureData' });
const secret = process.env.HMAC_SECRET;
const signature = generateHmacSignature(message, secret);
console.log('HMAC Signature:', signature);
```

Here, the signature ensures that any tampering with the data during transmission can be detected on the server side by recalculating the HMAC and comparing it with the provided value.

Securing data transmission also extends to the application's API endpoints. When handling sensitive transactions such as password updates or role modifications, endpoints should enforce strict CORS policies and authentication checks. This reduces the risk of unauthorized access by ensuring that only trusted origins are permitted to make requests. A secure CORS configuration in a Node.js Express application might be configured as follows:

```javascript
const express = require('express');
const cors = require('cors');

const app = express();

const corsOptions = {
    origin: 'https://your-app.com',
    optionsSuccessStatus: 200
};

app.use(cors(corsOptions));

// Define secure endpoints
app.post('/api/secure-endpoint', (req, res) => {
```

```
    // Handle request securely
    res.json({ message: 'Secure data transmitted' });
});

app.listen(3000, () => console.log('Server running on port 3000'));
```

Configuring CORS appropriately limits the potential for cross-site request forgery (CSRF) and other related attacks by ensuring that credentials are only transmitted between the expected origins.

Network-level security measures, such as using Virtual Private Networks (VPNs) or dedicated private connections, further enhance secure data transmission, particularly for administrative or inter-service communications. In cloud-based deployments, using Virtual Private Cloud (VPC) configurations can isolate sensitive components from public networks, thereby reducing exposure to external threats. By segmenting network access and enforcing strict firewall rules, organizations can ensure that only authorized traffic reaches sensitive endpoints.

Monitoring and logging are also critical elements in maintaining secure data transmission. By analyzing logs of TLS handshakes, certificate validations, and API requests, administrators can rapidly detect anomalous behavior or potential security breaches. Integrating these logs with a centralized security information and event management (SIEM) system enables real-time alerting and incident response. Properly configured logging not only helps in identifying vulnerabilities but also supports compliance with data protection regulations.

Error handling in secure data transmission is another critical factor. When an error occurs during cryptographic operations or secure communication, generic error messages should be returned to avoid leaking sensitive information. Instead, detailed error logs should be maintained server-side for debugging purposes. This approach mitigates the risk of attackers using error messages to infer system configurations or vulnerabilities.

Finally, staying abreast of emerging standards and vulnerabilities is essential. Regular security audits, penetration testing, and adherence to guidelines published by organizations such as OWASP (Open Web Application Security Project) help maintain robust defenses. Developers should periodically review and update TLS configurations, cipher suites, and certificate management practices in response to new threats. Applying patches and updating dependencies in client and server libraries reduces the risk of known vulnerabilities being exploited.

Ensuring secure data transmission is a multi-layered effort that spans across transport security, certificate validation, token protection, API endpoint configuration, network isolation, error handling, and active monitoring. By adhering to these best practices and employing rigorous security controls, developers can protect sensitive authentication and user management processes from interception and tampering. This layered approach not only safeguards data but also strengthens the overall security posture of Supabase-powered applications, ensuring a resilient and trustworthy user experience.

Chapter 5

Real-time Capabilities in Supabase

This chapter delves into Supabase's real-time features, explaining their setup and integration into applications. It covers listening to database changes, implementing real-time updates, and managing notifications. Strategies for optimizing performance and ensuring reliability are discussed, providing readers with the tools to create responsive, dynamic applications that efficiently leverage Supabase's real-time capabilities for enhanced user experiences.

5.1. Understanding Real-time Features

Supabase provides robust real-time functionalities that enable developers to create applications capable of dynamically reflecting data changes as they occur. The integration of real-time features within Supabase is critical for modern applications where immediacy of data

175

is essential for user engagement and operational efficiency. Real-time applications extend beyond simple static interactions by allowing users to experience dynamic data updates, interactive interfaces, and collaborative environments that adjust promptly to database modifications.

At its core, the real-time capabilities in Supabase are built upon PostgreSQL's replication features. Supabase leverages the Write-Ahead Log (WAL) produced by PostgreSQL to stream changes to connected clients as soon as they occur. This mechanism enables developers to subscribe to specific database events, such as inserts, updates, or deletes, and trigger corresponding actions in the user interface. By doing so, applications maintain consistent and immediate visibility of underlying data, thus reducing latency between events and their display.

The importance of real-time functionality is apparent in several modern application scenarios. For instance, collaborative platforms demand that changes made by one user are instantly communicated to other users in order to prevent data conflicts and ensure a synchronized interaction environment. Similarly, analytics dashboards benefit from real-time data visualization by providing stakeholders with continuously updated metrics that support timely decision-making. Supabase real-time features also prove beneficial in e-commerce platforms where inventory levels, pricing, and order statuses must be promptly updated to reflect recent transactions.

From an architectural perspective, the implementation of real-time features in Supabase introduces a new pattern of event-driven programming. Here, the emphasis is shifted towards subscribing to events rather than traditional polling techniques. Polling typically requires periodic checks for changes, which can lead to unnecessary overhead and delays. Conversely, an event-driven model reacts to changes as they happen, ensuring that applications remain both responsive and efficient in their use of resources. The decoupling of database operations from UI updates also facilitates scalability; as the number of clients increases, the system can continue handling notifications without the need for complex synchronization mechanisms or manual intervention.

To further illustrate the use of these features, consider the integration of Supabase's real-time subscription in a frontend application. Modern JavaScript frameworks can subscribe to database events using a dedicated client library provided by Supabase. Once a subscription is established, the application listens for specific types of changes and updates the state of the component accordingly. This model not only enhances the user experience but also simplifies the underlying logic needed for real-time updates.

```
import { createClient } from '@supabase/supabase-js';

// Initialize Supabase client
const supabaseUrl = 'https://your-project.supabase.co';
const supabaseKey = 'public-anon-key';
const supabase = createClient(supabaseUrl, supabaseKey);

// Subscribe to changes on a specific table
const subscription = supabase
  .from('messages')
  .on('INSERT', payload => {
    console.log('New message received:', payload.new);
    // Update application state or UI
  })
  .subscribe();
```

In this code snippet, the subscription listens for new records inserted into the messages table and triggers an update to the user interface as soon as a new message is detected. This approach eliminates the need for periodic checking of the database, thereby optimizing performance and ensuring that the application remains reactive.

The real-time capabilities are not restricted to small-scale applications only; they scale to meet the demands of complex systems. Applications handling large volumes of data or managing high-frequency transactions benefit significantly from Supabase's efficient data streaming

177

mechanism. The fluidity of real-time operations allows for prompt adjustments in the user interface, even in scenarios with substantial concurrent activity. Such efficiency is crucial when system responsiveness directly impacts user satisfaction or operational speed.

Historically, implementing real-time functionality required reliance on third-party services or extensive custom infrastructure. With Supabase, developers have access to a well-integrated system that combines the power of PostgreSQL with modern web technologies. This integration simplifies the process of achieving real-time synchronization between the client and the server. Furthermore, the platform's use of web sockets for channel communication presents a robust alternative to older, less efficient transport mechanisms such as long polling. Web sockets maintain a persistent connection between the client and the server, reducing connection overhead and enabling a more natural event-driven communication model.

An additional aspect worth noting is how real-time features contribute to enhanced application security and stability. With an event-driven architecture, applications can implement more granular control over data updates and user interactions. By enforcing real-time validations and immediate error handling, the system mitigates the risk of data conflicts, race conditions, or stale information. Developers can use triggers on the client side to ensure consistency of displayed data, thereby reducing the latency involved in communicating with the backend. This timely error detection supports both debugging and rapid adjustments in highly dynamic scenarios.

Real-time notifications further enrich the user experience by providing immediate alerts on significant activities. For example, in a multi-user application, real-time notifications can inform users about changes to shared resources, updates in discussion threads, or modifications to collaborative documents. As the application scales, these notifications ensure that every user remains informed about the current state of the system without having to manually refresh or check for updates.

The practical advantages of real-time systems can also be seen in workflow optimizations. Developers using Supabase can implement observer patterns where UI components automatically subscribe to changes happening in the backend. This pattern reduces the complexity of state management and minimizes the risk of discrepancies between the application's display and its underlying data. By centralizing event handling through Supabase's subscription channels, the responsibility of synchronizing state is shifted away from the application logic, allowing developers to focus on building sophisticated features and enhancing overall application robustness.

Moreover, the underlying technology that supports these real-time operations in Supabase is designed to be both reliable and resilient. The system is engineered to handle various failure conditions gracefully. For instance, in the event of network interruptions, Supabase's real-time connections are designed to attempt reconnections automatically. This built-in retry mechanism maintains the synchronization between the client and server with minimal intervention required by the developer. Such resilience is vital for applications that operate in environments with unreliable network conditions or where maintaining real-time integrity is critical.

Another dimension to consider is the ease of integration with serverless functions and third-party services. The flexibility of Supabase allows developers to combine real-time data subscriptions with cloud functions to execute complex business logic asynchronously. This fusion of real-time data streams with serverless compute resources expands the capabilities of the application, enabling complex workflows that depend on near-instantaneous state changes and computations.

The deployment of real-time features in Supabase is also supported by comprehensive documentation and a vibrant community. This ecosystem serves as a significant resource for developers aiming to extract maximum performance from their applications. Detailed guides, best practice recommendations, and community-contributed examples facilitate a smoother implementation process and encourage experimentation in diverse scenarios.

The analysis of real-time feature utilization leads to the broader understanding that modern applications must embrace reactivity to foster a responsive user experience. As user expectations evolve, the ability to deliver instant feedback and up-to-date information becomes a competitive advantage. Supabase's real-time framework equips developers with the tools necessary to create applications that are not only interactive but also scalable and efficient.

The shift from traditional request-response paradigms to event-driven models marks a significant advancement in web application development. Real-time functionalities provided by Supabase empower applications to move away from rigid data fetching techniques toward a more agile, context-aware approach. Applications become more intuitive, and user interactions more seamless, as the user interface evolves in tandem with the backend data modifications. This synchronous evolution between the server and client ensures that users always interact with the most current state of the application, thereby reinforcing trust and engagement.

Overall, understanding the real-time features within Supabase involves recognizing the underlying architectural components, the efficient data streaming methods, and the seamless integration with modern web protocols such as web sockets. Developers are encouraged to explore these capabilities to enhance the responsiveness of their applications, drive user interaction, and meet the demands of real-time data processing with precision and reliability.

5.2. Setting Up Real-time Functionality

Enabling real-time capabilities within your Supabase project involves a series of configuration steps that bridge the gap between your backend database and the client application. As described in the previous section, Supabase leverages PostgreSQL's inherent features to stream data changes instantaneously. The following discussion provides a detailed guide on configuring initial settings, integrating client libraries, and adjusting server configurations to ensure optimal performance of real-time features.

The initial step is to create a Supabase project via the platform's dashboard. When setting up your project, it is essential to verify that the real-time engine is enabled. This is controlled through the dashboard settings where the real-time functionality is usually activated by default. However, reviewing these settings ensures that all necessary endpoints, such as the web socket URL, are correctly established. This endpoint will serve as the communication bridge between your client and the server.

Before proceeding with client integration, it is crucial to confirm that your database has the appropriate replication settings activated. Supabase's real-time functionality uses PostgreSQL's replication mechanism to monitor database changes. In this context, ensuring that Write-Ahead Logging (WAL) is properly configured is an important prerequisite. This configuration is generally managed by Supabase automatically, but advanced users can inspect the WAL settings through the Postgres configuration menu if custom modifications are required.

Integration with client applications is streamlined through Supabase's official client library. For instance, when using the JavaScript client, the library handles both API requests and web socket connections seamlessly. The connection process requires the Supabase project URL and the corresponding API key. After initializing the client, developers can subscribe to database events by targeting specific tables and action types. The following code snippet demonstrates the process:

```
import { createClient } from '@supabase/supabase-js';

// Replace with your project-specific URL and anonymous key
const supabaseUrl = 'https://your-project.supabase.co';
const supabaseKey = 'your-anon-key';
const supabase = createClient(supabaseUrl, supabaseKey);

// Subscribing to 'INSERT' events in a designated table 'updates'
const realtimeSubscription = supabase
  .from('updates')
  .on('INSERT', payload => {
    console.log('New update received:', payload.new);
    // Handle the new data, e.g., refresh state in the UI
  })
  .subscribe();

// Logging connection status for diagnostic purposes
console.log('Real-time functionality has been initialized.');
```

In this example, the client is initialized with the project URL and an API key, after which a subscription is established on the table named updates. The subscription listens for INSERT events, meaning any new record inserted into the table will trigger the designated callback. Checking the connection status by logging to the console facilitates troubleshooting and confirms successful integration.

A critical aspect of setting up real-time functionality is the handling of client authentication and security. Supabase offers role-based access control (RBAC) through PostgreSQL's Row Level Security (RLS). When establishing real-time subscriptions, ensuring that RLS policies are correctly implemented is essential. Without appropriate RLS policies, even authenticated clients may receive insufficient or excessive access to the data stream. Developers must review and create policies in the Supabase dashboard to allow real-time subscriptions to function securely under the project's authentication scheme.

```
CREATE POLICY "Allow real-time access for authenticated users"
  ON public.updates
```

```
FOR SELECT
USING (auth.uid() IS NOT NULL);
```

The above SQL snippet demonstrates how to establish a basic policy wherein only authenticated users can access the updates table in real time. Integrating such security policies reinforces the integrity of the application and ensures that streaming data does not expose sensitive information inadvertently.

Following the configuration of client connectivity and security, attention must be paid to performance tuning parameters that support real-time operations. Network latency and connection stability are fundamental to delivering a seamless user experience. Supabase real-time connections are maintained via web sockets, which provide a persistent communication channel with minimal overhead compared to traditional HTTP polling. Developers should ensure that firewall settings, network proxies, or other intermediary devices do not disrupt these web socket connections. If issues arise, checking the browser console or network logs can provide insights into connectivity problems.

Apart from client side configurations, server side optimizations play a significant role. Supabase's underlying infrastructure is designed to handle high-frequency data events; however, the performance may be enhanced by fine-tuning database indexing and query optimizations. Since real-time subscriptions rely on immediate detection of changes, poorly optimized queries could introduce delay. Analyzing query execution plans and indexing relevant columns in the target tables can significantly reduce response times and ensure a faultless real-time experience.

Integrating real-time functionality with framework-specific components is straightforward with the Supabase library but may require additional adjustments depending on the framework in use. For example, when working with React, subscribing to a real-time data stream can be combined with state management libraries such as Redux or Context API. A typical integration pattern involves subscribing during the component's lifetime and ensuring that subscriptions are cleaned up appropriately to avoid memory leaks. The following code provides an example of such integration within a React component using hooks:

```
import React, { useState, useEffect } from 'react';
import { createClient } from '@supabase/supabase-js';

const supabaseUrl = 'https://your-project.supabase.co';
const supabaseKey = 'your-anon-key';
const supabase = createClient(supabaseUrl, supabaseKey);

const UpdatesComponent = () => {
  const [updates, setUpdates] = useState([]);

  useEffect(() => {
    const subscription = supabase
      .from('updates')
      .on('INSERT', payload => {
        setUpdates(current => [payload.new, ...current]);
      })
      .subscribe();

    return () => {
      supabase.removeSubscription(subscription);
    };
  }, []);

  return (
    <div>
      <h2>Real-time Updates</h2>
      {updates.map((update, index) => (
        <div key={index}>{update.content}</div>
      ))}
    </div>
  );
};

export default UpdatesComponent;
```

This React example demonstrates subscribing to a real-time data stream, managing state with the useState hook, and ensuring subscription cleanup using the useEffect hook. By removing the subscription when the component unmounts, the code avoids unnecessary resource consumption and potential memory leaks.

Another aspect of configuring real-time functionality is preparing for network failure scenarios. Given that real-time applications depend on persistent connections, it is advisable to implement reconnection strategies that can recover from temporary connectivity losses. Supabase's client library includes mechanisms to detect dropped connections and initiate reconnection protocols gracefully. Developers may also incorporate custom logic into their error handling routines to notify users of connection issues, thereby improving the overall robustness of the application.

Monitoring and logging are essential components of a successful real-time integration. Comprehensive logging of connection events, subscription actions, and data payloads assists in diagnosing issues during development and after production deployment. Setting up logging within the client code can be as simple as routing important events to a dedicated log service or displaying them via the browser console during debugging phases. For environments with strict production requirements, external logging solutions can capture these events for further analysis.

The overall process of setting up real-time functionality in Supabase is simplified by the platform's integrated tooling and extensive documentation. Comprehensive guides provided by Supabase ensure that even developers new to real-time web development can effectively configure and utilize these features. The ease of setup encourages rapid prototyping, allowing development teams to focus on implementing sophisticated business logic rather than managing underlying infrastructure complexities.

Additionally, the modular design of Supabase's real-time engine allows for future expansions. As applications scale and their requirements evolve, developers can extend the core functionalities by integrating with serverless functions or microservices. Such integrations can offer more customized data processing pipelines or aggregate data from multiple sources in real time. This flexibility signifies that the steps taken during the initial setup phase lay the groundwork for more elaborate real-time applications capable of handling diverse workloads.

Real-time functionality significantly enhances interactive user experiences by ensuring continuous data flow from the backend to the client. Establishing a robust installation and configuration process with Supabase sets the stage for dynamic, responsive applications. As demonstrated, configuring the dashboard settings, verifying database replication, integrating client libraries, securing data access, and optimizing performance combine to create a cohesive real-time data layer that underpins modern web applications.

Careful attention to these configuration details facilitates the leveraging of real-time features in scenarios ranging from collaborative tools to live data dashboards, ensuring that all components work harmoniously. The reliability and efficiency of these operations depend on both the correct setup and the ongoing monitoring of the system. Proper initial configuration minimizes potential pitfalls in data synchronization and performance, ensuring that the application maintains its responsiveness as it scales.

Successful implementation of real-time functionalities within Supabase requires not only technical precision in setting up system parameters but also an understanding of the overall application architecture. The steps described here create a foundation that enables the subsequent incorporation of advanced real-time features, ensuring that data remains accurate and the application is robust against unexpected failures.

186

5.3. Listening to Database Changes

Supabase implements an event-driven architecture that allows developers to subscribe directly to changes occurring within the database. This section elaborates on the mechanisms available for subscribing to database events, processing payloads, and integrating these updates seamlessly within an application. The subscription model in Supabase is designed to notify clients about modifications to data in near real-time, ensuring that applications remain synchronized with the latest dataset state without the need for periodic polling.

The core concept behind listening to database changes in Supabase is the usage of web socket connections, which facilitate persistent communication channels between the client and the server. Once a connection is established, the client can subscribe to specific events, such as record insertions, updates, or deletions. When any of these events occur, the Supabase backend immediately streams the change payload to the client. This event-driven paradigm minimizes latency and provides a responsive user experience, which is increasingly important in modern applications.

Consider the following example in JavaScript that demonstrates subscribing to the INSERT, UPDATE, and DELETE events for a database table named notifications. In this scenario, the client reacts to any change in the table, processes the payload, and adjusts the application state accordingly:

```
import { createClient } from '@supabase/supabase-js';

const supabaseUrl = 'https://your-project.supabase.co';
const supabaseKey = 'your-anon-key';
const supabase = createClient(supabaseUrl, supabaseKey);

const subscription = supabase
  .from('notifications')
  .on('INSERT', payload => {
    console.log('New notification:', payload.new);
```

```
    // Handle the new record
  })
  .on('UPDATE', payload => {
    console.log('Notification updated:', payload.new);
    // Update the record in the UI
  })
  .on('DELETE', payload => {
    console.log('Notification removed:', payload.old);
    // Remove the record from the display
  })
  .subscribe();
```

In this code, three distinct event paths are handled: when a new record is inserted, when an existing record is updated, and when a record is deleted. The `payload` object encapsulates the details of the event, where `payload.new` contains the new record data and `payload.old` contains the data from a deleted record. This model allows for a unified approach to data management across different types of operations.

The payload structure is designed to include contextual information about the event. For an `INSERT` event, for instance, the payload typically contains a `new` key that holds the complete record inserted into the database. In contrast, a `DELETE` event payload includes an `old` key representing the record that has been removed. The event type `UPDATE` typically provides both `old` and `new` keys, allowing the client to compare the previous state with the current state. The flexibility of the payload formats supports various application-specific requirements where conditional logic might be implemented, for example, by comparing previous and new values to determine the significance of a change.

In scenarios where multiple tables require monitoring, each subscription can be implemented separately to ensure modularity and clarity in the codebase. Developers might decide to create a dedicated module that manages all real-time subscriptions, abstracting the complexity of subscription management and providing a centralized error-handling mechanism. Such an approach reduces redundancy and simplifies debugging by consolidating all subscriptions in one location.

One important aspect of handling subscriptions in a production environment is the need to manage the lifecycle of these connections. It is essential to unsubscribe from events when they are no longer needed. Failure to do so can lead to memory leaks, unnecessary network traffic, and potential data inconsistency in the user interface. For instance, within a single-page application, developers should ensure that subscriptions are terminated when the relevant component is unmounted. The following code snippet demonstrates how to effectively clean up a subscription in a React component:

```
import React, { useEffect, useState } from 'react';
import { createClient } from '@supabase/supabase-js';

const supabaseUrl = 'https://your-project.supabase.co';
const supabaseKey = 'your-anon-key';
const supabase = createClient(supabaseUrl, supabaseKey);

const Notifications = () => {
  const [notifications, setNotifications] = useState([]);

  useEffect(() => {
    const subscription = supabase
      .from('notifications')
      .on('INSERT', payload => {
        setNotifications(prev => [payload.new, ...prev]);
      })
      .subscribe();

    return () => {
      supabase.removeSubscription(subscription);
    };
  }, []);

  return (
    <div>
      <h3>Live Notifications</h3>
      {notifications.map((note, idx) => (
        <div key={idx}>{note.message}</div>
      ))}
    </div>
  );
};

export default Notifications;
```

189

The above example emphasizes proper resource management. By removing the subscription when the component unmounts, the application avoids maintaining unnecessary connections, which can degrade performance over time. In addition, this practice improves the scalability of the application, especially when real-time functionalities are used extensively across various components.

Besides standard event subscriptions for table changes, Supabase allows for deeper integration with business logic through the use of server-side triggers. Developers can define triggers in PostgreSQL that not only log changes but also execute stored procedures or functions. This facility enables complex operations such as data validation, notification dispatch, or even synchronization with third-party services before the subscription payload is propagated to the client. These mechanisms further enhance the responsiveness and adaptability of real-time applications by embedding advanced data processing capabilities directly in the database layer.

When setting up subscriptions, it is also advisable to incorporate error handling and monitoring strategies. Network interruptions, invalid payloads, or unexpected errors may disrupt the continuous flow of data. Supabase's client library is designed to support reconnection protocols, but developers should implement their own notifications or logging mechanisms to capture and address errors during data streaming. Incorporating detailed logging facilitates debugging in live environments. Additionally, endpoints for subscriptions can be monitored using external tools that track connection statuses, latency, and data throughput, ensuring that the real-time system adheres to the performance benchmarks required by the application.

The configuration of Row Level Security (RLS) in Supabase further influences how and which data changes are observed through subscriptions. RLS policies ensure that only authorized data modifications trigger events to specific users or roles. For example, in multi-tenant applications or systems with varying levels of user access, using RLS policies helps in filtering out unwanted data from the subscriptions. A well-defined RLS policy not only secures the application but also reduces the volume of data transmitted through real-time channels, thereby optimizing overall performance.

```
CREATE POLICY "Allow only user-specific notifications"
  ON public.notifications
  FOR SELECT
  USING (user_id = auth.uid());
```

Implementing such a policy restricts the results delivered via the real-time subscription to those records that match the authenticated user's identifier. This selective approach to data propagation reinforces privacy and minimizes network overhead.

It is also useful to consider scalability practices when employing real-time subscriptions. As the frequency of data changes increases, the volume of events transmitted can grow rapidly. Efficient management of these events requires an architecture that is both horizontally scalable and resilient to high loads. Techniques such as aggregating events, debouncing rapid sequences of changes, or even implementing priority queues for critical updates can be employed to handle high volumes of real-time data without compromising the end-user experience.

Furthermore, developing a comprehensive testing strategy for real-time capabilities is imperative. Automated tests should verify that subscriptions respond as intended under various conditions, including high load, intermittent connectivity, and erroneous data updates. Integration tests can simulate sequences of database changes and validate that the correct payload is received by the client. Such tests ensure that the real-time mechanisms remain robust as the application evolves and new features are added.

Effective use of Supabase subscriptions also opens avenues for advanced analytics and user behavior metrics. By capturing events in real time, developers can analyze patterns, detect system anomalies, and implement adaptive features based on user interactions. For instance, logging the rate at which certain types of data are updated can yield insights into user activity, system performance, and potential areas for optimization. This continuous feedback loop between the database and the client not only enhances user satisfaction but also informs data-driven decision-making within the application.

Overall, listening to database changes using Supabase's subscription features encapsulates a mix of technical setup, security considerations, and performance tuning. The system's architecture is designed to support a wide range of applications, from simple notification systems to complex collaborative tools that require instant awareness of underlying data modifications. By subscribing to events, developers can implement dynamic interfaces that reflect changes immediately, ensuring that users interact with the latest and most accurate data available.

Such integration of real-time functionalities transforms the traditional request-response model into a more agile, event-propagation framework. This architecture enables the application to respond to data changes as they occur, thereby reducing lag and improving overall user engagement. Implementing efficient subscription management, ensuring data security, and optimizing for performance are key factors in leveraging the full potential of Supabase real-time capabilities, which ultimately contribute to the creation of robust, scalable, and user-friendly applications.

5.4. Implementing Real-time Updates in Applications

Integrating real-time updates in frontend applications is essential for achieving dynamic and responsive user interfaces. Building upon the previous discussions on subscribing to database changes and setting up real-time functionality, this section focuses on various techniques for implementing real-time updates in the frontend that contribute to a seamless user experience. The primary goal is to ensure that changes in the underlying data are immediately reflected against the user interface, thereby eliminating stale or inconsistent data views.

A typical approach to creating real-time experiences involves utilizing client libraries that interface with Supabase's web socket-based real-time engine. These libraries abstract much of the complexity involved in establishing persistent connections, handling reconnection scenarios, and parsing payloads arriving from the server. For instance, integrating the Supabase JavaScript client in a modern JavaScript framework like React or Vue simplifies the process by encapsulating the logic of subscribing to events and updating state accordingly.

Consider a scenario where an application is tasked with displaying a live feed of messages. Once a new message is inserted into the database, the corresponding visual component must update instantly to reflect the change. Below is an example of how real-time updates are implemented using React. The component initializes a subscription to the relevant table and updates its state, ensuring that each incoming message is rendered without the need for a manual refresh.

```
import React, { useState, useEffect } from 'react';
import { createClient } from '@supabase/supabase-js';

const supabaseUrl = 'https://your-project.supabase.co';
const supabaseKey = 'your-anon-key';
const supabase = createClient(supabaseUrl, supabaseKey);

const LiveFeed = () => {
  const [messages, setMessages] = useState([]);

  useEffect(() => {
    // Subscribe to the 'INSERT' event on the 'messages' table
    const subscription = supabase
      .from('messages')
      .on('INSERT', payload => {
```

```
      // Update state with the incoming new message
      setMessages(prevMessages => [payload.new, ...prevMessages]);
    })
    .subscribe();

  // Cleanup subscription when the component unmounts
  return () => {
    supabase.removeSubscription(subscription);
  };
}, []);

  return (
    <div>
      <h2>Live Feed</h2>
      {messages.map((message, index) => (
        <div key={index}>
          <p>{message.content}</p>
          <small>{new Date(message.created_at).toLocaleString()}</
    small>
        </div>
      ))}
    </div>
  );
};

export default LiveFeed;
```

In this example, the component leverages the useEffect hook to set up and later clean up the subscription. The state is managed with the useState hook, ensuring that incoming messages are prepended to the existing list. This approach minimizes latency between data change and UI update and preserves a smooth user experience by eliminating unnecessary re-renders.

Beyond React, similar techniques can be applied in other frameworks or vanilla JavaScript applications. Framework-agnostic approaches involve manually managing the connection's lifecycle, utilizing callback methods triggered by Supabase events, and updating the Document Object Model (DOM) accordingly. Although modern frameworks abstract many of the complexities involved in state management and component lifecycles, understanding the underlying mechanisms is valu-

194

able for optimizing performance and troubleshooting issues in production environments.

When designing applications with real-time updates, it is important to consider the strategies for efficient data handling. In scenarios where multiple types of events occur frequently, state management might become complex. In such cases, the use of centralized state management libraries, such as Redux for React or Vuex for Vue, is advisable. Centralized state management helps coordinate multiple real-time data streams by consolidating all updates into a single source of truth. This design pattern reduces redundancy and ensures consistency across different components that rely on the same data.

Incorporating real-time updates within the UI often necessitates additional user interface enhancements to visually communicate data changes. For example, when new content is added, developers can opt to animate the insertion of new items, highlight them briefly, or display a notification that draws the user's attention. These subtle user experience improvements contribute to a more engaging and intuitive interface. Animation libraries and CSS transitions can be integrated seamlessly into the application to provide visual cues without incurring significant performance costs.

Error handling and reconnection strategies are critical to maintaining a robust real-time experience. Network issues, server downtime, or interruptions in the web socket connection can temporarily disrupt the flow of data. Supabase's client library is designed to automatically handle reconnections, but implementing additional feedback mechanisms in the user interface is beneficial. For instance, a dropdown alert can inform users of connectivity issues, and a retry indicator can be displayed until the connection stabilizes. Monitoring connection status and logging events in a centralized manner aids developers in diagnosing issues and executing corrective measures promptly.

```
import React, { useState, useEffect } from 'react';
```

```
import { createClient } from '@supabase/supabase-js';

const supabaseUrl = 'https://your-project.supabase.co';
const supabaseKey = 'your-anon-key';
const supabase = createClient(supabaseUrl, supabaseKey);

const LiveNotifications = () => {
  const [notifications, setNotifications] = useState([]);
  const [connectionStatus, setConnectionStatus] = useState('Connected
    ');

  useEffect(() => {
    const subscription = supabase
      .from('notifications')
      .on('INSERT', payload => {
        setNotifications(current => [payload.new, ...current]);
      })
      .subscribe();

    const handleError = error => {
      console.error('Real-time error:', error);
      setConnectionStatus('Reconnecting');
    };

    // Simulate error handling (actual implementation may vary)
    supabase.on('error', handleError);

    return () => {
      supabase.removeSubscription(subscription);
      supabase.off('error', handleError);
    };
  }, []);

  return (
    <div>
      <h2>Notifications</h2>
      <p>Status: {connectionStatus}</p>
      {notifications.map((note, index) => (
        <div key={index}>{note.message}</div>
      ))}
    </div>
  );
};

export default LiveNotifications;
```

This snippet demonstrates a simple approach to error handling and

196

connection monitoring. Although the Supabase library may internally manage reconnect logic, exposing connection status in the user interface provides greater transparency and user confidence. An integrated feedback loop in the frontend ensures that users are aware of underlying connectivity issues, and developers can capture error events for future analysis.

Real-time updates extend beyond handling new inserts; they also encompass modifications and deletions. In applications such as collaborative workspaces or shared dashboards, updates must be propagated across multiple data operations. Developers can utilize similar subscription patterns to handle UPDATE and DELETE events. In practice, this involves comparing previous and new data states and categorizing the changes accordingly. For example, if an item is updated, the frontend can perform a diff comparison and only update the portions of the UI that have changed, thereby improving performance and reducing flicker.

An additional technique that can enhance the real-time experience is the batching of updates. In high-frequency systems, individual updates might overwhelm the rendering process if applied immediately. By implementing a mechanism to collect several events into a batch and then processing them in a single update cycle, the application can achieve a smoother visual transition. Debouncing and throttling strategies are often employed in these scenarios to limit state updates to manageable intervals, thereby ensuring that the interface does not freeze or become unresponsive during heavy data loads.

The architectural design of the frontend also plays a crucial role in effective real-time updates. Organizing components in a manner that localizes state changes minimizes the scope of re-rendering. This compartmentalization is particularly advantageous when only a subset of the application relies on real-time data. Optimizing component hierarchies to decouple real-time streams from static content ensures that only the necessary parts of the user interface refresh when updates occur.

In addition to performance considerations, the integration of real-time updates must adhere to best practices for user accessibility and interaction. For instance, dynamically updating content should be announced to assistive technologies, allowing users with disabilities to remain informed of changes. Adopting standards such as ARIA live regions can provide semantic cues to screen readers, ensuring that all users receive an equivalent experience regardless of their interaction modality.

Adopting these techniques across various frameworks and environments ensures that the benefits of real-time updates are fully realized. As applications become more data-intensive and user demands for seamless experiences increase, deploying an efficient strategy for real-time updates is rapidly becoming a necessity. By carefully managing subscriptions, optimizing state updates, and integrating UI enhancements, developers can build interfaces that feel instantaneous and intuitive.

Ultimately, the implementation of real-time updates in frontend applications using Supabase is a culmination of several interconnected practices. The process begins with proper setup and authentication, extends through efficient subscription management, and includes thoughtful state handling and error mitigation. Each element contributes to an overall strategy that ensures real-time data changes are propagated instantly and reliably, resulting in a dynamic and engaging user experience.

5.5. Handling Real-time Notifications and Alerts

Effectively informing users of key changes and events in real-time is critical in modern applications, where immediacy and user engagement are paramount. Real-time notifications and alerts provide an additional layer of interaction, ensuring that users are continuously aware of significant updates such as new messages, transaction changes, or system events, without having to manually refresh the interface. This section discusses techniques for setting up notifications and alerts using Supabase's real-time engine and integrating them into frontend applications to cultivate a responsive and informative user experience.

Real-time notification mechanisms are built upon the fundamental ability to listen to data changes in the database. By subscribing to specific events—such as inserts, updates, or deletions—developers can trigger alert systems in the client application. This enables a reactive design where alerts are generated only when specific conditions are met. Such selective notifications are beneficial in reducing notification fatigue, ensuring that only high-priority or critical events prompt user alerts. For instance, a collaborative editing platform might display notifications when significant changes are made by other users, prompting appropriate user acknowledgment or action.

A primary step in implementing notifications and alerts is to clearly define which events warrant a notification. This often involves establishing a set of business rules that filter out low-priority changes and focus on alerts that might disrupt or directly benefit the end user. Supabase's subscription model allows developers to tap into different database events and apply conditional logic to trigger notifications. In many cases, this functionality is combined with a dedicated user interface element such as a toast popup, modal alert, or an update counter in a navigation bar.

Consider an example where real-time subscriptions are used to notify users of new system alerts or messages. The following code snippet demonstrates how to subscribe to an INSERT event on a specific table, process the payload, and then trigger a notification in the user interface.

This integration is typically achieved by combining state management and UI frameworks to display notification components dynamically.

```
import { createClient } from '@supabase/supabase-js';
import { showToast } from './notificationUtils'; // Assume a helper
    for displaying UI alerts

const supabaseUrl = 'https://your-project.supabase.co';
const supabaseKey = 'your-anon-key';
const supabase = createClient(supabaseUrl, supabaseKey);

// Subscribe to 'INSERT' events in the 'alerts' table
const notificationSubscription = supabase
  .from('alerts')
  .on('INSERT', payload => {
    // Extract key information from the payload
    const { title, message, level } = payload.new;
    // Trigger a notification based on the alert level
    showToast({ title, message, level });
  })
  .subscribe();

console.log('Notification subscription established.');
```

In this example, the `alerts` table is monitored for new entries. When a new alert is inserted, the payload is processed to extract details such as `title`, `message`, and `level`. A helper function `showToast` is invoked to display an alert; this is typically implemented to render a visually distinct message that notifies the user of the update. The alert level can be used to categorize notifications, for example, highlighting error messages in red and informational messages in blue.

Customizing notifications based on the alert level is a common practice in contemporary interfaces. This categorization allows users to distinguish between different levels of urgency and respond accordingly. For example, a warning or error notification might prompt an immediate action, whereas an informational alert could be displayed less intrusively. Developers should strive for a balance in which notifications are noticeable without becoming intrusive or overwhelming the user interface.

Integrating notifications into the front-end architecture often involves utilizing a state management system that collects and organizes alert data. For instance, in a React application, developers can manage a list of active notifications using a global or component-level state. The following example demonstrates this approach using React hooks, where new notifications are appended to a state array and then rendered in a dedicated notification component.

```
import React, { useState, useEffect } from 'react';
import { createClient } from '@supabase/supabase-js';

const supabaseUrl = 'https://your-project.supabase.co';
const supabaseKey = 'your-anon-key';
const supabase = createClient(supabaseUrl, supabaseKey);

const NotificationCenter = () => {
  const [notifications, setNotifications] = useState([]);

  useEffect(() => {
    const subscription = supabase
      .from('alerts')
      .on('INSERT', payload => {
        // Append the new notification to the state
        setNotifications(currentAlerts => [payload.new, ...
      currentAlerts]);
      })
      .subscribe();

    // Clean up the subscription on component unmount
    return () => {
      supabase.removeSubscription(subscription);
    };
  }, []);

  return (
    <div className="notification-center">
      {notifications.map((alert, index) => (
        <div key={index} className={`notification ${alert.level}`}>
          <strong>{alert.title}</strong>
          <p>{alert.message}</p>
        </div>
      ))}
    </div>
  );
};
```

```
export default NotificationCenter;
```

In this component, the `NotificationCenter` manages an array of notifications using React's `useState` hook and subscribes to the `alerts` table. Each notification is rendered with a class corresponding to its level, allowing for flexible styling determined by urgency or type of alert. This dynamic update of the UI allows users to be continuously aware of critical changes, creating a seamless and interactive experience.

Beyond simple display, the handling of real-time notifications may also include marking notifications as read or dismissing them, which requires communication back to the Supabase backend. A common approach is to provide action buttons within each notification that trigger an update in the database. For example, when a user dismisses a notification, an `UPDATE` operation might flag the notification as read, thereby removing it from the active alert state. The following code snippet shows how such an update might be implemented:

```
function dismissNotification(notificationId) {
  supabase
    .from('alerts')
    .update({ dismissed: true })
    .eq('id', notificationId)
    .then(response => {
      if (response.error) {
        console.error('Error dismissing notification:', response.
    error);
      } else {
        console.log(`Notification ${notificationId} dismissed.`);
      }
    });
}
```

This function demonstrates the reverse flow where user actions on the frontend result in updates to the database. Once a notification is updated to a dismissed state, additional UI logic can remove it from the notification center, ensuring that the user interface remains clutter-free and focused on active alerts.

Integration of these notification and alert mechanisms into applications must also account for error handling and edge cases. Network connectivity issues or server-side errors may result in missed notifications or delayed updates. Implementing fallback strategies, such as periodic synchronization with the backend, can help mitigate such issues. Logging mechanisms should capture errors related to notifications, and user feedback should be provided to indicate if an alert might not have been delivered. This robustness in design ensures that the notification system remains reliable even under suboptimal conditions.

Design considerations for notifications also include the aesthetic and interactive aspects of alert components. Developers can take advantage of CSS transitions and animations to suavely introduce and remove notifications, thereby enhancing user engagement without compromising on performance. Accessibility also plays a crucial role; for instance, ensuring that notifications are readable by screen readers and that they conform to ARIA guidelines is essential for reaching all users. Implementing these best practices achieves a balance between functionality and user experience.

A further enhancement in notification handling involves the integration with external notification systems, such as email or mobile push notifications. While Supabase's real-time features offer in-app notifications, coupling them with external systems can extend the application's reach. In scenarios where it is critical that users receive an alert regardless of their current application usage, developers might trigger external notifications using Supabase functions or webhooks. Such multi-channel notification strategies ensure that critical alerts are delivered through the appropriate channel based on user preferences.

Apart from user-facing elements, analytics on notification delivery can contribute significantly to the long-term optimization of the alert system. Capturing data on when notifications are viewed, dismissed, or ignored can help developers fine-tune the criteria for which events trigger alerts. By integrating analytics modules, developers can quantitatively assess the effectiveness of the notification system and adjust thresholds, content, or display frequency accordingly. This datadriven approach leads to continuous improvement in how notifications contribute to overall user satisfaction and system responsiveness.

Managing subscription lifecycle consistency is critical when handling notifications. Unsubscribing properly from real-time updates when the notification module is no longer in use conserves resources and prevents memory leaks. This is particularly relevant in single-page applications where the notification component might be mounted and unmounted based on user navigation. Developers should ensure that subscriptions are cleaned up, as demonstrated in the previously provided React code examples, to maintain application performance and stability.

In essence, handling real-time notifications and alerts via Supabase involves a careful orchestration of backend subscriptions, frontend state management, conditional user interface rendering, and error handling. By utilizing structured subscription mechanisms provided by Supabase, developers can build alert systems that are both robust and user-friendly. Implementation details such as dynamically updating UI components, providing user interaction features for dismissing or marking notifications, and integrating system-wide logging and analytics allow the notifications to support both immediate user feedback and long-term insights into application performance.

The strategies discussed herein serve to empower developers with a comprehensive framework for building effective real-time notification systems. Such systems are instrumental in ensuring that users remain informed of key changes and events as they occur, thereby enhancing overall engagement and trust in the application's functionality.

5.6. Optimizing Performance for Real-time Operations

Optimizing performance in Supabase real-time operations is a multifaceted task that involves both backend and client-side strategies. Given that real-time applications depend on rapid data synchronization and low-latency communications, it is critical to adopt best practices that ensure efficient handling of high-frequency events. The following discussion covers strategies such as optimizing database queries, managing subscriptions thoughtfully, and incorporating performance-tuning techniques in client applications.

A foundational aspect of real-time operations is the efficient management of the underlying PostgreSQL database. Real-time features in Supabase rely on PostgreSQL's Write-Ahead Log (WAL) to capture database changes. However, if the database contains inefficient queries or lacks proper indexing, the resulting latency can undermine the responsiveness of real-time features. To mitigate such issues, developers should analyze query execution plans and create indexes on columns that are frequently monitored by subscriptions. For example, if a table `orders` is being heavily subscribed to for updates, creating indexes on key columns such as `order_status` and `customer_id` can drastically improve the speed of data retrieval and reduce overhead when notifications are broadcast.

```
CREATE INDEX idx_order_status ON orders(order_status);
CREATE INDEX idx_customer_id ON orders(customer_id);
```

In addition to indexing, careful design of database schemas can prevent redundant data processing. Normalizing data and structuring tables to reduce duplication can lead to a smaller volume of changes being propagated through the real-time engine. Efficient schema design minimizes the amount of information that must be transmitted and processed by subscribed clients.

205

On the client side, managing subscriptions efficiently is essential to prevent performance bottlenecks, especially in large-scale applications. Each active subscription consumes system resources and network bandwidth, so it is advantageous to avoid duplicating subscriptions for the same event or table. One effective approach is to implement a centralized subscription controller that manages multiple subscriptions and ensures that each event is processed only once per client session. By consolidating subscriptions, developers can reduce unnecessary network traffic and maintain a cleaner, more scalable codebase.

Moreover, debounce and throttle mechanisms are practical techniques for controlling the frequency of UI updates in response to real-time events. In scenarios where a high volume of changes occurs in rapid succession, immediately updating the user interface for every incoming event could overwhelm both the client and the network. Instead, grouping events or applying a debounce function to delay updates can yield a smoother user experience without noticeably sacrificing responsiveness.

```
import { debounce } from 'lodash';

const handleBatchUpdate = debounce((newData) => {
  // Update UI with batched data
  setData(prev => [...newData, ...prev]);
}, 300);

// Subscription callback that collects events and passes them for
    debouncing
supabase
  .from('updates')
  .on('INSERT', payload => {
    handleBatchUpdate([payload.new]);
  })
  .subscribe();
```

The example above uses the `debounce` function from Lodash to delay state updates by 300 milliseconds. This technique ensures that the client processes grouped data rather than every single update, thereby reducing the rendering load and enhancing overall performance.

Another critical consideration is the efficient use of network resources. Supabase real-time subscriptions are maintained over web sockets, which inherently provide a persistent and efficient connection. Despite the efficiency of web sockets, network latency and intermittent bandwidth fluctuations can impact the quality of real-time updates. To address these challenges, developers should ensure that their application includes robust error handling and reconnection strategies. By monitoring the status of web socket connections and implementing automatic retry logic, the application can recover gracefully from transient network issues.

```
let subscription = supabase
  .from('updates')
  .on('INSERT', payload => {
    // Process incoming payload
    console.log('New update:', payload.new);
  })
  .subscribe();

const reconnectSubscription = () => {
  if (!subscription) {
    subscription = supabase
      .from('updates')
      .on('INSERT', payload => {
        console.log('Reconnected update:', payload.new);
      })
      .subscribe();
  }
};

// Assuming a network monitoring function that triggers reconnection
      events
window.addEventListener('online', reconnectSubscription);
```

In optimizing performance, it is also crucial to consider the volume of real-time data being transmitted. In cases where real-time streams emit a large number of events, developers can implement filtering on the server side to ensure that only relevant events are forwarded to clients. Supabase allows developers to specify filtering conditions directly in the subscription query. For example, if only high-priority events are of interest, the subscription can be tailored to only capture those events, thereby reducing bandwidth usage and processing time on the client side.

```
const subscription = supabase
  .from('events:priority=eq.high')
  .on('INSERT', payload => {
    console.log('High-priority event:', payload.new);
  })
  .subscribe();
```

Implementing such filters ensures that clients are not burdened with processing low-priority or irrelevant data. Additionally, when updates are received, developers should implement efficient state management practices to avoid performance degradation. Using immutable data structures and functional updates within state management frameworks (such as Redux or the Context API in React) can limit unnecessary re-renders, thereby improving the overall responsiveness of the user interface.

Caching is another indispensable technique in the optimization arsenal. By caching frequently accessed data on the client side, applications can reduce the number of calls to the database and lower latency for read operations. While real-time subscriptions provide immediate updates, certain data that rarely changes or that can tolerate slight delays may be retrieved from a cache instead of being loaded repeatedly, thus conserving computational and network resources.

In addition to frontend optimizations, server-side performance tuning can provide substantial improvements. For instance, adjusting the PostgreSQL configuration parameters to better accommodate high-velocity real-time traffic can lead to more efficient throughput. Parameters such as `max_connections`, `shared_buffers`, and `wal_buffers` may require tuning based on the application's load profile. Although Supabase manages much of this transparently, users with advanced requirements can review and suggest configuration tuning to further enhance performance.

208

Monitoring and logging are also vital components of any performance optimization strategy. Continuous monitoring of real-time metrics, such as latency, throughput, and error rates, enables developers to detect performance bottlenecks early and address them proactively. Integrated logging can capture detailed information about subscription events, network anomalies, and database performance. This information is invaluable for iterative performance tuning and for scaling the application as usage increases.

Beyond the technical optimizations, design patterns play a key role in maintaining optimal real-time performance. For example, implementing a publish-subscribe pattern where a central broker handles event distribution can reduce the overhead on individual client components. This systemic design allows for better scaling since it localizes event handling and minimizes redundant processing across the application. Moreover, micro-optimizations such as lazy-loading non-critical components, postponing non-urgent updates, and offloading resource-intensive tasks to background processes can cumulatively enhance performance.

When performance optimizations are applied collectively, the result is an application that scales gracefully as the volume of real-time data grows. Each layer of optimization, from database schema improvements to client-side event handling, contributes to reducing latency and ensuring that data is propagated efficiently. By structuring subscriptions appropriately, applying filters, batching updates, and incorporating error handling, developers harness the full potential of Supabase's real-time capabilities while maintaining high performance under load.

Optimizing real-time operations is not a one-off task but requires continuous evaluation and refinement. As the application evolves and new features are introduced, it is imperative to re-assess the performance impact of these changes on the overall real-time infrastructure.

Regular performance audits, user feedback, and data-driven analyses help in identifying areas where further optimizations can be made. This proactive approach to performance management ensures that the application remains responsive and scalable even as usage patterns change over time.

The best practices outlined here are applicable across diverse real-time scenarios. Whether the application handles live notifications, collaborative data streams, or high-frequency updates, optimizing performance is central to providing a seamless user experience. The strategies encompass a holistic approach, from the efficient use of database resources to the thoughtful management of client-side updates, and they are designed to minimize latency, reduce unnecessary computations, and maximize the efficiency of data propagation through the real-time framework.

Implementing these practices ultimately leads to a robust, scalable, and efficient real-time system. As developers continue to iterate on these optimizations, the benefits become apparent in the form of reduced server load, faster response times, and a more engaging and fluid user experience. This commitment to performance optimization not only enhances the technical quality of the application but also aligns with the broader goals of reliability and user satisfaction in modern web development.

5.7. Ensuring Reliability and Resilience

Real-time systems must be designed to withstand a variety of failure modes, including network interruptions, server outages, and data inconsistencies. In the context of Supabase, ensuring reliability and resilience involves planning for transient failures, implementing robust error handling and reconnection strategies, and employing monitoring and logging to proactively detect and rectify issues. Understanding and preparing for these scenarios is essential to maintaining a responsive and stable user experience in applications that depend on continuous data synchronization.

A key consideration for achieving resilience in real-time features is the implementation of automatic reconnection mechanisms. Web socket connections, despite their efficiency, are susceptible to interruptions due to network fluctuations or server-side issues. Supabase's client library provides basic reconnection capabilities, but it is advisable for developers to layer additional logic into their applications. Custom reconnection strategies can include exponential backoff, user notifications about connection status, and a graceful degradation path that ensures minimal data loss. The following example illustrates a simple reconnection strategy using JavaScript:

```
let retryCount = 0;
const maxRetries = 5;

function subscribeToUpdates() {
  let subscription = supabase
    .from('updates')
    .on('INSERT', payload => {
      console.log('Received update:', payload.new);
      // Process the payload accordingly
    })
    .subscribe();

  subscription.on('error', error => {
    console.error('Subscription error:', error);
    retryCount++;

    if (retryCount <= maxRetries) {
      const delay = Math.pow(2, retryCount) * 1000;
      setTimeout(() => {
        console.log(`Attempting to resubscribe... (attempt ${
    retryCount})`);
        subscribeToUpdates();
      }, delay);
    } else {
      console.error('Max reconnection attempts reached.');
    }
  });
}
```

```
subscribeToUpdates();
```

In this sample, an exponential backoff mechanism is used to attempt a reconnection. Each failure increases the delay before the next reconnection attempt, reducing the load on the server during network instability and mitigating the risk of repeated connection failures. Such strategies ensure that temporary issues do not result in prolonged downtime.

Reliability also depends on comprehensive error handling. When using real-time subscriptions, developers should anticipate and catch possible exceptions that might arise from processing incoming data. For example, changes in database schema, malformed payloads, or unauthorized data access can all trigger errors. Implementing try-catch blocks or promise rejection handlers around critical code paths aids in capturing these exceptions. Once captured, errors should be logged for later analysis, and appropriate measures should be taken to rectify them or notify the user. The following code snippet demonstrates how error handling might be incorporated into a subscription callback:

```
supabase
  .from('notifications')
  .on('INSERT', payload => {
    try {
      if (!payload.new) {
        throw new Error('Payload is missing new data');
      }
      console.log('Notification received:', payload.new);
      // Further processing of notification
    } catch (error) {
      console.error('Error processing notification:', error);
      // Optionally, display an error message or trigger a fallback
      mechanism
    }
  })
  .subscribe();
```

By incorporating detailed error handling, applications can avoid swapping a faulty data state into the user interface, thus preventing data inconsistencies. Logging errors to a centralized monitoring system further supports long-term reliability, as recurring issues can be identified and addressed in future iterations of the application.

Another strategy to increase reliability involves setting up fallback mechanisms. In scenarios where real-time connections are completely interrupted or when reconnections fail, it is advisable to implement alternative data-fetching strategies, such as periodic polling. Although polling is less efficient than event-driven updates, it can serve as a temporary fallback to ensure that the application remains at least partially operational. A hybrid approach that combines real-time subscriptions with scheduled polling can be particularly effective. Consider the following example:

```
function fetchLatestData() {
  supabase
    .from('updates')
    .select('*')
    .then(response => {
      if (response.data) {
        console.log('Polled latest data:', response.data);
        // Update UI with polled data
      }
    })
    .catch(error => {
      console.error('Polling error:', error);
    });
}

const pollingInterval = setInterval(() => {
  if (connectionLost) {  // connectionLost being a flag updated via
    connection monitoring
    fetchLatestData();
  }
}, 10000);
```

Here, the application checks for lost connections by monitoring a flag (e.g., connectionLost). If a disruption is detected, the fallback polling mechanism is triggered at fixed intervals to ensure that critical data continues to refresh. This hybrid model reduces the risk of prolonged downtime and guarantees that users are presented with the most recent data possible during outages.

The reliability of any real-time system is also affected by the infrastructure supporting the database and client applications. Optimizing database configurations is critical for ensuring that the system handles high volumes of write and read operations correctly. Tuning PostgreSQL parameters such as `max_connections`, `shared_buffers`, and `wal_level` can help maintain performance and reliability under heavy load. Regular monitoring of database performance metrics and resource usage can highlight potential bottlenecks that may lead to data inconsistencies or delayed propagation of changes.

In addition to infrastructural configurations, implementing redundancy can greatly enhance system resilience. Deploying multiple instances of any service—be it the database server, application server, or real-time communication layer—ensures that the failure of a single node does not result in a total system outage. Load balancers, replication mechanisms, and backup servers provide the necessary redundancy that allows real-time features to continue operating seamlessly even under extreme load or in the event of hardware failures.

Monitoring forms an integral part of maintaining reliability and resilience. Detailed performance and error metrics should be collected and analyzed continuously in production environments. Tools like Prometheus, Grafana, or built-in logging solutions provided by cloud platforms enable developers to track the health of the system, monitor real-time subscription latency, and detect anomalies. An effective monitoring setup might include alerts based on specific error thresholds, such as a sudden spike in failed subscription attempts or increased reconnection intervals, so that the development team is rapidly notified of potential issues.

```
function logEvent(eventType, details) {
```

```
  // Log the event details to an external monitoring service
  console.log(`Event: ${eventType}`, details);
}

supabase
  .from('updates')
  .on('INSERT', payload => {
    logEvent('INSERT_EVENT', payload);
    // Process the insertion event
  })
  .subscribe();

window.addEventListener('error', (e) => {
  logEvent('GLOBAL_ERROR', e.message);
});
```

This approach enables constant insight into the operational status of the application. When integrated with alerting systems, these logs inform developers of unusual patterns before they escalate into significant outages.

Data consistency is another key aspect of resilience. Real-time operations must ensure that users receive a consistent view of the data, even when multiple concurrent updates occur. Techniques such as optimistic concurrency control or using version numbers can help detect and resolve conflicts. When multiple real-time updates overlap, implementing a reconciliation mechanism on the client or server side ensures that the final state is accurate and free from partial or duplicate updates. By maintaining a controlled and systematic approach to conflict resolution, developers can minimize discrepancies in the presented data.

Lastly, designing real-time features with scalability in mind further reinforces system resilience. As the number of active users and real-time events grow, the underlying architecture must be able to distribute the load evenly. Microservices architecture and the use of message brokers to decouple event processing from user-facing updates can achieve high levels of scalability. This design approach ensures that even if the real-time traffic surges due to a sudden event, the system can absorb and process the load without hindering the overall user experience.

Each of these strategies—automatic reconnection with exponential backoff, robust error handling, fallback mechanisms, optimized infrastructure, redundancy, comprehensive monitoring, consistency checks, and scalable architecture—contributes to the overall goal of creating a reliable and resilient real-time application. As real-time capabilities become an integral part of modern web applications, incorporating these principles is crucial to maintain uptime, prevent data inconsistencies, and deliver a seamless user experience.

By integrating these best practices, developers can build real-time features on Supabase that are not only fast and dynamic but also robust against the challenges of real-world network and infrastructure variability. These measures ensure that even under adverse conditions, real-time operations remain dependable, thereby fostering trust and satisfaction among end users.

Chapter 6

Integrating Supabase with Frontend Frameworks

This chapter discusses the integration of Supabase with popular frontend frameworks like React, Angular, and Vue.js. It provides guidance on setting up development environments, managing authentication, and implementing real-time data. Emphasizing seamless integration, the chapter equips developers with the skills to build responsive applications that effectively utilize Supabase's backend capabilities, enhancing both performance and user experience.

6.1. Choosing the Right Frontend Framework

When designing a Supabase project that leverages a scalable backend solution, the selection of an appropriate frontend framework is pivotal.

Popular frontend frameworks such as React, Angular, and Vue.js have emerged as robust choices due to their community support, ease of integration with RESTful or real-time APIs, and the distinct philosophies that underpin their design. This section examines the characteristics of these frameworks and offers a set of criteria to aid developers in making an informed decision that aligns with the architectural and performance requirements of their Supabase project.

Among the primary considerations is the architectural paradigm of the framework. React, for instance, emphasizes a component-based approach with a one-way data flow, which facilitates a predictable state mechanism. Its simplicity and modular design make it ideal for applications where a high degree of interactivity is required. Angular, on the other hand, is more opinionated. Built around a Model-View-Controller (MVC) pattern, Angular provides an integrated suite of tools including dependency injection, powerful templating features, and end-to-end tooling, making it suitable for large-scale enterprise applications. Vue.js offers a balance between flexibility and simplicity. Its gradual adoption model allows developers to incrementally enhance an existing project, making it a viable option for both small- and medium-sized projects that may eventually scale.

In addition to architectural paradigms, several technical criteria should be considered. Firstly, the maturity and stability of the framework can significantly impact the long-term maintainability of the project. A well-established framework typically comes with extensive documentation, a vibrant developer community, and a plethora of third-party libraries. On the performance front, the efficiency of the virtual DOM implementation in frameworks such as React or the reactive data-binding employed by Vue.js can contribute to superior user experience, particularly in applications that demand real-time updates—a common requirement when interacting with Supabase's real-time synchronization capabilities.

218

Another fundamental criterion is the learning curve associated with the framework. Angular's comprehensive feature set may require a steeper learning curve, which is a critical factor for teams with limited experience in modern frontend development paradigms. Conversely, React's emphasis on a functional programming style along with its unidirectional data flow leads to simpler state management when used in conjunction with libraries such as Redux. Vue.js tends to present an even gentler approach with a syntax that is both intuitive and flexible, making it accessible to newcomers while still offering advanced features for experienced developers.

The ecosystem surrounding each framework also provides essential insights. React's vast ecosystem includes a variety of libraries for state management, routing, and API integration, which simplifies tasks such as integrating Supabase authentication and real-time data updates. Angular provides an integrated solution with built-in services that streamline many of these tasks, albeit at the cost of requiring adherence to its prescribed structure. Vue.js, with its growing ecosystem, offers a wealth of plugins and community-driven solutions that can bridge certain gaps and expedite integration efforts, especially when rapid prototyping is a requirement.

The performance benchmarks and the inherent scalability of the framework should also be accounted for. React applications that leverage virtual DOM diffing strategies typically perform well under conditions where dynamic user interfaces are prevalent. Angular's change detection mechanisms and dependency injection promote efficient data flow in large-scale applications. Likewise, Vue.js's reactivity system is designed to optimize rendering and render only what is necessary, a feature that becomes critical when dealing with applications that continuously interact with Supabase's real-time data streams.

In the context of Supabase projects, integration simplicity is another decisive factor. Each framework has its own method of initializ-

ing and interacting with Supabase's API. For example, initializing
the Supabase client in a React application is straightforward, usually
achieved by creating a dedicated context or hook that encapsulates API
calls. Consider the following code snippet that demonstrates the initialization and basic usage within a React component:

```
import React, { useEffect, useState } from 'react';
import { createClient } from '@supabase/supabase-js';

const supabaseUrl = 'https://your-project.supabase.co';
const supabaseKey = 'your-anon-key';
const supabase = createClient(supabaseUrl, supabaseKey);

const DataDisplay = () => {
    const [data, setData] = useState([]);

    useEffect(() => {
        let isMounted = true;
        supabase
            .from('example-table')
            .select('*')
            .then((response) => {
                if (isMounted) {
                    setData(response.data);
                }
            });
        return () => { isMounted = false; };
    }, []);

    return (
        <div>
            {data.map((item) => (
                <div key={item.id}>{item.name}</div>
            ))}
        </div>
    );
};

export default DataDisplay;
```

In Angular applications, the integration often involves configuring
modules and services to encapsulate the Supabase client. This abstraction not only aids in managing API calls but also in ensuring that
changes in the backend or authentication mechanisms are localized

within the service layer. A minimal service configuration might appear as follows:

```
import { Injectable } from '@angular/core';
import { createClient, SupabaseClient } from '@supabase/supabase-js';

@Injectable({
  providedIn: 'root'
})
export class SupabaseService {
  private supabase: SupabaseClient;
  private readonly supabaseUrl = 'https://your-project.supabase.co';
  private readonly supabaseKey = 'your-anon-key';

  constructor() {
    this.supabase = createClient(this.supabaseUrl, this.supabaseKey);
  }

  getData() {
    return this.supabase.from('example-table').select('*');
  }
}
```

Vue.js offers a flexible integration approach where a dedicated plugin or simply a centralized module in the Vue instance can be utilized to manage the Supabase client. Given the reactive nature of Vue, the integration with Supabase can be achieved also by employing the framework's composition API for more refined control over reactive data:

```
<script setup>
import { ref, onMounted } from 'vue';
import { createClient } from '@supabase/supabase-js';

const supabaseUrl = 'https://your-project.supabase.co';
const supabaseKey = 'your-anon-key';
const supabase = createClient(supabaseUrl, supabaseKey);

const data = ref([]);

onMounted(async () => {
  const { data: response } = await supabase.from('example-table').
    select('*');
  data.value = response;
});
</script>
```

```
<template>
  <div>
    <div v-for="item in data" :key="item.id">{{ item.name }}</div>
  </div>
</template>
```

In comparing these frameworks for Supabase integration, developers should weigh the complexity of their application against the inherent strengths and limitations of each framework. For applications with heavy real-time interactions, the efficient rendering and state management mechanisms of React and Vue might offer superior performance. Conversely, projects that require a strong architectural discipline and built-in functionalities for routing, form handling, and HTTP communication may benefit more from Angular's comprehensive framework structure.

Beyond the technical capabilities, the long-term viability of a frontend framework within a Supabase project is also influenced by the surrounding tools and community resources. Frequent updates, extensive documentation, and active community support contribute to the robustness of the development process. A well-documented framework will not only provide a faster development cycle but will also reduce the likelihood of encountering integration obstacles when dealing with evolving backend APIs such as those provided by Supabase.

The criteria for selecting a frontend framework also incorporate the level of control required over the application state and the ease of adopting modern development practices such as test-driven development (TDD) and component isolation. Frameworks like React facilitate testing through isolated components and predictable state patterns. Tools such as Jest or React Testing Library integrate seamlessly with React applications, ensuring that both unit and integration tests can be conducted efficiently. Angular's dependency injection and modular architecture further support scalable testing practices, while Vue's simplicity and clear patterns make it relatively easy to implement both unit tests and end-to-end tests using tools like Mocha and Cypress.

Considering the interplay between these factors—architectural paradigms, performance benchmarks, learning curves, ecosystem maturity, and testing infrastructure—provides a rigorous foundation for choosing the framework that best aligns with project goals. Developers should evaluate the inherent trade-offs; for example, while Angular offers an all-inclusive environment that reduces the reliance on external libraries, its complexity may not be warranted for projects with simpler requirements. In such cases, the minimalistic approach of Vue or the flexibility of React may prove more advantageous.

The decision process can also be informed by prototyping. A brief proof-of-concept using a lightweight application to assess the ease of integrating Supabase's functionalities can reveal practical insights specific to the team's workflow and project constraints. Additionally, community forums and case studies are valuable resources for understanding real-world issues encountered by developers integrating Supabase with these frameworks. Engaging with these resources can help to identify potential pitfalls and performance bottlenecks.

The integration of Supabase with a frontend framework is not solely a matter of technical compatibility but is deeply intertwined with developer productivity and long-term project sustainability. A developer's familiarity with a particular framework, or the willingness to learn new paradigms, will significantly influence the successful adoption of the framework for Supabase-centric projects. Therefore, an assessment that includes both technical benchmarks and soft factors such as developer expertise is imperative.

The criteria outlined above serve as a guide for selecting the optimal frontend framework for Supabase integration. The decision should be based on the specific requirements of your project, balancing performance, scalability, maintainability, and developer proficiency. A careful examination of these factors ensures that the chosen framework will not only meet the immediate demands of integrating with Supabase but also support the evolution of the application over time.

6.2. Setting Up Project Environments

Creating a robust development environment is critical for ensuring seamless integration between Supabase and frontend frameworks. This section discusses best practices and practical steps to establish an environment that supports efficient development, testing, and deployment. Emphasis is placed on automating repetitive tasks, managing dependencies, and configuring environment variables, which collectively help in creating a stable connection between your Supabase backend and the chosen frontend framework.

An effective development setup begins with ensuring that the fundamental tools are installed. Package managers such as npm and yarn are essential for JavaScript-based frontend projects. Equally, ensuring that Node.js is present in its latest Long Term Support (LTS) version will help maintain consistency across different development machines. Version control systems, primarily Git, should be set up early in the project lifecycle. The following commands install dependencies and clone a project repository, setting the stage for subsequent configuration:

```
# Ensure Node.js and package manager are installed
node --version
npm --version

# Clone the project repository
git clone https://github.com/your-org/your-supabase-project.git
cd your-supabase-project

# Install dependencies
npm install
```

Following the installation of core development tools, configuring environment variables is a critical step. Environment variables store configuration settings that differ between development, staging, and production environments, such as your Supabase project URL and the anonymous key. To maintain security and flexibility, environment-specific parameters should not be hard-coded within the project's source code. Instead, a configuration file (commonly .env) can be created at the project's root, and a package such as dotenv can be integrated to load these variables into the runtime. A sample .env file might appear as follows:

```
SUPABASE_URL=https://your-project.supabase.co
SUPABASE_ANON_KEY=your-anon-key
NODE_ENV=development
```

In a React project, integration of these environment variables is straightforward. By installing the dotenv package and configuring the application entry point, the project can securely access the necessary keys. An initialization snippet in a React application may be structured like this:

```
import React from 'react';
import ReactDOM from 'react-dom';
import App from './App';
import { createClient } from '@supabase/supabase-js';

// Load environment variables
const supabaseUrl = process.env.REACT_APP_SUPABASE_URL;
const supabaseAnonKey = process.env.REACT_APP_SUPABASE_ANON_KEY;

// Create Supabase client
const supabase = createClient(supabaseUrl, supabaseAnonKey);

ReactDOM.render(
  <React.StrictMode>
    <App supabase={supabase} />
  </React.StrictMode>,
  document.getElementById('root')
);
```

When dealing with Angular, environment configurations are typically managed via dedicated environment files. The Angular CLI provides `environment.ts` and `environment.prod.ts` files that facilitate switching between configurations. The developer can create a service that abstracts the connection to Supabase. An example service in Angular might be structured as follows:

```
import { Injectable } from '@angular/core';
import { createClient, SupabaseClient } from '@supabase/supabase-js';
import { environment } from '../environments/environment';

@Injectable({
  providedIn: 'root'
})
export class SupabaseService {
  private supabase: SupabaseClient;

  constructor() {
    this.supabase = createClient(environment.supabaseUrl, environment
    .supabaseAnonKey);
  }

  getSupabaseClient(): SupabaseClient {
    return this.supabase;
  }
}
```

Vue.js projects typically handle environment variables using the same `.env` convention as React. Vue applications often adopt the Vue CLI, which automatically integrates environment variables provided they adhere to the naming convention of prefixing with `VUE_APP_`. A sample integration using the Composition API might look like this:

```
<script setup>
import { ref, onMounted } from 'vue';
import { createClient } from '@supabase/supabase-js';

const supabaseUrl = import.meta.env.VITE_SUPABASE_URL;
const supabaseAnonKey = import.meta.env.VITE_SUPABASE_ANON_KEY;
const supabase = createClient(supabaseUrl, supabaseAnonKey);

const data = ref([]);

onMounted(async () => {
  const { data: response } = await supabase.from('example-table').
    select('*');
```

```
    data.value = response;
});
</script>

<template>
  <div>
    <div v-for="item in data" :key="item.id">{{ item.name }}</div>
  </div>
</template>
```

Managing dependencies efficiently is another cornerstone for a streamlined development environment. Consistent use of package-lock files or yarn.lock files guarantees that all developers use the same package versions, reducing potential conflicts. Automated dependency updates, combined with rigorous version control, maintain the health of the codebase over time. Additionally, integrating a linter such as ESLint and a formatter like Prettier ensures code uniformity across various components and modules.

Integrating testing frameworks into the development environment is equally important. For frontend projects, frameworks like Jest for React, Jasmine or Karma for Angular, and Mocha with Chai for Vue can be configured to work seamlessly. Testing not only validates individual components but also checks interactions with Supabase services. Continuous integration systems that run tests on every push help catch issues early and support rapid iteration cycles. A simple example of a test case in a React project using Jest might be:

```
import { createClient } from '@supabase/supabase-js';

const supabaseUrl = process.env.REACT_APP_SUPABASE_URL;
const supabaseAnonKey = process.env.REACT_APP_SUPABASE_ANON_KEY;
const supabase = createClient(supabaseUrl, supabaseAnonKey);

test('fetches data from Supabase example-table', async () => {
  const { data, error } = await supabase.from('example-table').select
    ('*');
  expect(error).toBeNull();
  expect(data).not.toBeNull();
});
```

To further optimize the development ecosystem, consider incorporating containerization with Docker. This approach simplifies dependencies management and minimizes configuration discrepancies between development, staging, and production environments. A Dockerfile for a Node.js project can package the application along with all its dependencies and ensure that the environment remains consistent irrespective of the host system. An example Dockerfile might be:

```
FROM node:14-alpine
WORKDIR /app
COPY package*.json ./
RUN npm install --silent
COPY . .
EXPOSE 3000
CMD ["npm", "start"]
```

Ensuring smooth integration also involves configuring secure connections between the frontend and Supabase. HTTPS should be enabled in all communications, leveraging certificates and secure protocols to protect sensitive user data. When working in a local development environment, tools such as mkcert can help generate valid SSL certificates, thereby simulating production-level security measures during development.

Another important aspect is setting up debugging tools. Modern browser developer tools, along with dedicated debug libraries, assist in monitoring API calls, tracking state changes, and inspecting real-time interactions with Supabase. Integrated development environments (IDEs) such as Visual Studio Code support various plugins that facilitate debugging and code navigation. For instance, the ability to set breakpoints and inspect environment variables within the IDE enhances the troubleshooting process when issues arise.

The adoption of task runners, such as npm scripts or Gulp, can further streamline the workflow by automating tasks like code compilation, testing, and deployment. These tools help reduce manual overhead, allowing developers to focus on writing code rather than managing routine operational tasks. A sample npm script setup might look like:

```
{
  "scripts": {
    "start": "react-scripts start",
    "build": "react-scripts build",
    "test": "react-scripts test",
    "lint": "eslint src/**",
    "predeploy": "npm run build",
    "deploy": "netlify deploy --prod"
  }
}
```

Beyond local development, integrating continuous integration/continuous deployment (CI/CD) pipelines ensures that every commit undergoes a series of tests before being integrated into the main branch. Services such as GitHub Actions, Travis CI, and CircleCI can be configured to run a complete suite of tests, build the application, and deploy it automatically. This automation reduces the risk of human error and allows for rapid, reliable updates to both the frontend and the Supabase backend.

Developers are encouraged to document their environment setup process. Comprehensive documentation not only aids new team members but also serves as a reference for troubleshooting configuration issues. Keeping configuration details, dependency versions, and custom scripts in version control is crucial for maintaining reproducibility and facilitates smoother onboarding processes for new contributors.

Building a resilient development environment requires careful consideration of security, automation, and scalability. By using tools that manage dependencies, configure secure connections, and facilitate debugging, developers ensure that integration between frontend frameworks and Supabase is both efficient and maintainable. Balancing manual configuration with automated processes creates an environment that supports rapid development cycles and minimizes integration challenges as the project scales over time.

6.3.   Connecting Supabase with React

Integrating Supabase with a React application requires a clear understanding of both the Supabase client and React's state management
paradigms. The process begins by setting up the Supabase client in the
React ecosystem, managing API calls, and maintaining state efficiently
to reflect real-time changes. This section details these processes and
provides concrete coding examples to facilitate a smooth integration.

The first step is to initialize the Supabase client. React applications typically employ environment variables to store sensitive data such as the
Supabase project URL and anonymous key. Using these environment
variables ensures that API credentials are not exposed directly in the
codebase. The following code snippet demonstrates how to create the
Supabase client and inject it into the application using React's context
mechanism:

```
import React, { createContext, useContext } from 'react';
import { createClient } from '@supabase/supabase-js';

const SupabaseContext = createContext(null);

export const SupabaseProvider = ({ children }) => {
  const supabaseUrl = process.env.REACT_APP_SUPABASE_URL;
  const supabaseAnonKey = process.env.REACT_APP_SUPABASE_ANON_KEY;
  const supabase = createClient(supabaseUrl, supabaseAnonKey);

  return (
    <SupabaseContext.Provider value={supabase}>
      {children}
    </SupabaseContext.Provider>
  );
};

export const useSupabase = () => {
  const context = useContext(SupabaseContext);
  if (!context) {
    throw new Error('useSupabase must be used within a
```

```
      SupabaseProvider ') ;
   }
   return context;
};
```

The above initialization encapsulates the Supabase client within a context that can be consumed by any descendant component. This design pattern promotes modularity and reusability, which are critical in larger React applications. Incorporating a context provider into the application's root component ensures that all components have seamless access to Supabase's functions.

Following client initialization, the next step involves managing state in relation to API calls. React's built-in hooks, such as useState and useEffect, can be used effectively to track and update state based on data retrieved from Supabase. For instance, a component that fetches data from a specific table in Supabase might be integrated as follows:

```
import React, { useState, useEffect } from 'react';
import { useSupabase } from './SupabaseProvider';

const DataFetcher = () => {
  const supabase = useSupabase();
  const [data, setData] = useState([]);
  const [loading, setLoading] = useState(true);
  const [error, setError] = useState(null);

  useEffect(() => {
    const fetchData = async () => {
      setLoading(true);
      const { data: response, error } = await supabase
        .from('example_table')
        .select('*');
      if (error) {
        setError(error);
      } else {
        setData(response);
      }
      setLoading(false);
    };

    fetchData();
  }, [supabase]);
```

231

```
if (loading) {
  return <div>Loading...</div>;
}

if (error) {
  return <div>Error fetching data: {error.message}</div>;
}

return (
  <div>
    {data.map((item) => (
      <div key={item.id}>
        <strong>{item.name}</strong>: {item.description}
      </div>
    ))}
  </div>
);
};

export default DataFetcher;
```

This example demonstrates how to handle asynchronous API calls within a React component while managing loading states and errors. The use of useEffect ensures that the API call is executed only once when the component mounts, and state variables (data, loading, and error) are updated accordingly.

State management becomes even more significant when components must handle updates in real time. Supabase offers real-time functionalities that can be integrated with React's state updates. The following code illustrates how to subscribe to changes in a specific Supabase table and update the component's state dynamically:

```
import React, { useState, useEffect } from 'react';
import { useSupabase } from './SupabaseProvider';

const RealTimeData = () => {
  const supabase = useSupabase();
  const [data, setData] = useState([]);

  useEffect(() => {
    // Initial fetch of data
    const loadData = async () => {
```

```
    const { data: initialData, error } = await supabase
      .from('example_table')
      .select('*');
    if (!error) {
      setData(initialData);
    }
  };

  loadData();

  // Subscribe to real-time updates
  const subscription = supabase
    .from('example_table')
    .on('*', payload => {
      // Update local state based on payload event
      if (payload.eventType === 'INSERT') {
        setData(prevData => [...prevData, payload.new]);
      }
      if (payload.eventType === 'UPDATE') {
        setData(prevData =>
          prevData.map(item =>
            item.id === payload.new.id ? payload.new : item
          )
        );
      }
      if (payload.eventType === 'DELETE') {
        setData(prevData =>
          prevData.filter(item => item.id !== payload.old.id)
        );
      }
    })
    .subscribe();

  // Cleanup subscription on unmount
  return () => {
    supabase.removeSubscription(subscription);
  };
}, [supabase]);

return (
  <div>
    {data.map((item) => (
      <div key={item.id}>
        {item.name}: {item.value}
      </div>
    ))}
  </div>
);
```

```
};

export default RealTimeData;
```

This implementation leverages Supabase's real-time capabilities by subscribing to any changes in the data. The component begins by fetching an initial dataset and then sets up a subscription to listen for events such as inserts, updates, and deletes. Whenever such an event occurs, the state is updated accordingly, ensuring that the UI reflects the most recent data.

Efficient integration also necessitates robust error handling and user feedback. When making API calls, it is essential to handle unexpected errors gracefully. Enriching the user experience with loading indicators and error messages can be achieved through conditional rendering. The code examples provided illustrate simple error checks and conditional views; however, more comprehensive error management might include logging to services and displaying notifications via libraries such as react-toastify.

For applications that require more sophisticated state management, libraries such as Redux or Recoil can be integrated with the Supabase client. These libraries facilitate global state management and can be particularly useful when multiple components depend on shared data. An example of integrating Redux with a Supabase data fetch might include asynchronous actions via Redux Thunk. The following code snippet demonstrates a simplified version of a Redux action that fetches data from Supabase:

```
export const fetchExampleData = () => async (dispatch, getState, {
    supabase }) => {
  dispatch({ type: 'FETCH_DATA_START' });
  const { data, error } = await supabase.from('example_table').select
    ('*');

  if (error) {
    dispatch({ type: 'FETCH_DATA_ERROR', payload: error });
  } else {
```

```
      dispatch({ type: 'FETCH_DATA_SUCCESS', payload: data });
   }
};
```

In the Redux setup, middleware is configured to pass the Supabase client into the action creators. This approach separates business logic from the UI layer and standardizes state interactions across the application. While Redux introduces additional complexity, it also provides powerful mechanisms for debugging and scaling state management in larger projects.

Another crucial aspect is orchestrating component lifecycle with data fetching processes. As React evolves, hooks such as useReducer provide an alternative to useState for more complex state logic. The useReducer hook can centralize state transitions and make the logic behind API call responses and state changes more transparent. For example, integrating useReducer into a Supabase data fetching component can lead to more predictable state transitions:

```
import React, { useReducer, useEffect } from 'react';
import { useSupabase } from './SupabaseProvider';

const initialState = {
  data: [],
  loading: true,
  error: null,
};

function reducer(state, action) {
  switch (action.type) {
    case 'FETCH_INIT':
      return { ...state, loading: true, error: null };
    case 'FETCH_SUCCESS':
      return { ...state, loading: false, data: action.payload };
    case 'FETCH_FAILURE':
      return { ...state, loading: false, error: action.payload };
    default:
      throw new Error();
  }
}

const DataComponent = () => {
```

```
const supabase = useSupabase();
const [state, dispatch] = useReducer(reducer, initialState);

useEffect(() => {
  const fetchData = async () => {
    dispatch({ type: 'FETCH_INIT' });
    const { data, error } = await supabase.from('example_table').
  select('*');
    if (error) {
      dispatch({ type: 'FETCH_FAILURE', payload: error });
    } else {
      dispatch({ type: 'FETCH_SUCCESS', payload: data });
    }
  };

  fetchData();
}, [supabase]);

if (state.loading) {
  return <div>Loading...</div>;
}

if (state.error) {
  return <div>Error: {state.error.message}</div>;
}

return (
  <div>
    {state.data.map((item) => (
      <div key={item.id}>{item.name}</div>
    ))}
  </div>
);
};

export default DataComponent;
```

This implementation clearly separates the different states of data fetching and provides more robust state management than simple `useState` hooks in scenarios that involve multiple state transitions or complex data manipulations.

Integrating state management and API calls using Supabase in a React application forms the backbone of modern, data-driven web applications. Developers are encouraged to modularize logic related to

Supabase interaction by encapsulating API calls in custom hooks or context providers. This approach isolates side effects and simplifies testing. Custom hooks not only promote reusability but also improve code readability by abstracting complex logic into dedicated functions.

It is also advisable to implement caching mechanisms where appropriate to reduce redundant API calls. Utilizing libraries such as React Query can help manage caching, background data synchronization, and provide powerful tools for handling asynchronous state updates. The incorporation of such libraries ensures that the application remains responsive even under variable network conditions and high data load.

Integrating Supabase with React requires careful consideration of initialization, state management, API handling, and error recovery. By strategically leveraging React's context, hooks, and potentially state management libraries, developers can build scalable applications that respond dynamically to real-time data changes provided by Supabase. This robust integration not only improves efficiency during development but also enhances user experience by ensuring that data is consistently in sync with the backend.

6.4. Integrating with Angular

Integrating Supabase with an Angular application requires a systematic configuration of modules, services, and environment management. This section explains the key steps necessary to create a robust Angular integration, including setting up environment files, creating dedicated services for Supabase interaction, and incorporating these services into Angular modules and components to ensure seamless communication with the Supabase backend.

The process begins with configuring environment variables.

Angular CLI uses designated files such as `environment.ts` and `environment.prod.ts` to distinguish between development and production settings. In these files, values for the Supabase project URL and anonymous key are defined. For instance, the `environment.ts` file may appear as follows:

```
export const environment = {
  production: false,
  supabaseUrl: 'https://your-project.supabase.co',
  supabaseAnonKey: 'your-anon-key'
};
```

Such configuration ensures that sensitive data is managed externally and can be replaced during the build process for different environments. This separation is critical to maintain security and flexibility in the deployment pipeline.

The central piece of integration lies within the creation of an Angular service that encapsulates all interactions with the Supabase API. Leveraging Angular's dependency injection system, a dedicated service is developed to instantiate and maintain a connection with Supabase. The following service example demonstrates how to import the Supabase client, initialize it with environment variables, and expose methods for data retrieval and management:

```
import { Injectable } from '@angular/core';
import { createClient, SupabaseClient } from '@supabase/supabase-js';
import { environment } from '../environments/environment';

@Injectable({
  providedIn: 'root'
})
export class SupabaseService {
  private supabase: SupabaseClient;

  constructor() {
    this.supabase = createClient(environment.supabaseUrl, environment
      .supabaseAnonKey);
  }

  // Method to fetch data from a table
  fetchData(table: string) {
```

238

```
    return this.supabase.from(table).select('*');
}

// Method to insert data into a table
insertData(table: string, payload: any) {
  return this.supabase.from(table).insert(payload);
}

// Method to update data in a table
updateData(table: string, payload: any, id: number) {
  return this.supabase.from(table).update(payload).eq('id', id);
}

// Method to delete data from a table
deleteData(table: string, id: number) {
  return this.supabase.from(table).delete().eq('id', id);
}

// Method to subscribe to real-time updates
subscribeToTable(table: string, callback: (payload: any) => void) {
  const subscription = this.supabase
    .from(table)
    .on('*', callback)
    .subscribe();

  return subscription;
}

// Method to remove a subscription
removeSubscription(subscription: any) {
  this.supabase.removeSubscription(subscription);
}
}
```

This service abstracts the raw Supabase API, offering an intuitive interface for other parts of the Angular application to interact with the backend. Key methods such as fetchData, insertData, updateData, and deleteData centralize database operations. Additionally, real-time subscriptions can be established and managed through dedicated methods, enabling live updates to be reflected in the user interface.

Once the service is in place, it must be registered in the Angular module. Although services provided in the root (using providedIn: 'root') are automatically available throughout the application, incorporating the service into the module structure highlights its central role in data management. A typical module configuration in Angular might appear as follows:

```
import { BrowserModule } from '@angular/platform-browser';
import { NgModule } from '@angular/core';
import { AppComponent } from './app.component';
import { HttpClientModule } from '@angular/common/http';
import { SupabaseService } from './services/supabase.service';

@NgModule({
  declarations: [
    AppComponent
  ],
  imports: [
    BrowserModule,
    HttpClientModule
  ],
  providers: [SupabaseService],
  bootstrap: [AppComponent]
})
export class AppModule { }
```

With the service in place and registered, Angular components can now leverage dependency injection to request Supabase functionality. To illustrate how this works, consider a component tasked with displaying data from a Supabase table. In its lifecycle, the component initiates an API call to retrieve data, manages state accordingly, and optionally subscribes to real-time updates:

```
import { Component, OnInit, OnDestroy } from '@angular/core';
import { SupabaseService } from './services/supabase.service';
import { Subscription } from 'rxjs';

@Component({
  selector: 'app-data-display',
  template: `
    <div *ngIf="loading">Loading data...</div>
    <div *ngIf="error">Error retrieving data: {{ error }}</div>
    <div *ngIf="data">
      <div *ngFor="let item of data">
        <strong>{{ item.name }}</strong>: {{ item.description }}
      </div>
    </div>
  `
```

240

```
})
export class DataDisplayComponent implements OnInit, OnDestroy {
  data: any[] = [];
  loading = false;
  error: string | null = null;
  private subscription: any;

  constructor(private supabaseService: SupabaseService) { }

  ngOnInit() {
    this.loadData();

    // Subscribe to real-time updates for the 'example_table'
    this.subscription = this.supabaseService.subscribeToTable('
     example_table', (payload: any) => {
      if (payload.eventType === 'INSERT') {
        this.data.push(payload.new);
      } else if (payload.eventType === 'UPDATE') {
        this.data = this.data.map(item => item.id === payload.new.id
     ? payload.new : item);
      } else if (payload.eventType === 'DELETE') {
        this.data = this.data.filter(item => item.id !== payload.old.
     id);
      }
    });
  }

  loadData() {
    this.loading = true;
    this.supabaseService.fetchData('example_table').then((response:
     any) => {
      if (response.error) {
        this.error = response.error.message;
      } else {
        this.data = response.data;
      }
      this.loading = false;
    }).catch((err: any) => {
      this.error = err.message;
      this.loading = false;
    });
  }

  ngOnDestroy() {
    // Unsubscribe from real-time updates when the component is
     destroyed
    if (this.subscription) {
      this.supabaseService.removeSubscription(this.subscription);
```

```
        }
    }
}
```

This component demonstrates practical integration points. The ngOnInit method calls loadData to retrieve initial data and then updates the local state based on incoming real-time events via the Supabase service. The component implements error handling and a loading indicator for an improved user experience. Moreover, the ngOnDestroy lifecycle hook ensures that real-time subscriptions are cleaned up, preventing potential memory leaks.

The integration also benefits from Angular's reactive programming paradigm. While the Supabase service in the preceding example uses promise-based APIs, Angular developers might prefer incorporating Observables for more reactive data handling. Converting Supabase API calls to Observables can be accomplished using Angular's from utility, which allows for more flexible integration with Angular's change detection. For example, a modified version of the data fetching method within the service using Observables might be defined as follows:

```
import { from, Observable } from 'rxjs';

fetchDataObservable(table: string): Observable<any> {
  return from(this.supabase.from(table).select('*'));
}
```

The use of Observables integrates well with Angular's async pipe in templates, which automatically subscribes to and unsubscribes from Observables. This method reduces boilerplate code in components and simplifies asynchronous data handling. The corresponding component template might then leverage the async pipe:

```
<div *ngIf="(data$ | async) as data; else loading">
  <div *ngFor="let item of data">
    <strong>{{ item.name }}</strong>: {{ item.description }}
  </div>
</div>
<ng-template #loading>
```

242

```
  <div>Loading data...</div>
</ng-template>
```

And in the component class, the Observable is assigned as follows:

```
import { Component, OnInit } from '@angular/core';
import { SupabaseService } from './services/supabase.service';
import { Observable } from 'rxjs';

@Component({
  selector: 'app-data-display',
  templateUrl: './data-display.component.html'
})
export class DataDisplayComponent implements OnInit {
  data$: Observable<any>;

  constructor(private supabaseService: SupabaseService) { }

  ngOnInit() {
    this.data$ = this.supabaseService.fetchDataObservable('
    example_table');
  }
}
```

This refactoring not only simplifies the data flow but also leverages Angular's reactive patterns, which can be especially beneficial when handling complex state changes or integrating with additional reactive libraries.

In addition to data fetching and subscription management, the Angular integration must consider error handling and security. Comprehensive error handling should be implemented in both the service and components to catch and log errors consistently. Utilizing Angular's HttpInterceptor alongside the Supabase service can centralize error logging and provide customized responses or notifications to end users. This approach guarantees that any issues arising from API calls are captured and addressed promptly, preserving application resilience.

Finally, documentation and modular design remain cornerstones of a maintainable integration. Grouping Supabase-related functionalities into dedicated modules, services, and components allows developers

243

to extend or modify the integration with minimal disruption to the rest of the application. Consistent naming conventions, well-documented code, and separation of concerns greatly improve team collaboration and ease future scalability.

The steps outlined above establish a comprehensive framework for integrating Supabase into an Angular application. By configuring environment variables, encapsulating the Supabase client within Angular services, and leveraging Angular's reactive programming features, developers can create a robust and scalable data layer that bridges the backend and frontend efficiently. This integration methodology not only streamlines development but also provides a solid foundation for handling real-time data and managing complex state interactions, ensuring a seamless user experience and a maintainable codebase.

6.5.   Using Supabase with Vue.js

Integrating Supabase into a Vue.js application is a multifaceted process that leverages the inherent strengths of Vue's component-based architecture. This section provides an in-depth exploration of configuring Supabase in Vue.js, focusing on environment management, component integration, state handling, and real-time data synchronization. The discussion is supported by detailed code examples that demonstrate practical approaches to building scalable applications.

The initial step involves configuring environment variables to securely handle sensitive credentials such as the Supabase URL and anonymous key. In Vue.js projects created with the Vue CLI or Vite, environment variables are defined in a .env file. For instance, one can create a file with the following structure:

```
VUE_APP_SUPABASE_URL=https://your-project.supabase.co
VUE_APP_SUPABASE_ANON_KEY=your-anon-key
```

This configuration allows the application to access these variables securely at runtime. The Vue project automatically exposes variables prefixed with VUE_APP_ when built, ensuring that sensitive information is managed externally and can be replaced based on different deployment environments.

With environment variables in place, the next step is to initialize the Supabase client within the Vue.js application. The process can be accomplished by creating a dedicated module that initializes and exports the Supabase client. The following code snippet demonstrates how to achieve this:

```
import { createClient } from '@supabase/supabase-js';

const supabaseUrl = process.env.VUE_APP_SUPABASE_URL;
const supabaseAnonKey = process.env.VUE_APP_SUPABASE_ANON_KEY;

const supabase = createClient(supabaseUrl, supabaseAnonKey);

export default supabase;
```

By abstracting the Supabase client initialization in its own module, the code becomes more modular and reusable, which is a central tenet of the component-based architecture in Vue.js. This module can be imported into any component or service that requires access to the Supabase API.

Vue.js offers two primary paradigms for component creation: the Options API and the Composition API. The Composition API, in particular, provides fine-grained control over reactivity, which can be advantageous when integrating with real-time systems like Supabase. Using the Composition API, developers can encapsulate data fetching, subscriptions, and state updates into composable functions. Consider the following example that demonstrates how to fetch data from a Supabase table and display it in a Vue component:

```
<script setup>
import { ref, onMounted } from 'vue';
```

```
import supabase from '@/supabaseClient';

const data = ref([]);
const loading = ref(true);
const error = ref(null);

const fetchData = async () => {
  const { data: fetchedData, error: fetchError } = await supabase
    .from('example_table')
    .select('*');
  if (fetchError) {
    error.value = fetchError;
  } else {
    data.value = fetchedData;
  }
  loading.value = false;
};

onMounted(() => {
  fetchData();
});
</script>

<template>
  <div>
    <div v-if="loading">Loading data from Supabase...</div>
    <div v-if="error">Error: {{ error.message }}</div>
    <div v-else>
      <ul>
        <li v-for="item in data" :key="item.id">
          <strong>{{ item.name }}</strong>: {{ item.description }}
        </li>
      </ul>
    </div>
  </div>
</template>
```

This component uses the Composition API to manage state through reactive references. The onMounted lifecycle hook triggers data fetching once the component has been mounted, ensuring that the API call occurs only once per component lifecycle. The reactive approach guarantees that any change to the state, such as the arrival of data or an error, is instantly reflected in the user interface.

Handling real-time subscriptions with Supabase in Vue.js further

246

demonstrates the power of Vue's reactivity. By subscribing to changes on a specific table, the application can dynamically update the UI in response to real-time events. The following code example illustrates how to set up a real-time listener within a Vue component:

```
<script setup>
import { ref, onMounted, onBeforeUnmount } from 'vue';
import supabase from '@/supabaseClient';

const realtimeData = ref([]);

const subscribeToRealtimeUpdates = () => {
  const mySubscription = supabase
    .from('example_table')
    .on('*', payload => {
      if (payload.eventType === 'INSERT') {
        realtimeData.value.push(payload.new);
      } else if (payload.eventType === 'UPDATE') {
        realtimeData.value = realtimeData.value.map(item =>
          item.id === payload.new.id ? payload.new : item
        );
      } else if (payload.eventType === 'DELETE') {
        realtimeData.value = realtimeData.value.filter(
          item => item.id !== payload.old.id
        );
      }
    })
    .subscribe();

  return mySubscription;
};

let subscription;

onMounted(async () => {
  // Initial data load
  const { data: initialData } = await supabase
    .from('example_table')
    .select('*');
  realtimeData.value = initialData;
  // Subscribe to real-time events
  subscription = subscribeToRealtimeUpdates();
});

onBeforeUnmount(() => {
  // Clean up the subscription
  supabase.removeSubscription(subscription);
```

247

```
});
</script>

<template>
  <div>
    <div v-if="realtimeData.length === 0">No data available yet.</div
    >
    <ul v-else>
      <li v-for="item in realtimeData" :key="item.id">
        <strong>{{ item.name }}</strong>: {{ item.description }}
      </li>
    </ul>
  </div>
</template>
```

In this example, the component sets up a real-time subscription through Supabase and updates a reactive reference whenever an event occurs. The `onBeforeUnmount` lifecycle hook is used to remove the subscription when the component is destroyed, preventing memory leaks. The reactive nature of the Vue component ensures that any addition, update, or deletion in the Supabase table is immediately visible in the interface.

An important aspect of integrating Supabase with Vue.js is managing application state that spans multiple components. As applications grow, it may become necessary to implement a centralized state management solution such as Vuex or Pinia. These tools help manage shared state in a predictable manner. For example, Vuex can be configured to store data retrieved from Supabase, which can then be accessed and mutated by any component. A simple Vuex store module might look like this:

```
import { createStore } from 'vuex';
import supabase from '@/supabaseClient';

export default createStore({
  state: {
    items: [],
    loading: false,
    error: null
  },
```

```
mutations: {
  setLoading(state, payload) {
    state.loading = payload;
  },
  setItems(state, items) {
    state.items = items;
  },
  setError(state, error) {
    state.error = error;
  },
  addItem(state, newItem) {
    state.items.push(newItem);
  },
  updateItem(state, updatedItem) {
    state.items = state.items.map(item =>
      item.id === updatedItem.id ? updatedItem : item
    );
  },
  removeItem(state, id) {
    state.items = state.items.filter(item => item.id !== id);
  }
},
actions: {
  async fetchItems({ commit }) {
    commit('setLoading', true);
    const { data, error } = await supabase.from('example_table').
    select('*');
    if (error) {
      commit('setError', error.message);
    } else {
      commit('setItems', data);
    }
    commit('setLoading', false);
  },
  subscribeToItems({ commit }) {
    const subscription = supabase
      .from('example_table')
      .on('*', payload => {
        if (payload.eventType === 'INSERT') {
          commit('addItem', payload.new);
        } else if (payload.eventType === 'UPDATE') {
          commit('updateItem', payload.new);
        } else if (payload.eventType === 'DELETE') {
          commit('removeItem', payload.old.id);
        }
      })
      .subscribe();
    return subscription;
```

```
    }
  },
  getters: {
    allItems: state => state.items,
    isLoading: state => state.loading,
    errorMessage: state => state.error
  }
});
```

This Vuex module not only handles data fetching but also manages real-time updates via mutations. Using a state management system like Vuex allows developers to centralize Supabase operations, ensuring consistency and reusability across the application. Components can then subscribe to the store and automatically receive updates through computed properties and reactive bindings.

Additionally, developers can further encapsulate Supabase operations within composable functions to enhance code reuse and separation of concerns. Encapsulating logic in composables isolates data-fetching and subscription logic from presentation components, making unit testing more straightforward. An example of a composable for Supabase data might be as follows:

```
import { ref, onMounted, onBeforeUnmount } from 'vue';
import supabase from '@/supabaseClient';

export function useSupabaseData(table) {
  const records = ref([]);
  const loading = ref(true);
  const error = ref(null);
  let subscription = null;

  const fetchData = async () => {
    const { data, error: err } = await supabase.from(table).select
    ('*');
    if (err) {
      error.value = err;
    } else {
      records.value = data;
    }
    loading.value = false;
  };
```

```
const subscribeToUpdates = () => {
  subscription = supabase
    .from(table)
    .on('*', payload => {
      if (payload.eventType === 'INSERT') {
        records.value.push(payload.new);
      } else if (payload.eventType === 'UPDATE') {
        records.value = records.value.map(item =>
          item.id === payload.new.id ? payload.new : item
        );
      } else if (payload.eventType === 'DELETE') {
        records.value = records.value.filter(item => item.id !==
    payload.old.id);
      }
    })
    .subscribe();
};

onMounted(() => {
  fetchData();
  subscribeToUpdates();
});

onBeforeUnmount(() => {
  supabase.removeSubscription(subscription);
});

return {
  records,
  loading,
  error
};
}
```

This composable function abstracts common Supabase operations, enabling any Vue component to incorporate data-fetching and real-time updates by simply importing and invoking useSupabaseData. Utilizing composables results in a cleaner and more maintainable codebase that adheres to Vue's emphasis on modularity.

To summarize the integration strategy, using Supabase with Vue.js involves configuring environment variables properly, initializing the Supabase client in a dedicated module, developing components that leverage Vue's reactive capabilities, and considering centralized state man-

agement or composable functions for advanced use cases. By following these practices, developers benefit from a streamlined workflow in
which the separation of concerns and component reusability are maintained throughout the application architecture.

Employing Vue.js's component-based structure in combination with
Supabase APIs not only simplifies development but also ensures that
the application remains scalable and responsive to real-time data
changes. The outlined approaches and code examples in this section
serve as a comprehensive guide for integrating Supabase into Vue.js
projects, ensuring that developers can efficiently manage data interactions within a clean and modular architectural framework.

6.6. Handling Authentication in the Frontend

A secure and intuitive user authentication process is paramount when
integrating Supabase into modern frontend applications. Supabase
provides a comprehensive authentication system that supports email/-
password login, social login providers, and multi-factor authentication.
This section details techniques for managing user authentication in the
frontend, outlining secure interactions, proper state handling, and error management. The integration pattern is consistent across frameworks, though examples here are provided in a JavaScript context that
can be adapted for React, Angular, Vue.js, or plain JavaScript applications.

The authentication flow begins with user registration and login. Supabase offers convenient methods such as `signUp` and `signIn` which return a session object upon successful authentication. The initial step is
to securely capture user credentials via input forms and then pass these
credentials to the appropriate Supabase API calls. To ensure secure interactions, it is important to manage authentication state using robust
state management practices, often combined with context providers or

centralized state stores.

A simple user registration process using Supabase credentials can look like the following example. In this React component snippet, a registration form collects user email and password, calls the `signUp` method, and handles the resulting session or error:

```javascript
import React, { useState } from 'react';
import { createClient } from '@supabase/supabase-js';

const supabaseUrl = process.env.REACT_APP_SUPABASE_URL;
const supabaseAnonKey = process.env.REACT_APP_SUPABASE_ANON_KEY;
const supabase = createClient(supabaseUrl, supabaseAnonKey);

const Register = () => {
  const [email, setEmail] = useState('');
  const [password, setPassword] = useState('');
  const [message, setMessage] = useState(null);

  const handleSignUp = async (e) => {
    e.preventDefault();
    const { user, session, error } = await supabase.auth.signUp({
      email: email,
      password: password
    });
    if (error) {
      setMessage(error.message);
    } else {
      setMessage('Confirmation email sent. Check your inbox.');
    }
  };

  return (
    <form onSubmit={handleSignUp}>
      <label>Email:
        <input type="email" value={email} onChange={(e) => setEmail(e
.target.value)} required />
      </label>
      <label>Password:
        <input type="password" value={password} onChange={(e) =>
      setPassword(e.target.value)} required />
      </label>
      <button type="submit">Register</button>
      {message && <p>{message}</p>}
    </form>
  );
};
```

```
export default Register;
```

The above component demonstrates secure form handling that avoids storing passwords in plain text and does not expose any sensitive data in the frontend code. The use of environment variables for the Supabase credentials further enhances security by ensuring sensitive keys are not hard-coded.

Following user registration, implementing sign-in is similar to registration but focused on verifying credentials and retrieving a session token. The session token returned by Supabase should ideally be stored in a secure manner, such as in-memory state or secure cookies, rather than local storage, which is susceptible to cross-site scripting (XSS) attacks. A sample sign-in component is shown below:

```
import React, { useState } from 'react';
import { createClient } from '@supabase/supabase-js';

const supabaseUrl = process.env.REACT_APP_SUPABASE_URL;
const supabaseAnonKey = process.env.REACT_APP_SUPABASE_ANON_KEY;
const supabase = createClient(supabaseUrl, supabaseAnonKey);

const Login = () => {
  const [email, setEmail] = useState('');
  const [password, setPassword] = useState('');
  const [errorMessage, setErrorMessage] = useState(null);

  const handleSignIn = async (e) => {
    e.preventDefault();
    const { user, session, error } = await supabase.auth.signIn({
      email: email,
      password: password
    });
    if (error) {
      setErrorMessage(error.message);
    } else {
      // Use session to set a secure authentication state in your app
      context
      setErrorMessage(null);
      console.log('Logged in user:', user);
    }
  };
```

```
  return (
    <form onSubmit={handleSignIn}>
      <label>Email:
        <input type="email" value={email} onChange={(e) => setEmail(e
.target.value)} required />
      </label>
      <label>Password:
        <input type="password" value={password} onChange={(e) =>
setPassword(e.target.value)} required />
      </label>
      <button type="submit">Login</button>
      {errorMessage && <p>{errorMessage}</p>}
    </form>
  );
};

export default Login;
```

In this example, error handling is critical. Any authentication error is captured and displayed to the user to guide corrective actions. This approach helps in identifying issues such as incorrect credentials or network errors, ensuring that users receive appropriate feedback.

An effective frontend authentication system not only handles login and registration but also monitors user session state. Supabase provides methods to track authentication state changes via subscription. By setting up listeners that trigger on session changes, the application can react dynamically to events such as token expiration or user logout. Consider the following authentication context provider for a React application:

```
import React, { createContext, useContext, useState, useEffect } from
    'react';
import { createClient } from '@supabase/supabase-js';

const supabaseUrl = process.env.REACT_APP_SUPABASE_URL;
const supabaseAnonKey = process.env.REACT_APP_SUPABASE_ANON_KEY;
const supabase = createClient(supabaseUrl, supabaseAnonKey);

const AuthContext = createContext();

export const AuthProvider = ({ children }) => {
```

```
const [session, setSession] = useState(null);

useEffect(() => {
  setSession(supabase.auth.session());

  const { data: listener } = supabase.auth.onAuthStateChange((event
    , session) => {
    setSession(session);
  });

  return () => {
    listener.unsubscribe();
  };
}, []);

const value = { session, supabase };

return <AuthContext.Provider value={value}>{children}</AuthContext.
  Provider>;
};

export const useAuth = () => {
  return useContext(AuthContext);
};
```

This provider wraps the application and exposes the current session along with the Supabase client. By updating the session state on authentication state changes, the application can automatically redirect users, display protected routes, and manage token refresh cycles seamlessly.

Secure handling of authentication also involves implementing a sign-out mechanism. Logging out should invalidate the session both on the client side and on Supabase, making sure that no residual credentials remain accessible. A simple implementation for a logout button within a React component is shown here:

```
import React from 'react';
import { useAuth } from './AuthProvider';

const Logout = () => {
  const { supabase } = useAuth();

  const handleLogout = async () => {
```

```
   const { error } = await supabase.auth.signOut();
   if (error) {
     console.error('Error logging out:', error.message);
   }
 };

 return <button onClick={handleLogout}>Logout</button>;
};

export default Logout;
```

In addition to traditional email/password schemes, Supabase supports
authentication with third-party providers such as Google, GitHub, and
Facebook. The frontend implementation of social sign-in involves redi-
recting the user to the provider's authentication interface and handling
the callback. The following code snippet outlines a basic third-party
login approach:

```
import React from 'react';
import { useAuth } from './AuthProvider';

const SocialLogin = () => {
  const { supabase } = useAuth();

  const handleSocialLogin = async (provider) => {
    const { error } = await supabase.auth.signIn({ provider });
    if (error) {
      console.error('Social login error:', error.message);
    }
  };

  return (
    <div>
      <button onClick={() => handleSocialLogin('google')}>Sign in
      with Google</button>
      <button onClick={() => handleSocialLogin('github')}>Sign in
      with GitHub</button>
    </div>
  );
};

export default SocialLogin;
```

Security considerations must extend to the management of tokens and

257

user data. Typically, session tokens are stored securely in HttpOnly cookies when using server-side rendering or API proxies, rather than in local storage, which is susceptible to cross-site scripting (XSS) attacks. When designing the frontend, it is critical to ensure that tokens are transmitted only over HTTPS connections and that the backend validates these tokens correctly.

Another important aspect of authentication is error handling and user feedback. Clear error messages help users address issues such as network errors, invalid credentials, or account lockouts. Additionally, logging errors centrally using client-side logging tools or integrating with remote logging services can improve the responsiveness of maintenance and support teams. Furthermore, implementing rate limiting or other anti-abuse mechanisms at the API level reinforces the security posture during authentication attempts.

Implementing frontend authentication with Supabase requires diligent management of authentication flows throughout the user journey. This includes protecting routes in single-page applications by checking whether a user is authenticated before granting access to secure pages. Frameworks often provide routing guards, which can be harnessed to verify the session stored in the authentication context. For example, a route guard in React might redirect unauthorized users to a login page if no active session exists.

In building the overall authentication workflow, it is advisable to compartmentalize authentication logic into dedicated components or composable functions. This modularization simplifies testing and maintenance while ensuring separation of concerns. A well-structured authentication module allows frontend developers to extend functionality to include password reset flows, account verification, and two-factor authentication without disrupting the core application logic.

The techniques discussed here—ranging from registration and login to state management and secure token handling—form a comprehensive blueprint for managing user authentication in the frontend. By leveraging Supabase's robust authentication APIs and integrating them with modern frontend state management tools, developers can build secure, responsive, and user-friendly applications that maintain a high standard of data integrity and application security throughout the user lifecycle.

6.7. Real-time Data Integration in the Frontend

Implementing real-time data updates in frontend applications is essential for building interactive and responsive user experiences. Supabase leverages PostgreSQL's replication and subscription mechanisms to deliver real-time capabilities, enabling developers to subscribe to changes in database tables. This section outlines strategies for integrating real-time data into frontend applications, detailing best practices for managing subscriptions, handling different event types, and optimizing performance. The discussion also includes comprehensive code examples to demonstrate how to subscribe to data changes and update application state accordingly.

Real-time updates are achieved through Supabase's ability to listen for table events such as insertions, updates, and deletions. By establishing a subscription, the client application can receive notifications as soon as data changes occur in the backend. The benefits include instant UI updates without requiring the user to refresh the page and a seamless communication channel between the server and the client for highly dynamic applications.

One common strategy is to encapsulate the logic for real-time subscriptions within a dedicated module or service. This abstraction promotes code reuse and simplifies the management of subscription lifecycles. Developers can utilize this module to subscribe to changes when a com-

ponent mounts and to clean up subscriptions when the component is
no longer in use. It is important to consider managing the subscription's state to prevent memory leaks and ensure that the application
does not continue to listen for changes when the data is no longer
needed.

The following example demonstrates how to implement real-time data
updates in a React application using Supabase. In this code snippet, the component initializes a subscription to a specific table called
example_table. The subscription listens for three types of events—
INSERT, UPDATE, and DELETE—and updates the component's state
accordingly:

```
import React, { useState, useEffect } from 'react';
import { useSupabase } from './SupabaseProvider';

const RealTimeComponent = () => {
  const supabase = useSupabase();
  const [data, setData] = useState([]);
  const [error, setError] = useState(null);

  useEffect(() => {
    // Initial fetch of data
    const fetchData = async () => {
      const { data: initialData, error } = await supabase.from('
      example_table').select('*');
      if (error) {
        setError(error);
      } else {
        setData(initialData);
      }
    };

    fetchData();

    // Subscribe to real-time events
    const subscription = supabase
      .from('example_table')
      .on('*', (payload) => {
        if (payload.eventType === 'INSERT') {
          setData((prevData) => [...prevData, payload.new]);
        }
        if (payload.eventType === 'UPDATE') {
          setData((prevData) =>
```

```
            prevData.map((item) =>
                item.id === payload.new.id ? payload.new : item
            )
          );
        }
        if (payload.eventType === 'DELETE') {
          setData((prevData) =>
            prevData.filter((item) => item.id !== payload.old.id)
          );
        }
      })
      .subscribe();

    return () => {
      supabase.removeSubscription(subscription);
    };
  }, [supabase]);

  if (error) {
    return <div>Error: {error.message}</div>;
  }

  return (
    <div>
      {data.length === 0 ? (
        <div>No data available</div>
      ) : (
        data.map((item) => (
          <div key={item.id}>
            <strong>{item.name}</strong>: {item.description}
          </div>
        ))
      )}
    </div>
  );
};

export default RealTimeComponent;
```

In this implementation, the `useEffect` hook is used to set up the subscription when the component mounts and to tear it down during un-
mounting. The subscription listens to all changes (denoted by `'*'`) on
the `example_table` table. For each event, the component's state is updated using functional updates to maintain immutability and preserve
previous state values. This design pattern ensures that the UI is always

261

synchronized with changes in the database.

For Angular applications, the process follows a similar pattern. Angular developers can encapsulate real-time data logic within services, leveraging dependency injection to inject the Supabase service into components. The following example illustrates the implementation of real-time data integration in an Angular component:

```
/* SupabaseService.ts */
import { Injectable } from '@angular/core';
import { createClient, SupabaseClient } from '@supabase/supabase-js';
import { environment } from '../environments/environment';

@Injectable({
  providedIn: 'root'
})
export class SupabaseService {
  private supabase: SupabaseClient;

  constructor() {
    this.supabase = createClient(environment.supabaseUrl, environment
      .supabaseAnonKey);
  }

  subscribeToTable(table: string, callback: (payload: any) => void) {
    const subscription = this.supabase
      .from(table)
      .on('*', callback)
      .subscribe();

    return subscription;
  }

  removeSubscription(subscription: any) {
    this.supabase.removeSubscription(subscription);
  }

  async fetchData(table: string) {
    return await this.supabase.from(table).select('*');
  }
}

/* data-display.component.ts */
import { Component, OnInit, OnDestroy } from '@angular/core';
import { SupabaseService } from './supabase.service';

@Component({
```

```
  selector: 'app-data-display',
  template: `
    <div *ngIf="error">{{ error }}</div>
    <div *ngIf="loading">Loading data...</div>
    <div *ngIf="!loading">
      <div *ngFor="let item of data">
        <strong>{{ item.name }}</strong>: {{ item.description }}
      </div>
    </div>
  `
})
export class DataDisplayComponent implements OnInit, OnDestroy {
  data: any[] = [];
  loading = false;
  error: string | null = null;
  private subscription: any;

  constructor(private supabaseService: SupabaseService) {}

  async ngOnInit() {
    this.loading = true;
    const response = await this.supabaseService.fetchData('
     example_table');
    if (response.error) {
      this.error = response.error.message;
    } else {
      this.data = response.data;
    }
    this.loading = false;

    this.subscription = this.supabaseService.subscribeToTable('
     example_table', (payload: any) => {
      if (payload.eventType === 'INSERT') {
        this.data.push(payload.new);
      } else if (payload.eventType === 'UPDATE') {
        this.data = this.data.map(item =>
          item.id === payload.new.id ? payload.new : item
        );
      } else if (payload.eventType === 'DELETE') {
        this.data = this.data.filter(item => item.id !== payload.old.
     id);
      }
    });
  }

  ngOnDestroy() {
    if (this.subscription) {
      this.supabaseService.removeSubscription(this.subscription);
```

```
    }
  }
}
```

In this Angular example, the service handles both fetching initial data and managing the real-time subscription. The component calls these service functions during lifecycle hooks (ngOnInit and ngOnDestroy). The inline template efficiently displays loading states, error messages, and live data updates. This approach benefits from Angular's strong dependency injection and modular design principles, ensuring that real-time logic is decoupled from UI representation.

Vue.js utilizes a similar approach using the Composition API or Options API to integrate real-time subscriptions. The reactive nature of Vue makes it particularly suited for real-time updates. The following example demonstrates a Vue component that subscribes to real-time updates using the Composition API:

```
<script setup>
import { ref, onMounted, onBeforeUnmount } from 'vue';
import supabase from '@/supabaseClient';

const data = ref([]);
const loading = ref(true);
const error = ref(null);
let subscription = null;

const fetchData = async () => {
  const { data: fetchedData, error: fetchError } = await supabase
    .from('example_table')
    .select('*');
  if (fetchError) {
    error.value = fetchError;
  } else {
    data.value = fetchedData;
  }
  loading.value = false;
};

const subscribeToUpdates = () => {
  subscription = supabase
    .from('example_table')
    .on('*', (payload) => {
```

```
      if (payload.eventType === 'INSERT') {
        data.value.push(payload.new);
      } else if (payload.eventType === 'UPDATE') {
        data.value = data.value.map(item =>
          item.id === payload.new.id ? payload.new : item
        );
      } else if (payload.eventType === 'DELETE') {
        data.value = data.value.filter(item => item.id !== payload.
    old.id);
      }
    })
    .subscribe();
};

onMounted(async () => {
  await fetchData();
  subscribeToUpdates();
});

onBeforeUnmount(() => {
  supabase.removeSubscription(subscription);
});
</script>

<template>
  <div>
    <div v-if="loading">Loading data...</div>
    <div v-if="error">Error: {{ error.message }}</div>
    <ul v-if="!loading && data.length">
      <li v-for="item in data" :key="item.id">
        <strong>{{ item.name }}</strong>: {{ item.description }}
      </li>
    </ul>
    <div v-else-if="!loading && !data.length">No data available</div>
  </div>
</template>
```

In this Vue component, the reactive references (data, loading, and error) ensure the UI updates automatically when the data store changes. The onMounted hook starts the data fetching and subscription process, and the onBeforeUnmount hook ensures that the subscription is properly removed to avoid unnecessary resource usage.

Managing real-time data integration involves more than subscribing

265

and updating state. Developers should also consider performance optimizations, such as debouncing rapid updates, reducing unnecessary re-renders, and aggregating data changes where possible. In applications with complex data flows, it can be advantageous to implement throttling mechanisms that limit how frequently state updates are applied. Advanced state management libraries like Redux, Vuex, or NgRx can be integrated with real-time subscriptions to centralize data management and optimize rendering performance by isolating changes to specific parts of the state tree.

Furthermore, error handling and reconnection strategies are critical when dealing with real-time data. Network interruptions or server-side issues can cause subscriptions to drop. The application should gracefully handle these scenarios by providing fallback mechanisms, such as a reconnection routine that attempts to re-establish the subscription after a delay, or by notifying the user of temporary connectivity issues. Logging such errors for later diagnosis can also improve system reliability.

The integration of Supabase's real-time capabilities also benefits from careful testing and debugging practices. Developers are encouraged to use browser developer tools and logging mechanisms to inspect real-time events as they occur and to monitor application performance. Simulating high-frequency update scenarios can help identify potential bottlenecks and guide the development of more efficient handling strategies.

The techniques outlined in this section demonstrate that real-time data integration in frontend applications is achievable through careful planning, clear separation of concerns, and effective use of modern frontend frameworks. By abstracting subscription management within dedicated modules or services, maintaining clear and reactive state flows, and ensuring proper cleanup and error handling, developers can build applications that react instantaneously to backend changes. This results in dynamic, engaging user interfaces that fully leverage the potential of Supabase's real-time data capabilities, providing an optimal blend of performance, reliability, and user experience.

Chapter 7

Storage Solutions with Supabase

This chapter explores Supabase's storage solutions, detailing the setup and configuration of storage buckets. It covers file management, access control, and integrating storage into applications. Emphasizing performance optimization, it presents strategies for efficient storage use and discusses backup and disaster recovery. Readers gain a comprehensive understanding of leveraging Supabase for secure and scalable file storage within their applications.

7.1. Understanding Supabase Storage Options

Supabase provides a robust set of storage solutions that integrate seamlessly with its suite of developer tools. Its two primary storage paradigms include database storage and file storage. Both systems are

269

designed to work in concert with the underlying PostgreSQL database, while addressing distinct use cases through tailored interfaces and performance optimizations.

Database storage in Supabase refers primarily to the relational storage of structured data. This capability leverages PostgreSQL's rich features including ACID compliance, advanced query processing, and extensive indexing options. Relational storage is ideal for data that demands strong consistency, complex querying, and transactional integrity. Typical examples include user information, application metadata, or any dataset where relationships and constraints are crucial. Developers can define tables, foreign keys, and triggers directly through SQL, harnessing the full power of PostgreSQL in a serverless architecture. In practice, interacting with the database storage is accomplished through direct SQL queries or via Supabase's auto-generated RESTful and GraphQL APIs.

File storage, on the other hand, is engineered to manage unstructured data such as images, videos, documents, and other media files. This system abstracts away the complexities of file handling by providing a simple bucket-based approach. Files are stored in designated buckets, which can be configured with diverse access permissions based on project requirements. The file storage solution ensures scalability, security, and efficient retrieval of assets by employing content-delivery strategies and caching mechanisms. In addition, it integrates with the Supabase ecosystem, allowing seamless combination of file metadata stored in the database with physical files stored in buckets.

A direct point of differentiation between database and file storage lies in their suitability for various data types and application patterns. While relational storage supports fine-grained queries, indexing, and transactions, file storage is optimized for large object storage, offering features such as resumable file uploads and direct URL-based file access. The choice between these two typically involves considering the nature of the data: for instance, a text-based user comment might be best stored in a relational table, whereas an image associated with that comment would be stored in a dedicated file bucket.

Supabase's comprehensive API interfaces enable developers to query and manipulate both data types with relative ease. Invoking database operations typically involves making use of SQL commands embedded in application logic. Consider the example below that demonstrates a simple query using a Supabase client for retrieving user records:

```
const { data, error } = await supabase
  .from('users')
  .select('*')
  .eq('status', 'active');
if (error) {
  console.error('Database error:', error);
} else {
  console.log('Active users:', data);
}
```

The above snippet illustrates a basic database operation where an active subset of user records is fetched based on their status. This example harnesses Supabase's fluent API for streamlined access to the PostgreSQL database.

Interactions with Supabase file storage are equally straightforward. Files are typically uploaded to and retrieved from predefined buckets using Supabase's dedicated storage API. When uploading files, considerations such as file size, type, and access permissions are taken into account. The API abstracts these complexities into an intuitive interface. The following example demonstrates how one might upload a file to a bucket and then retrieve the corresponding public URL for access:

```
const file = document.getElementById('fileInput').files[0];
const { data, error } = await supabase.storage
  .from('user-uploads')
  .upload(`public/${file.name}`, file);
if (error) {
  console.error('Upload error:', error);
} else {
```

```
const { publicURL, error: urlError } = supabase.storage
  .from('user-uploads')
  .getPublicUrl(`public/${file.name}`);
if (urlError) {
  console.error('URL error:', urlError);
} else {
  console.log('File public URL:', publicURL);
}
}
```

This code snippet illustrates a typical file storage operation by handling file selection, upload, and public URL retrieval. The bucket user-uploads is configured to allow public access to files stored under the public/ directory. This separation of file paths provides a straightforward mechanism for managing permissions and allows for scalable file management across different buckets.

A further dimension that differentiates file storage from traditional database storage is the handling of access control and permissions. Supabase supports granular access policies for files stored in buckets, enabling developers to restrict file access based on user roles or group membership. This security model ensures that only authenticated and authorized users can retrieve sensitive data. It is common for developers to store file metadata, such as its association with a specific user or related content, in the relational database, while the actual file resides in storage. Such a model facilitates efficient queries that join metadata with file storage, ensuring consistency and security.

Performance optimization is another critical aspect of Supabase's storage solutions. For database storage, standard PostgreSQL optimizations apply. Indexing strategies, query rewriting, and partitioning are available to balance load and ensure rapid query times even with large datasets. On the file storage side, Supabase employs caching, parallel file upload capabilities, and integration with content delivery networks (CDNs) to enhance retrieval speeds and reduce latency. By leveraging these optimizations, applications can scale efficiently without compromising on access speed or data consistency.

Managing large volumes of data in both paradigms requires careful planning. For database storage, maintaining normalized structures with proper constraints and indexes is paramount. For file storage, developers must evaluate bucket organization, file naming conventions, and strategies for archiving less frequently accessed files. These considerations are integral to sustaining performance over time. Additionally, Supabase's backup and disaster recovery protocols extend to both the database and file storage systems, ensuring that data is resilient against accidental deletion or corruption. Backup strategies typically involve periodic snapshots and replication, providing multiple layers of data protection.

The combination of database and file storage in Supabase offers a unified solution for modern applications. Developers have the flexibility to design architectures where high-volume file storage is complemented by relational datasets that enforce business logic and data integrity. This hybrid structure is particularly beneficial for applications such as social networks, content management systems, and e-commerce platforms, where media assets and transactional data coexist. For example, a social media application may store user posts and comments in relational tables, while profile pictures or shared media files are stored in distinct file storage buckets. The ability to reference these files within the database by storing URLs or metadata creates a cohesive data management system that is both robust and scalable.

Integrating these storage solutions requires adherence to best practices. It is advisable to enforce strict type definitions when designing schemas to minimize runtime errors. Similarly, access policies must be rigorously defined and tested under various scenarios, ensuring that unauthorized access is effectively mitigated. Inefficiencies or misconfigurations in either database or file storage may lead to performance degradation or security vulnerabilities. Therefore, developers should make use of Supabase's monitoring and logging features to continuously track usage patterns and automate alerts for suspicious activities.

In practice, the synergy between the two storage solutions fosters a development environment where applications can efficiently navigate between structured and unstructured data. For instance, a typical implementation might involve a workflow where a user first uploads a file to a designated bucket, after which an entry is created in a relational table linking that file to the user's profile or post. A transaction that spans multiple components ensures that the process either completes fully or aborts without leaving inconsistent states. This transactional integrity is fundamental to building reliable applications.

Future enhancements to Supabase's storage capabilities are likely to focus on further integration and performance improvements. Emerging trends in data management, such as serverless functions and edge computing, are expected to be incorporated, allowing developers to harness real-time data processing and geographically distributed storage without significant overhead. As these advancements take hold, the interaction between database storage and file storage will likely become even more seamless, providing developers with greater flexibility in designing distributed systems.

Robust documentation and community support underpin Supabase's storage approach, allowing developers at all levels to quickly adapt and solve complex problems. The platform's open source nature not only promotes transparency but also accelerates innovation by enabling contributions from a diverse ecosystem of developers. Enhanced developer experience is achieved through intuitive interfaces, comprehensive SDKs, and extensive examples that demonstrate the best practices in migrating from traditional storage systems to Supabase's integrated environment.

The dual-storage infrastructure offered by Supabase exemplifies a mature approach to modern data management. Each storage system is optimized for its respective data types and operational requirements while maintaining interoperability through shared authentication, access control, and API designs. This coherence across storage types simplifies the development process and contributes to the overall scalability and security of applications built on the Supabase platform.

7.2. Setting Up and Configuring Storage Buckets

Creating and configuring storage buckets in Supabase is a systematic process that empowers developers to effectively manage unstructured data alongside relational data. The process involves multiple steps, starting from bucket creation through the Supabase dashboard or API, followed by configuring access levels, defining naming conventions, and implementing policies that govern file operations.

The initial step in setting up a storage bucket is to determine its purpose and scope. Developers must decide whether the bucket is intended for public or private access. Public buckets allow file retrieval without authentication, making them suitable for assets like images or public documents, while private buckets restrict file access through authentication, a necessity for sensitive or user-specific data. Using the Supabase dashboard, a developer can navigate to the Storage section and initiate the bucket creation process. Alternatively, the Supabase client libraries offer programmatic methods to create buckets.

For instance, the following code snippet demonstrates the creation of a public bucket using JavaScript:

```
const { data, error } = await supabase.storage.createBucket('public-
    assets', { public: true });
if (error) {
  console.error('Error creating bucket:', error);
} else {
  console.log('Bucket created successfully:', data);
}
```

275

In this example, the bucket named `public-assets` is established with public access. Developers must choose a unique bucket name and set the appropriate access parameter. For private buckets, the access parameter should be set to `false`, ensuring that authentication is required for any file interaction.

Once the bucket is created, further configuration is essential to maintain an organized and scalable file management system. Naming conventions are critical; a consistent naming strategy that incorporates prefixes or environment-specific identifiers (such as `dev-`, `staging-`, or `prod-`) assists in distinguishing buckets across multiple deployment stages. Organizing files within buckets can be further refined by creating subdirectories or using naming patterns that categorize files by type, such as `avatars`, `documents`, or `media`. This approach simplifies file retrieval and enhances overall maintainability.

Security is a primary concern when configuring storage buckets. Supabase offers granular access control mechanisms that enable developers to define permissions for file uploads, downloads, and modifications. For public buckets, while the files are accessible to external users, it is important to implement rules that govern file types and sizes. In contrast, private buckets benefit from Row Level Security (RLS) policies that integrate with the Supabase authentication system. Such policies can restrict file operations to specific users or user roles, thereby minimizing the risk of unauthorized access.

Developers can extend these permissions by programmatically defining policies based on application logic. A common pattern involves tagging file metadata with user identifiers upon upload. This metadata can later be used by the Supabase API or SQL-based RLS policies to enforce access control. Configuring these settings requires both frontend and backend considerations.

276

Integration tests for bucket configuration often include file upload, retrieval, and deletion operations. The following code example illustrates
how to upload a file to a private bucket and subsequently generate a
signed URL for temporary access:

```
const file = document.getElementById('fileInput').files[0];
const { data: uploadData, error: uploadError } = await supabase.
    storage
  .from('private-files')
  .upload(`documents/${file.name}`, file);
if (uploadError) {
  console.error('Upload error:', uploadError);
} else {
  const { data: signedUrlData, error: signedUrlError } = await
    supabase.storage
    .from('private-files')
    .createSignedUrl(`documents/${file.name}`, 60);
  if (signedUrlError) {
    console.error('Error generating signed URL:', signedUrlError);
  } else {
    console.log('Signed URL (valid for 60 seconds):', signedUrlData.
    signedUrl);
  }
}
```

Here, the file is stored in the `private-files` bucket under a
`documents/` subdirectory. A signed URL is then created, which
provides temporary access to the file for 60 seconds. This method is
particularly useful when files need to be secured yet accessible for a
limited duration.

Access policies for buckets can also be configured via the Supabase
dashboard. The dashboard provides an interface where developers
can manage bucket-level settings, such as enabling or disabling public access, setting file size restrictions, or configuring allowed file types.
For advanced configurations, bucket policies may be dynamically adjusted using SQL commands that modify the underlying PostgreSQL
RLS settings. Although such configurations are often handled through
the dashboard, knowledge of instructing these changes programmatically is advantageous for complex applications.

Another aspect to consider is integrating automation for bucket management. In multi-tenant applications or environments where files are organized per user or group, automating bucket creation based on specific triggers or events becomes vital. For example, the following function demonstrates how to automatically create a storage bucket for each new tenant:

```
async function createTenantBucket(tenantId) {
  const bucketName = `tenant-${tenantId}`;
  const { data, error } = await supabase.storage.createBucket(
    bucketName, { public: false });
  if (error) {
    console.error('Error creating tenant bucket:', error);
    return null;
  }
  console.log('Bucket created for tenant:', data);
  return bucketName;
}
```

This function emphasizes the utility of programmatically managing storage buckets by ensuring that each tenant's data is isolated and secured. Automation reduces manual errors and streamlines deployment in applications with dynamic user bases.

Performance considerations also play a role when setting up and configuring storage buckets. Supabase optimizes file retrieval with caching mechanisms, which reduce latency, particularly for frequently accessed files. However, developers must also account for the costs associated with storage, especially when dealing with large-scale data. Monitoring bucket usage through Supabase's analytics tools helps in identifying growth trends and potential inefficiencies. In cases where storage quotas are a concern, implementing life-cycle rules that automate the archival or deletion of old files can be managed through scheduled tasks or external integrations, thereby optimizing storage utilization.

In terms of security updates, regularly auditing bucket permissions and access logs is crucial. The Supabase platform provides detailed logging capabilities that allow developers to track file interactions and monitor for any irregularities. By incorporating such logs into external monitoring systems, one can construct a comprehensive security framework that proactively identifies and addresses potential vulnerabilities.

Furthermore, Cross-Origin Resource Sharing (CORS) configurations should be considered, especially if client-side applications from different domains interact with the storage buckets. Properly configured CORS headers ensure that authorized domains can access the bucket resources, while unauthorized domains remain restricted. This configuration is typically managed on the server-side but benefits from clear documentation within the bucket setup process.

The detailed configuration process of storage buckets in Supabase involves not only setting up the buckets but also continuously refining them. Developers are encouraged to document every configuration detail — from bucket names to access policies — and maintain this documentation as part of the project's technical reference. Such documentation aids in troubleshooting, onboarding new team members, and ensuring that the storage strategy aligns with evolving application requirements. Regular reviews and updates to both the documentation and the bucket configurations help maintain a secure, efficient, and scalable environment.

Ensuring compatibility between storage buckets and the application's authentication mechanisms further reinforces security. Supabase offers tight integration between the storage service and its authentication system, allowing developers to tie file access directly to user sessions. This integration is achieved by embedding user metadata with files during upload and enforcing access controls on subsequent file operations. Proper implementation of these best practices protects against unauthorized file access while ensuring that legitimate users experience minimal friction.

The comprehensive process of setting up and configuring storage buckets in Supabase is designed to be both accessible for new users and robust enough for advanced applications. By following a step-by-step approach—first determining the bucket's purpose, then choosing the appropriate access level, and finally integrating automated processes and strict security measures—developers can build a file storage system that not only supports current application needs but is also flexible enough to accommodate future growth. This methodical attention to detail in configuration underpins an efficient, secure, and scalable file management system tailored to the demands of modern web and mobile applications.

7.3. Uploading and Managing Files

Supabase facilitates effective file management via a dedicated storage API that abstracts many of the complexities associated with handling unstructured data. This section outlines the processes for uploading, organizing, and maintaining files within Supabase, building on previous concepts such as storage bucket configuration and access control. A disciplined approach to file management is essential to maintain performance, ensure security, and enable straightforward retrieval of assets when needed.

Uploading files to Supabase is achieved through streamlined API calls that handle file transfers, metadata association, and error checking. When a file is uploaded, it is stored in a designated bucket according to the directory structure prearranged during bucket configuration. Developers are encouraged to implement best practices such as organizing files based on type, origin, or user identifiers. The organization can be augmented by employing naming conventions that include timestamps or unique identifiers to prevent name collisions and facilitate efficient indexing.

A typical process to upload a file involves capturing the file from a user interface element or a server-side process, then using the Supabase storage client to transmit the file to the backend. The following example demonstrates a standard file upload in JavaScript:

```
const file = document.getElementById('fileInput').files[0];
const filePath = `uploads/${Date.now()}_${file.name}`;
const { data, error } = await supabase.storage
  .from('user-uploads')
  .upload(filePath, file);
if (error) {
  console.error('Upload failed:', error);
} else {
  console.log('File uploaded:', data);
}
```

In this example, a file is selected by the user and renamed dynamically using the current timestamp concatenated with the original filename. This strategy helps avoid overwriting any existing files and simplifies file retrieval based on upload time. The file is then uploaded into the user-uploads bucket, where directory organization is achieved by placing files in an uploads directory.

Beyond simple file uploads, effective management includes organizing files into directories or categorizing file types. Developers should design a logical structure, potentially incorporating subdirectories to segregate content (such as images, documents, or videos). The structure not only aids in maintenance but also streamlines programmatic access when querying for files. For example, predictable directory paths allow application logic to efficiently infer the correct file location without executing extraneous queries.

Managing files in Supabase storage extends to operations such as listing, updating metadata, and deletion. To list all files in a specific directory, a developer can utilize the API to retrieve file information. The API returns not only the filenames but also additional metadata that can be used to further categorize or filter files. The code snippet below shows how to list files within a designated directory:

```
const { data: fileList, error } = await supabase.storage
  .from('user-uploads')
  .list('uploads', {
    limit: 100,  // or any appropriate pagination limit
    offset: 0,
    sortBy: { column: 'name', order: 'asc' }
  });
if (error) {
  console.error('Error listing files:', error);
} else {
  console.log('List of files:', fileList);
}
```

In this example, the list operation is paginated to handle scenarios involving large volumes of files. Developers can sort the file list and use additional parameters such as offset to navigate through multiple pages, ensuring that the file management system is scalable as file volumes grow.

File metadata plays a significant role in organizing and retrieving files effectively. Metadata can include file size, type, upload time, and custom parameters that the application associates with the file. By storing structured metadata either directly within file properties or as related entries in the relational database, developers can implement complex queries and filtering mechanisms. Metadata can be updated post-upload to reflect changes or to store additional details. A typical operation to update file metadata might involve modifying a relational table that tracks file details, linking a URL or bucket path with descriptive attributes.

File deletion is another crucial aspect of file management. Removing files that are no longer needed helps maintain an optimized storage environment and reduce associated costs. Deleting a file follows a similar pattern to uploading, where the file is identified by its path, and the API call removes the file from the bucket. The following example shows how to safely delete a file:

```
const filePath = 'uploads/1623070800000_example.jpg';
const { error } = await supabase.storage
  .from('user-uploads')
  .remove([filePath]);
if (error) {
  console.error('Delete operation failed:', error);
} else {
  console.log('File successfully deleted:', filePath);
}
```

Supabase supports batch deletion, which can be particularly useful when purging directories or handling cleanup tasks during maintenance routines. By invoking the removal method with an array of file paths, developers ensure efficient bulk operations.

Managing files effectively also requires careful attention to error handling and monitoring. Uploads, deletions, and file modifications should be executed with robust error-checking mechanisms to gracefully handle transient network issues or permission-related errors. Logging errors to a centralized monitoring system facilitates proactive troubleshooting and reinforces the overall security posture of the application. Additionally, developers are encouraged to implement retry logic in scenarios where file operations encounter temporary failures.

In addition to API-driven file management, integrating scheduled maintenance routines can streamline the archival process for older or less frequently accessed files. Developing a lifecycle policy that determines when files should be archived or purged helps in managing storage costs and performance. Such policies may be implemented using serverless functions or scheduled scripts that periodically query metadata to identify stale files. These scripts then move files to a designated archival bucket or mark them for deletion. Automation of these routine tasks reduces manual intervention and minimizes the risks associated with human error.

Organizational strategies for managing files in Supabase may benefit from incorporating tagging or categorization schemes. Tags can be applied during upload and stored as part of the file's metadata, providing enhanced searchability and filtering within the storage system. For example, files uploaded via a photo-sharing application might be tagged with identifiers corresponding to locations, events, or user-generated labels. When integrated with a relational database, these tags facilitate complex queries that span both file storage and structured data.

In a multi-user environment, associating file uploads with specific users is paramount to ensuring data isolation and personalized access control. This is achieved by embedding user identifiers within the file paths or metadata. For instance, files uploaded by a particular user may reside in a subdirectory named after the user's unique ID. This practice not only aids in organizing files but also simplifies access control enforcement. Supabase's Row Level Security policies can further restrict file operations based on these identifiers, ensuring that users can only interact with content that they have uploaded.

The management of file versions is another consideration for applications that require iterative file updates. Version control for files can be implemented by appending version identifiers to filenames or directories. This method allows the application to maintain historical versions of a file, which is particularly important in collaborative environments or applications that require audit trails. Versioning can be further enhanced by linking file versions to records in the database, thereby providing a comprehensive view that spans both file storage and structured data.

When dealing with media files, performance optimization is enhanced by leveraging content delivery networks (CDNs). Although Supabase file storage is capable of handling file distribution efficiently, integrating a CDN can significantly reduce latency for end users geographically distant from the primary hosting location. The integration is transparent to the application logic, with Supabase providing direct URL access that can be cached and distributed via a CDN. Detailed logging and analytics in Supabase assist in monitoring usage patterns and determining the effectiveness of CDN strategies.

Security considerations remain central to managing file uploads and storage. Developers are advised to validate file types and sizes before accepting uploads to prevent the storage of malicious or unnecessarily large files. Client-side validations, combined with server-side checks, create a defense in depth against potential exploits. In addition, where file uploads expose sensitive information, encryption strategies may be employed. While Supabase does not automatically encrypt files at rest, developers can integrate encryption routines within the application layer before uploading the file to further secure the data.

The overall process of uploading and managing files within Supabase requires an integrated approach where frontend operations, backend validations, metadata management, and security practices function in unison. By adopting a strategy that emphasizes methodical organization, consistent naming conventions, and robust error handling, developers can construct a file management system that is both scalable and secure.

To further illustrate the interplay between file management operations, consider an application scenario where a user uploads an image that must be processed, tagged, and associated with a user account. The procedure begins with image selection and client-side validation. Once the image is deemed valid, it is uploaded to a specific bucket using a reliable API call, as shown in the earlier example. On successful upload, a reference to the file, including its URL and metadata such as upload time and user ID, is stored in a dedicated database table. This database record serves as the central point for future retrieval, updating, or deletion operations. Integrated monitoring ensures that anomalies in the file lifecycle – such as uploads that fail or files that remain unused – are logged and addressed promptly.

The comprehensive management of files in Supabase is not an isolated task but intimately tied to overall application architecture. A well-designed file management system supports the broader goals of scalability, maintainability, and security. The dynamic nature of modern applications necessitates that file operations be agile, accommodating rapid changes in usage patterns and storage requirements. Supabase provides a flexible yet powerful environment to address these needs through its storage API, detailed logging facilities, and seamless integration with relational database components. By following the detailed practices outlined herein, developers can confidently implement systems that support robust file management and offer a solid foundation for future expansion.

7.4. Implementing Access Control for Stored Data

Securing stored files is a critical aspect of developing applications with Supabase, and it requires a robust access control mechanism that operates at multiple levels. Leveraging integrated features such as Row Level Security (RLS) in PostgreSQL, Supabase enables fine-grained permissions for both file storage and associated metadata in the database. This section discusses how to set up and configure access control to secure files stored in Supabase, detailing both conceptual guidance and implementation practices through code examples.

Access control in Supabase is primarily achieved by integrating authentication with resource-level permissions. Developers have the flexibility to enforce different levels of access based on user roles, ensuring that only authenticated and authorized users can perform file operations. Two primary paradigms exist: public access, where files are accessible to all users, and private access, where files are restricted to authenticated users or users with specific associations. In private storage buckets, Supabase recommends using signed URLs to grant time-limited access to resources. This practice protects files from unauthorized access while allowing controlled sharing.

When configuring access control, a common approach is to utilize Supabase's RLS policies on relational tables that store file metadata and additional context. By linking file records to a user identifier, developers can enforce policies that ensure a user may only access files they own. For example, consider a table user_files with a column user_id corresponding to the owner. The following SQL policy can be established to allow access solely to the file owner:

```
-- Enable RLS on the table
ALTER TABLE user_files ENABLE ROW LEVEL SECURITY;

-- Create a policy that allows a user to select only their own
    records
CREATE POLICY "Allow user access to own files"
ON user_files
FOR SELECT
USING (auth.uid() = user_id);

-- Create policies for insert and update operations if necessary
CREATE POLICY "Allow user to insert files"
ON user_files
FOR INSERT
WITH CHECK (auth.uid() = user_id);
```

The above policy ensures that only the user whose unique identifier matches the user_id field can query or insert new records. Developers should replicate similar policies for update and delete operations to secure full data integrity. Furthermore, the coupling of file metadata with corresponding file storage paths in buckets allows these RLS policies to serve as an additional safeguard when fetching files via signed URLs.

When building a secure application, it is recommended to manage file access through a two-step process. First, file uploads and downloads occur through the Supabase Storage API. Second, the file metadata is

287

concurrently stored in the database, enabling the enforcement of RLS policies. An example is shown below where a file is uploaded and a corresponding metadata record is created with an associated user identifier:

```
async function uploadUserFile(file, userId) {
  const filePath = `private/${userId}/${Date.now()}_${file.name}`;
  const { data: uploadData, error: uploadError } = await supabase.
    storage
    .from('user-files')
    .upload(filePath, file);

  if (uploadError) {
    console.error('File upload failed:', uploadError);
    return;
  }

  // Insert file metadata into user_files table
  const { data: fileRecord, error: dbError } = await supabase
    .from('user_files')
    .insert([{ user_id: userId, file_path: filePath, file_name: file.
    name, uploaded_at: new Date() }]);

  if (dbError) {
    console.error('Metadata insertion failed:', dbError);
  } else {
    console.log('File uploaded and metadata stored:', fileRecord);
  }
}
```

In this code, the file is stored in a private bucket structured by user identifier. Immediately after the upload, a metadata record is inserted into the user_files table. The metadata record, containing both the file path and the user identifier, enforces the link between the physical file and its owner. This linkage is critical for applying RLS policies and ensuring that file access operations are tightly controlled.

For downloading files, creating signed URLs is a secure method to allow temporary access to files stored in private buckets. Signed URLs ensure that the recipient has access only for a predetermined time window, thus minimizing the risk of exposure. The code snippet below illustrates this process:

```
async function getSignedFileUrl(filePath) {
  const { data, error } = await supabase.storage
    .from('user-files')
    .createSignedUrl(filePath, 120); // URL valid for 120 seconds

  if (error) {
    console.error('Error generating signed URL:', error);
    return null;
  }

  return data.signedUrl;
}
```

The function getSignedFileUrl generates a URL that is valid for a specified duration. This practice is particularly useful when files need to be displayed to authenticated users without permanently exposing the storage path. The temporary nature of signed URLs becomes a vital component in a comprehensive access control strategy, especially when coupled with RLS policies on metadata records.

Access control must also consider the distinction between various roles within an application. Most applications will have more than one type of user—administrators, regular users, or even guests—each requiring different levels of file access. Supabase allows custom claims to be added to user tokens, which can then be used in RLS policies to further differentiate permissions. For instance, administrators might be granted the ability to access files across all user accounts. An exemplary SQL policy might resemble the following:

```
CREATE POLICY "Allow admin access to all files"
ON user_files
FOR SELECT
USING (auth.role() = 'admin' OR auth.uid() = user_id);
```

This policy permits users with an admin role to bypass the usual restrictions, thus facilitating administrative tasks such as auditing or troubleshooting across user accounts. It is essential to carefully manage these elevated permissions to ensure they are granted only under secure circumstances.

In addition to RLS for relational metadata, Supabase Storage itself supports bucket-level configurations that control file access. When creating a bucket, setting the `public` parameter determines its default access state. Public buckets are useful for non-sensitive data, but when confidentiality is required, private buckets should be the default. Access mechanisms such as signed URLs mitigate risks while retaining flexibility.

Furthermore, developers are encouraged to audit access logs regularly. Supabase provides logging mechanisms that can be integrated with external monitoring tools, ensuring that any anomalous access or unauthorized attempts are detected promptly. Combining these logging capabilities with automated alerting systems builds a defensive layer that reinforces overall security.

It is advisable to implement additional client-side checks to enforce file security before initiating file operations. For instance, verifying the user's session status and role before allowing file uploads or downloads not only helps prevent inadvertent security breaches but also enhances the user experience by ensuring that restricted operations are disabled at the interface level. Complementing API-level security with client-side checks forms a defense-in-depth strategy.

It is worth noting that dynamic file access control is applicable to advanced use cases, such as multi-tenant environments. In such systems, each tenant's file storage is contextualized by unique identifiers and isolated within discrete buckets or directory structures. Access control logic must carefully validate user affiliation with the tenant to prevent cross-tenant data leakage. Automation of these checks via middleware functions enhances security while making the system scalable and easier to manage in the long term.

Finally, a comprehensive security approach includes rigorous testing of access control configurations. Simulation of various access scenarios—involving both legitimate and malicious requests—ensures that policies function as intended. Penetration testing and vulnerability assessments provide insight into potential weaknesses in the system and guide remedial actions. Continuous integration pipelines should include automated tests that validate access control, ensuring that policy modifications do not inadvertently introduce new vulnerabilities.

The implementation of access control for stored data in Supabase is not static. As applications evolve, file access policies must be regularly reviewed, updated, and documented. Best practices include maintaining version-controlled SQL scripts for RLS policies and regular audits of file and metadata access logs. The iterative refinement of access control strategies is essential to protect both user data and application integrity.

By combining Supabase's built-in authentication, storage API, and PostgreSQL's robust RLS features, developers can construct a secure, scalable system for handling stored files. This integrated approach to access control ensures that sensitive data is protected at every stage—from initial upload through dynamic retrieval via signed URLs—while granting controlled access to authorized users according to well-defined policies.

7.5. Integrating File Storage in Applications

Integrating Supabase's file storage capabilities into applications involves combining frontend user interfaces, backend endpoints, and Supabase's RESTful and JavaScript APIs to create seamless file upload and download workflows. Developers can leverage the previously discussed storage bucket configurations, file management techniques, and access control measures to build robust systems that handle media and document storage efficiently. This section examines techniques for integration, including client-side interactions, server-side synchronization, and the use of secure download mechanisms.

A common task in modern applications is enabling users to upload files from the client interface. Integration begins on the client-side by capturing file input, validating the file type and size, and providing clear feedback to the user during the upload process. After the file selection, the application invokes Supabase storage functions to upload the file to a specific bucket. A typical integration in JavaScript is as follows:

```
async function handleFileUpload(event) {
  const file = event.target.files[0];
  if (!file) return;
  // Validate file size and type before upload
  const maxSize = 5 * 1024 * 1024; // 5 MB
  if (file.size > maxSize) {
    alert('File size exceeds 5 MB limit.');
    return;
  }
  const filePath = `user_uploads/${Date.now()}_${file.name}`;
  const { data, error } = await supabase.storage
    .from('user-files')
    .upload(filePath, file);
  if (error) {
    console.error('Upload failed:', error);
    alert('Upload failed. Please try again.');
    return;
  }
  console.log('File uploaded successfully:', data);
  // Optionally store file metadata in application state or database
}
```

The function above illustrates key integration points: validating the file, dynamically generating a unique file path, and executing the upload request to a designated bucket. The user interface should remain responsive during this process, providing visual cues (such as a progress bar or spinner) that indicate the state of the upload.

Beyond client-side operations, integrating file storage into applications also necessitates synchronizing file metadata with backend data stores. Frequently, file uploads are accompanied by a corresponding record in a relational database. This ensures that the files are easily tracked and associated with user information, events, or other application-specific entities. The following snippet demonstrates how to combine a file upload with metadata insertion:

```
async function uploadFileWithMetadata(file, userId) {
  const filePath = `private/${userId}/${Date.now()}_${file.name}`;
  const { data, error } = await supabase.storage
    .from('user-files')
    .upload(filePath, file);
  if (error) {
    console.error('Upload error:', error);
    return;
  }
  // Save metadata to database table (e.g., user_files)
  const { data: record, error: dbError } = await supabase
    .from('user_files')
    .insert([{ user_id: userId, file_path: filePath, file_name: file.
    name, uploaded_at: new Date() }]);
  if (dbError) {
    console.error('Database insertion error:', dbError);
  } else {
    console.log('Metadata stored successfully:', record);
  }
}
```

This integrated approach ensures that the file storage and the database remain synchronized. By storing metadata, features such as search, filtering, and user-specific file retrieval can be implemented more efficiently. The two-step process outlined in the example also facilitates the enforcement of access control; policies on the user_files table can restrict access based on the stored associations.

Downloading files is another critical aspect of integrating Supabase's storage service into an application. In many cases, files stored in private buckets require secure access. Generating signed URLs is an effective method to grant temporary access to files, ensuring that file paths remain protected. The following function demonstrates the generation of a signed URL:

```
async function fetchFileUrl(filePath) {
  const { data, error } = await supabase.storage
```

```
  .from('user-files')
  .createSignedUrl(filePath, 120); // URL valid for 120 seconds
if (error) {
  console.error('Error generating signed URL:', error);
  return null;
}
return data.signedUrl;
}
```

The temporary nature of a signed URL ensures that access to the file is limited to a short timeframe, mitigating the risks of unauthorized distribution. Developers can incorporate this functionality within download buttons or automated refresh tasks, providing seamless access in a user-friendly manner.

Integrating file storage into applications also involves handling different user roles and permissions. Access control mechanisms, as discussed in previous sections, can determine which users are allowed to upload, view, or delete files. On the client side, application logic should query the user's authorization status before displaying certain file operations. For example, an administrator dashboard might display comprehensive file listings and editing options, while standard users only see files they have uploaded. Custom claims within user tokens can be used for role differentiation:

```
if (user.role === 'admin') {
  // Render admin-specific file management controls
  console.log('Display full file management interface');
} else {
  // Render limited interface for standard user
  console.log('Display user-specific file operations');
}
```

This approach makes sure that the user interface adheres to backend security policies, thereby ensuring a cohesive security strategy across the application.

In addition to file upload and download functionalities, integrating file storage includes monitoring file operations and ensuring performance

294

optimization. Logging each file interaction is essential for diagnostic and security purposes. Developers can integrate logging mechanisms into both upload and download processes. Using serverless functions or middleware layers to capture these events can provide a centralized view of file activity. Such logs can be augmented with metadata from Supabase's analytics tools, offering insights into usage patterns and potential performance bottlenecks.

Error handling is another pillar of integration. Each API call to Supabase should include robust error-checking logic to address issues like network failures, permission errors, or interruptions during file transfers. Implementing retry logic, displaying descriptive error messages, and alerting users when operations fail are key to ensuring a smooth user experience. For instance, consider an extended version of the file upload function that incorporates retry attempts:

```
async function robustUpload(file, userId, retries = 3) {
  const filePath = `private/${userId}/${Date.now()}_${file.name}`;
  try {
    const { data, error } = await supabase.storage
      .from('user-files')
      .upload(filePath, file);
    if (error) throw error;
    // Insert metadata if upload is successful
    const { data: record, error: dbError } = await supabase
      .from('user_files')
      .insert([{ user_id: userId, file_path: filePath, file_name:
    file.name, uploaded_at: new Date() }]);
    if (dbError) throw dbError;
    console.log('Upload and metadata insertion successful:', record);
  } catch (err) {
    if (retries > 0) {
      console.warn('Retrying upload due to error:', err);
      await robustUpload(file, userId, retries - 1);
    } else {
      console.error('Final upload attempt failed:', err);
      alert('Upload failed after multiple attempts.');
    }
  }
}
```

This example demonstrates how the integration can be made more resilient by implementing retry mechanisms, ensuring that transient errors do not result in a poor user experience.

Another consideration is the integration of file storage with third-party tools, such as content delivery networks (CDNs) and image processing services. After uploading media, an application might need to process the file (e.g., generating thumbnails) or serve it via a CDN to reduce latency. Supabase's file storage provides direct URLs that can be cached or transformed by external services. Integration may involve invoking an API endpoint after a successful file upload to trigger image processing jobs, and then updating the file metadata with URLs for the processed images. This layered approach ensures that file storage is not an isolated component, but rather an integrated part of a larger media management strategy.

Lastly, it is important to incorporate testing and monitoring into the integration process. Automated tests should verify that file uploads, downloads, and metadata synchronizations work as expected under various scenarios, including high traffic and network instability. End-to-end tests that simulate user interactions can help identify potential issues in the workflow before deployment. Monitoring tools can track the performance and usage of file storage operations, alerting developers to anomalies such as unusual access patterns or repeated errors. Integrating these practices not only stabilizes application performance but also enhances security and reliability.

Integrating file storage in applications thus requires a multi-faceted approach that spans both frontend and backend components. Techniques such as dynamic file path generation, metadata synchronization, signed URL generation, and role-based access control work together to establish a secure and user-friendly file management system. The Supabase storage API, coupled with PostgreSQL's robust security features, provides developers with all the necessary tools to integrate file storage capabilities seamlessly into their applications. Through thoughtful implementation and rigorous testing, developers can build applications that not only handle file uploads and downloads efficiently but also ensure that these operations are secure, scalable, and well integrated with the overall application architecture.

7.6. Optimizing Storage Performance and Efficiency

Optimizing storage performance and efficiency in Supabase requires a multi-layered approach that encompasses both file storage and underlying database operations. Developers can enhance performance by implementing best practices designed to reduce latency, manage costs, and maintain scalability. This section details techniques for optimizing storage usage, including effective bucket organization, caching strategies, lifecycle management, and database optimization strategies for file metadata.

A foundational strategy in performance optimization is the rational organization of storage buckets. When configuring buckets, developers should choose between public and private settings based on the usage pattern. Public buckets, while offering low latency for frequently accessed static assets, can potentially incur excessive bandwidth costs if not monitored carefully. Private buckets, in contrast, may impose an overhead due to generating signed URLs, but they offer stringent access controls. A hybrid approach using both types is often advisable. For example, static assets that require global availability can be stored in a public bucket and served via a Content Delivery Network (CDN) to ensure minimal latency, while sensitive files remain in private buckets reserved for authenticated access.

Efficient naming conventions and directory structures provide an additional layer of optimization by supporting faster file retrieval and easier maintenance. A well-structured storage scheme organizes files into directories based on criteria such as file type, upload date, or owner. This not only simplifies programmatic access but also reduces the complexity of listing operations in large buckets. In practice, developers may employ timestamp-based or hash-based prefixes to ensure unique file paths, which aids in both load distribution and debugging processes. A consistent naming strategy can be implemented as follows:

```
function generateFilePath(userId, fileName) {
  const timestamp = Date.now();
  return `private/${userId}/${timestamp}_${fileName}`;
}
```

Beyond bucket configuration, optimizing the file upload process itself is crucial for performance. Large files should be broken into manageable chunks to allow parallel uploads when network reliability is an issue. Developers can integrate retry logic to handle transient network errors to avoid prolonging downtime. Advanced file upload routines may also include pre-upload compression or format conversion, reducing file size and thus saving storage costs and reducing upload latency.

There is considerable value in implementing caching strategies for frequently accessed files. When files are delivered through public buckets or signed URL mechanisms, integrating a CDN can significantly reduce latency by caching content closer to the end user. In addition to CDN caching, local browser caching mechanisms can be utilized to avoid repeated network requests for static content. Developers should set appropriate cache-control headers within the file serving infrastructure and configure these settings in conjunction with Supabase's URL generation process. For example, after generating a public URL, a developer might append caching parameters:

```
// Example function to modify URL with caching parameters
function getCachedFileUrl(url) {
  const cacheDuration = 3600; // Cache for one hour
  return `${url}?cache-control=max-age=${cacheDuration}`;
}
```

For applications with high volumes of file storage, periodic auditing and file lifecycle management are essential for controlling costs and maintaining performance. Developers can design and implement automated routines that archive or delete obsolete files based on criteria such as last-accessed timestamps or custom retention policies. Archival strategies might involve moving less-frequently accessed files to a separate archival bucket or employing a scheduled script that purges files older than a predefined threshold. The following example illustrates an automated cleanup function that interacts with Supabase storage:

```
async function cleanupOldFiles(bucketName, directory, olderThanDate)
  {
  const { data: fileList, error: listError } = await supabase.storage
    .from(bucketName)
    .list(directory);

  if (listError) {
    console.error('Error listing files:', listError);
    return;
  }

  const filesToDelete = fileList.filter(file => new Date(file.
    last_modified) < olderThanDate);
  const filePaths = filesToDelete.map(file => `${directory}/${file.
    name}`);

  if (filePaths.length > 0) {
    const { error: deleteError } = await supabase.storage
      .from(bucketName)
      .remove(filePaths);
    if (deleteError) {
      console.error('Error deleting files:', deleteError);
    } else {
      console.log('Old files deleted:', filePaths);
    }
  } else {
    console.log('No files to delete in the specified timeframe.');
  }
}
```

Such automated lifecycle management routines contribute to cost-effective storage solutions by reducing the accumulation of outdated data. In addition, incorporating alerts into these processes can enable developers to track storage usage patterns and adjust policies proactively.

Optimizing the performance of file metadata stored in a relational database is equally important. File metadata tables, which track properties like file names, upload timestamps, and user associations, benefit from proper indexing. Indexes on frequently queried columns, such as user identifiers or upload dates, can drastically reduce query execution times. For instance, a compressed composite index on the columns user_id and uploaded_at can speed up queries that retrieve files for a specific user in a given time range. Database maintenance routines, including periodic vacuuming and reindexing, support optimal performance as the volume of stored metadata increases.

Another aspect of database optimization is partitioning large tables that store file records. Partitioning by date or user identifier can distribute the load and improve the manageability of the data set. This strategy is particularly useful when dealing with applications that see a high frequency of file uploads and deletions. Well-partitioned tables facilitate faster scans and reduce the computational overhead on query execution, thus leading to a more responsive application overall.

Cost-effective storage management in Supabase not only emphasizes performance improvements but also addresses the economic implications of storing large volumes of data. Continuous monitoring of storage usage and bandwidth consumption is essential. Supabase provides analytics tools that allow developers to track file accesses, storage growth, and associated costs. Utilizing these analytics, teams can optimize their storage strategy by identifying unused or redundant files. Moreover, balancing between high-performance storage for active data and lower-cost archival storage for inactive data ensures that financial resources are allocated efficiently.

Batch processing is a recommended approach to manage bulk file operations that may otherwise lead to performance bottlenecks. For instance, updating metadata for a large number of files or cleaning up obsolete files is more efficient when performed in a single batch operation rather than individual API calls for each file. This not only reduces the number of transactions on the server but also minimizes network overhead. Developers can design batch operations that group similar files together and process them asynchronously to avoid blocking the main execution thread.

Efficient error handling and logging practices are integral to optimization. Detailed logs that capture file operation metrics—such as upload times, error rates, and response times—can provide invaluable insights during performance tuning. Instruments integrated within Supabase's diagnostic tools and external monitoring solutions can highlight areas of improvement, enabling developers to iteratively refine their storage strategies.

In scenarios involving large-scale file operations, parallel processing can offer substantial performance gains. By partitioning large upload tasks into smaller, concurrent units, an application can leverage multi-threading or asynchronous programming patterns to expedite file transfers. Care must be taken to balance concurrency with resource limitations, ensuring that the system does not become overwhelmed by too many simultaneous operations. Developers should implement a concurrency control mechanism that limits the number of parallel uploads or downloads to an optimal level, dynamically adjusting based on current system load.

Lastly, applying best practices for both client and server-side operations guarantees the overall efficiency of the storage subsystem. On the client side, reducing file size through compression or leveraging progressive file upload patterns can alleviate bandwidth pressures. On the server side, deploying robust caching layers and fine-tuning database queries can further cut down on response times. In a comprehensive system, each layer from the user interface to the backend storage contributes to delivering a high-performance, cost-effective solution.

By combining sound architectural decisions with targeted performance tuning, developers can harness the full potential of Supabase's storage solutions. The techniques detailed in this section provide a framework for optimizing both storage performance and overall cost-efficiency. Through continued monitoring, iterative improvements, and the implementation of industry best practices, applications can achieve high scalability while remaining responsive to end user demands and cost constraints.

7.7. Backup and Disaster Recovery for Storage

Ensuring data resilience in modern applications involves a well-defined backup and disaster recovery strategy for both file storage and associated metadata. Supabase offers mechanisms that, when integrated with external tools and scheduled automation, enable robust data protection and rapid recovery from accidental deletions, malicious actions, or system failures. This section details strategies for implementing backup and recovery plans, emphasizing the importance of continuous data protection, redundancy, and streamlined recovery procedures.

A critical component of data resilience is establishing a backup strategy that addresses both the file storage—the physical files stored in buckets—and the metadata maintained in relational databases. File backups should preserve the current state of files, including their organizational structure, access control settings, and timestamps. Similarly, backup routines for metadata must capture the relationships between files and users, file naming conventions, and other attributes critical for restoring application state.

302

Replication is a fundamental method for enhancing data resilience. Supabase's underlying PostgreSQL environment supports replication and point-in-time recovery, ensuring that changes to metadata can be restored to a previous state in cases of data corruption or accidental deletion. In parallel, file replication can be achieved through periodic exports of file buckets to an external backup system or a secondary storage location. Developers are encouraged to leverage both built-in and external tools to replicate and archive data.

Automating backups is essential for minimizing human error and ensuring consistency. Scheduled tasks that execute backup routines can help maintain an up-to-date archive of files and metadata. For instance, a scheduled serverless function or a cron job can trigger backups during off-peak hours, reducing the operational load during high-traffic periods. A typical backup process might involve listing the contents of a storage bucket, downloading the files, and then uploading them to a designated backup bucket or external storage service. The following example demonstrates a simple automated backup function using JavaScript:

```
async function backupFiles(sourceBucket, backupBucket, directory) {
  // List files in the source bucket directory
  const { data: fileList, error: listError } = await supabase.storage
    .from(sourceBucket)
    .list(directory);
  if (listError) {
    console.error('Error listing files:', listError);
    return;
  }

  // Iterate through file list to backup each file
  for (const file of fileList) {
    const filePath = `${directory}/${file.name}`;
    // Download file from source bucket
    const { data: fileData, error: downloadError } = await supabase.
    storage
      .from(sourceBucket)
      .download(filePath);
    if (downloadError) {
      console.error('Error downloading file:', filePath,
      downloadError);
```

```
      continue;
    }

    // Upload file to backup bucket preserving the directory
      structure
    const { error: uploadError } = await supabase.storage
      .from(backupBucket)
      .upload(filePath, fileData);
    if (uploadError) {
      console.error('Error uploading backup file:', filePath,
      uploadError);
    } else {
      console.log('Backed up file:', filePath);
    }
  }
}
```

In this example, the function backupFiles lists files in a specified directory of a source bucket, downloads each file, and uploads them to a backup bucket. Implementing such a function as part of a scheduled task provides continuous protection against data loss. It is important to implement error handling and logging mechanisms in production systems to monitor backup success and identify potential issues.

Redundancy across multiple geographic regions further enhances data resilience. Storing backups in diverse locations mitigates the risk of data loss due to localized failures, natural disasters, or network outages. Many backup strategies incorporate offsite storage, where backups are transferred to cloud storage services provided by third-party vendors. Utilizing such multi-region strategies ensures that a single point of failure does not compromise the entire system.

Versioning is another essential element of an effective backup strategy. Maintaining multiple versions of files can be invaluable in scenarios where data corruption or accidental overwrites occur. Supabase's file storage can be supplemented with version control mechanisms by incorporating version identifiers in file names or maintaining version histories in database records. For example, a versioned naming scheme might append a version number or a commit hash to the file name, which then can be stored alongside metadata:

```
async function uploadVersionedFile(file, userId, version) {
  const filePath = `private/${userId}/${Date.now()}_v${version}_${
    file.name}`;
  const { data, error } = await supabase.storage
    .from('user-files')
    .upload(filePath, file);
  if (error) {
    console.error('Upload error:', error);
    return;
  }
  console.log('Versioned file uploaded:', data);
}
```

This versioned approach allows applications to roll back to an earlier, uncorrupted state if a file becomes compromised. Maintaining a detailed version history in the metadata database further reinforces resilience by enabling precise tracking of file changes over time.

Recovery planning must be documented and routinely tested to ensure that data can be effectively restored when needed. Regular drills that simulate data loss events and subsequent recovery processes help to identify weaknesses in the backup system before they manifest in production. Recovery plans should outline the steps to restore both file storage and database states. This might include instructions on how to select a backup point, procedures for verifying data integrity post-recovery, and steps for resynchronizing metadata with physical files.

In addition to server-side backup routines, database backups are equally important. Supabase provides mechanisms for taking full and incremental backups of PostgreSQL databases. These backups can be automated via the platform or through third-party database management tools. Adopting incremental backups, which capture only the changes since the last full backup, can reduce storage and time overhead while still providing comprehensive data recovery options. Coupling database backups with file backups creates a dual-layered

305

approach that addresses both structured and unstructured data.

Monitoring and alerting systems play a critical role in backup and disaster recovery. Automated monitoring scripts can check the status of backup routines, validate file integrity, and ensure that backups are being executed at scheduled intervals. Alerts sent via email or integrated with incident management systems prompt immediate attention when backups fail or fall behind schedule. Implementing comprehensive monitoring reduces the risk that unnoticed backup failures may compromise the overall recovery strategy.

The design of an effective backup and disaster recovery plan must also consider regulatory and compliance requirements. Many industries mandate specific backup retention periods, encryption standards, and recovery time objectives (RTOs). Developers must configure backup strategies in line with these requirements, ensuring that data is not only secure but also meets the necessary legal and compliance standards. Encryption of backups, for example, adds an extra layer of security, protecting sensitive data even if backup files are compromised during transmission or storage.

Furthermore, integrating recovery testing into continuous integration pipelines assists in maintaining a resilient backup system. Simulated recovery scenarios can be executed as part of regular testing routines. This proactive testing helps to ensure that every component of the backup solution—from file replication to database restoration—operates as expected. Implementing mock disaster recovery scenarios assures that dependencies, such as network bandwidth and service availability, are sufficient to support a full restoration under adverse conditions.

A robust backup and disaster recovery strategy is inherently iterative. As applications evolve and data volumes grow, backup methods must be periodically reviewed and updated to address new risks and requirements. Documentation and version control of backup procedures are crucial for maintaining an accurate and effective recovery plan. Regular reviews of backup logs and recovery metrics provide insights that drive improvements in the backup strategy, ensuring that the system remains resilient in the face of emerging threats.

By combining automated replication, geographic redundancy, version control, and rigorous testing, developers can build a data resilience strategy that minimizes downtime and prevents data loss even under the most challenging circumstances. Supabase provides the core infrastructure needed to manage file storage and metadata, while integrating with external tools and best practices furthers the resilience of the entire storage system.

Continuous improvement in backup and disaster recovery practices is a key element of an operational strategy designed to handle worst-case scenarios. The techniques highlighted in this section provide a blueprint for constructing a comprehensive backup system that not only secures data but also facilitates rapid recovery. With well-defined processes, automated routines, and thorough testing, applications can achieve a level of resilience that minimizes risk and ensures continuity of service even in the event of catastrophic failures.

Chapter 8

Using Supabase for API Development

This chapter offers a comprehensive look at developing APIs with Supabase, covering endpoint configuration, CRUD operations, and security measures. It discusses integrating APIs into web applications, ensuring efficient data interaction. The chapter also addresses best practices for testing, debugging, and maintaining APIs, equipping developers with the skills to create robust and secure application interfaces using Supabase.

8.1. Exploring Supabase API Capabilities

Supabase provides developers with a versatile backend platform that centers on a PostgreSQL database while exposing its capabilities through a RESTful API which conforms to the PostgREST specification. This design grants developers the ability to perform sophisticated data operations with minimal configuration, thus aligning with modern web development practices and reducing the complexity of connecting client-side applications to dynamic data.

Supabase automatically generates API endpoints based on the defined database schema, which streamlines data access and manipulation. This generation process means that every table and view in the PostgreSQL database is directly accessible as an API endpoint. Developers can perform operations such as filtering, pagination, and ordering directly through URL query parameters, adhering to standard HTTP practices. For instance, retrieving a full record set while applying a simple filter is achieved by appending specific parameters to the URL. This native integration reduces the need for additional middleware and enables rapid prototyping.

The API capabilities extend to full CRUD (Create, Read, Update, Delete) operations by mapping HTTP methods to database actions. A POST request creates new records, a GET request retrieves data, a PATCH request applies updates, and a DELETE request removes records. Each operation is executed using simple HTTP calls. Below is an example of a POST request to insert a new record:

```
curl -X POST -H "apikey: YOUR_SUPABASE_KEY" \
    -H "Authorization: Bearer YOUR_JWT_TOKEN" \
    -H "Content-Type: application/json" \
    -d '{"column1": "value1", "column2": "value2"}' \
    https://your-project.supabase.co/rest/v1/your_table
```

Handling data through these endpoints is straightforward due to the consistent response structure provided by Supabase. Status codes, headers, and JSON payloads work together to offer transparent feedback on the success or failure of a transaction. Such uniformity ensures that developers can integrate error handling and logging mechanisms without extensive customization.

A notable feature of the Supabase API is its support for advanced query

310

parameters. These parameters allow developers to execute complex queries directly via the API. For example, a developer can request data that satisfies multiple conditions, apply sorting parameters, and limit the number of returned records. An example request for retrieving records with a price greater than 100 and sorting the results in descending order is shown below:

```
curl -H "apikey: YOUR_SUPABASE_KEY" \
    -H "Authorization: Bearer YOUR_JWT_TOKEN" \
    "https://your-project.supabase.co/rest/v1/your_table?select=*&
    price=gt.100&order=price.desc"
```

These advanced querying capabilities allow applications to offload complex data filtering and sorting to the backend, reducing the processing load on the client side. This is particularly important in modern web applications, where performance and efficiency are critical factors.

In addition to traditional CRUD operations, Supabase extends its API capabilities to support real-time functionality. By leveraging PostgreSQL's replication features along with WebSocket connections, Supabase enables real-time data updates. This means that any database changes, such as insertions or updates, can be immediately communicated to subscribed clients. Real-time subscriptions are essential for applications such as collaborative tools, live dashboards, and chat applications where low-latency data reflection is required.

Real-time functionality is accessed via a WebSocket client that subscribes to changes on specified tables or channels. Once a change occurs, the server pushes the new data to connected clients without necessitating the overhead of continuous polling. The enhanced efficiency and responsiveness provided by this feature are well-suited to develop interactive and data-intensive web applications.

Beyond the basic operations, Supabase allows for the customization of API functionality through Remote Procedure Calls (RPCs). RPCs enable the execution of custom server-side functions encapsulated within

311

the PostgreSQL database. This means developers can perform operations that go beyond simple CRUD functions and incorporate business logic or perform complex data aggregations directly in the database. The use of RPC endpoints provides an additional layer of flexibility when standard API endpoints do not suffice.

The configuration of RPC endpoints is accomplished by defining SQL functions within the backend database. Once defined, these functions are exposed as new endpoints that accept parameters and return results as JSON. This feature allows developers to create modular, reusable components that encapsulate both data access and computation, effectively bridging the gap between raw database operations and application-specific requirements.

A critical consideration when exploring the API capabilities of Supabase is its integrated security framework. The API endpoints enforce authentication using JSON Web Tokens (JWTs) and API keys. Authentication and authorization are managed at the database level using PostgreSQL's row-level security (RLS) policies, which restrict data access based on predefined user roles and conditions. This integration ensures that only authenticated and authorized users can execute sensitive operations, thus meeting the stringent security requirements of modern web applications.

The API responses provided by Supabase are designed for clarity and ease of debugging. Detailed error messages, HTTP status codes, and metadata within the responses help developers quickly identify issues and adjust their requests accordingly. When combined with comprehensive logging and monitoring practices, these capabilities contribute to more robust and resilient application development.

Developers benefit further from the standardized implementation of CORS policies on the API endpoints. These policies restrict resource sharing based on defined origins, providing an additional layer of security for cross-domain communications. Such measures are indispensable in web environments where external scripts or third-party services interact with the backend.

Supabase's API design also encourages integration with modern framework ecosystems. Popular frontend frameworks and libraries are well-equipped to interact with RESTful APIs, which simplifies the integration process. The consistency of the API structure allows developers to use state management tools and asynchronous data fetching libraries without incurring the overhead of adapting to diverse backend protocols. Thus, the Supabase API becomes a natural extension for building responsive single-page applications.

Furthermore, the modular architecture inherent in Supabase promotes the extension of functionalities via custom middleware and hooks. Developers can insert pre-processing or post-processing stages that run before data is transmitted over the API or after a response is received. This modularity not only increases the flexibility of the deployment but also ensures that common tasks such as logging, error processing, or data sanitization are centrally managed. Custom hooks and middleware complement the core functionality, ensuring that complex business processes remain decoupled from the essential data operations.

The robustness of the Supabase API is complemented by extensive documentation, which is continuously updated by the community and the core development team. Detailed explanations of API parameters, security practices, and usage examples facilitate quick onboarding and promote best practices among users. Such documentation is invaluable in bridging the gap between high-level concepts and practical, implementable solutions.

The overall design philosophy of Supabase emphasizes a uniform and scalable API that minimizes the gap between database operations and application development. It efficiently handles the demands of modern web applications by providing a secure, reliable, and flexible interface. Developers can leverage the API to manage data interactions, implement real-time updates, and enforce security protocols—all through a single, cohesive platform.

By focusing on both ease of use and the depth of functionality, Supabase addresses the core requirements of modern web development. Its architecture streamlines backend operations while offering enough customization to handle complex application scenarios. The combination of automatic endpoint generation, real-time data synchronization, advanced querying, and integrated security measures empowers developers to create scalable and maintainable applications. This depth of functionality ensures that Supabase remains a compelling option for developers seeking to build data-driven applications that are both agile and secure.

8.2.   Setting Up API Endpoints

Supabase simplifies the process of establishing API endpoints by automating the exposure of PostgreSQL tables and views as RESTful endpoints. This process is designed to reduce the complexity associated with backend configurations while offering a flexible and secure interface for data manipulation. In the context of modern web development, where applications require efficient data access and robust security, setting up API endpoints with Supabase provides a streamlined method for connecting client-side interactions with server-side data.

The initial step in creating an API endpoint involves defining the database schema. Tables, views, and relationships must be structured carefully since the resulting endpoints mirror these database objects. Once the schema is established, Supabase uses the PostgREST specification to map each table to a corresponding endpoint. For instance, a table named users automatically results in an endpoint such as

314

`https://your-project.supabase.co/rest/v1/users`. The automation of endpoint creation not only accelerates development but also ensures that the API remains consistent with the underlying data model.

Configuration of these endpoints is largely managed through the Supabase dashboard, which offers an interface to adjust settings such as column-level permissions, row-level security policies, and CORS configurations. Developers can integrate these settings with the database's role-based access control policies. Row-Level Security (RLS) is particularly useful in ensuring that data access is restricted appropriately; policies can be defined so that only users with specific roles have access to sensitive data. These configurations are implemented using SQL commands directly within the database environment. For example, enabling RLS on a table is as straightforward as executing the following command:

```
ALTER TABLE users ENABLE ROW LEVEL SECURITY;
```

Once RLS is enabled, policies must be created to define the allowable operations. A typical policy might allow users to update their own records while preventing modifications to data belonging to others. Consider the example below which sets a policy on the users table to permit updates only when the authenticated user matches the record's owner:

```
CREATE POLICY "Allow owners to update their own data"
  ON users
  FOR UPDATE
  USING (auth.uid() = id);
```

API endpoints also support rich query parameters that can be used for filtering, sorting, and paginating results. Developers can append specific query operators directly to the URL. For example, to fetch all records from a `products` table where the `price` exceeds a certain value and the results are sorted in descending order, one might use the following query:

315

```
curl -H "apikey: YOUR_SUPABASE_KEY" \
    -H "Authorization: Bearer YOUR_JWT_TOKEN" \
    "https://your-project.supabase.co/rest/v1/products?price=gt.50&
    order=price.desc"
```

This level of configurability at the endpoint allows developers to directly manage how data is retrieved and manipulated, offloading much of the workload from the client side. The reliance on URL parameters to control data operations means that both simple and complex queries can be executed without additional server-side logic, thereby streamlining the overall application architecture.

The setup process extends to support for data insertion, updating, and deletion through the corresponding HTTP methods. For example, a POST request allows for the creation of new records, bypassing the need for writing custom insert functions. Using cURL, one can insert a record into a table as shown below:

```
curl -X POST -H "apikey: YOUR_SUPABASE_KEY" \
    -H "Authorization: Bearer YOUR_JWT_TOKEN" \
    -H "Content-Type: application/json" \
    -d '{"name": "Sample Product", "price": 99.99}' \
    https://your-project.supabase.co/rest/v1/products
```

Each endpoint follows a consistent pattern based on the HTTP method invoked. A GET request retrieves data, PATCH updates existing records, and DELETE removes records. Parsing and formatting of the response data are handled automatically by Supabase, which returns data in JSON format. This standardization is critical for client-side applications relying on predictable structures and error codes to manage user interactions.

Developers should be aware that the act of setting up API endpoints is not limited solely to data manipulation; it also encompasses configuration instrumental to ensuring secure, reliable operations. Supabase provides comprehensive controls over CORS settings to limit cross-origin requests. This is particularly essential for applications that interact with external services or are accessed via the web. For example, specifying trusted domains in the dashboard prevents unauthorized web pages from making requests to the API, enhancing the security posture of the application.

Furthermore, the Supabase environment supports the establishment of dynamic endpoint behaviors through the use of Remote Procedure Calls (RPCs). An RPC endpoint is created by defining a custom SQL function that encapsulates complex operations beyond the basic CRUD patterns. Once the function is established, Supabase exposes it as an endpoint accessible through an RPC call. A simple RPC function might be used to perform a complex aggregation, as illustrated in this example:

```
CREATE FUNCTION get_monthly_sales(month INTEGER)
RETURNS TABLE(product_id INTEGER, total_sales NUMERIC) AS $$
  SELECT product_id, SUM(sales)
  FROM sales_data
  WHERE EXTRACT(MONTH FROM sale_date) = month
  GROUP BY product_id;
$$ LANGUAGE SQL;
```

An RPC call can then be made using a POST request to the designated endpoint. This approach enables developers to encapsulate business logic within the database and maintain performance by reducing the need for additional server-side logic.

The process of setting up API endpoints is further augmented by Supabase's emphasis on ease of testing and debugging. Tooling is provided within the Supabase ecosystem to simulate different conditions and invoke endpoints with varied payloads. Integrated logging helps trace each API request, providing detailed insights into query performance, potential errors, and security incidents. These logs, combined with extensive API documentation, form a critical resource for maintaining a healthy and secure application architecture.

Customizing the behavior of API endpoints does not stop at data retrieval and manipulation. Supabase supports the integration of custom middleware, allowing pre-processing of API requests and post-processing of API responses. This capability is especially useful when additional validation or transformation tasks are required. For example, middleware can be used to validate incoming JSON payloads before they reach the database, ensuring data integrity. While these transformations are executed on the client side or via additional server functions, the integration points provided by Supabase make it easy to interlace these processes with API calls.

It is also important to consider performance optimization during setup. With increasing data volumes and more complex queries, developers must ensure that endpoints remain responsive. Supabase recommends the use of database indexes, query optimization, and caching strategies where applicable. The configuration of resource-intensive endpoints can be managed through careful analysis of query plans and periodic monitoring. The performance enhancements, coupled with Supabase's auto-scaling capabilities, ensure that the API endpoints perform reliably under varying load conditions.

Developers are encouraged to take advantage of Supabase's comprehensive online documentation, which provides step-by-step guidance and best practices for creating secure and efficient API endpoints. These resources are designed to cater to both novice and experienced developers, ensuring that all users can configure endpoints suitable for their specific requirements. Detailed walkthroughs demonstrate how to integrate endpoints with various frontend frameworks, ensuring seamless data flows and minimizing development overhead.

In modern web development, the ability to rapidly deploy and configure API endpoints has a direct impact on the agility of the development process. The simplicity and power afforded by Supabase allow developers to focus on building application logic rather than wrestling with backend complexities. The platform's design encourages incremental development; endpoints can be configured, tested, and refined contin-uously as the project scales and requirements evolve. This modular ap-proach results in systems that are both flexible and resilient to changes in business logic or data structures.

The systematic approach to setting up API endpoints ensures that each component of the data access layer is robust, secure, and optimized for performance. The interplay between automatic endpoint generation, customizable security policies, rich query capabilities, and support for procedural extensions positions Supabase as a powerful tool for mod-ern backend development. The holistic integration of these elements within the Supabase ecosystem creates a platform that simplifies the entire process of API development, from initial configuration to deploy-ment and maintenance.

By leveraging the automatic generation of CRUD endpoints, develop-ers can reduce the time required to build and deploy complex applica-tions. The strategic use of SQL functions for RPCs further empowers developers to implement tailored business logic, ensuring that data op-erations are performed in a manner consistent with the application's requirements. This comprehensive approach results in a cohesive and scalable API infrastructure that can handle a variety of data-intensive operations while maintaining high standards of security and perfor-mance.

8.3. Handling CRUD Operations

Implementing CRUD operations through Supabase APIs is a straight-forward process that leverages the inherent RESTful design of the plat-form. Each operation in CRUD—Create, Read, Update, and Delete—maps directly to an HTTP method. Supabase automatically creates and manages these endpoints based on the underlying PostgreSQL schema while integrating robust security policies and advanced query function-

ality. This section provides detailed guidance on using these operations to manipulate data effectively via Supabase APIs.

The Create operation corresponds with HTTP POST requests. By issu-
ing a POST request to a designated endpoint, a developer can insert
new records into a database table. The process entails constructing a
JSON payload that represents the new record. Developers must ensure
that the payload adheres to the table's schema, enforcing data types
and constraints defined during the table creation. For example, when
adding a new record to a table called items, the following cURL command can be used:

```
curl -X POST -H "apikey: YOUR_SUPABASE_KEY" \
    -H "Authorization: Bearer YOUR_JWT_TOKEN" \
    -H "Content-Type: application/json" \
    -d '{"name": "New Item", "description": "Item description", "
    price": 49.99}' \
    https://your-project.supabase.co/rest/v1/items
```

In this code example, the JSON payload includes fields that match the
column names of the items table. The use of proper headers is essential to ensure that the request is authenticated and the data format is
correctly identified as JSON. This command creates a new record and
returns a response that details the inserted data, confirming the success or failure of the operation.

The Read operation is designed to retrieve records and is implemented
using HTTP GET requests. Supabase's API supports a variety of query
parameters that facilitate filtering, ordering, and limiting the data returned. This allows developers to execute refined queries directly from
the URL without the need for complicated server-side logic. For instance, to retrieve a list of items where the price is greater than 25,
sorted in ascending order by name, a GET request can be structured
as follows:

```
curl -H "apikey: YOUR_SUPABASE_KEY" \
    -H "Authorization: Bearer YOUR_JWT_TOKEN" \
    "https://your-project.supabase.co/rest/v1/items?price=gt.25&
```

```
order=name.asc"
```

This command sends a request that leverages query operators to filter out records with a price below 25. The ordering parameter order=name.asc ensures that the results are alphabetically sorted by the name column. The response is returned in JSON format, containing an array of records that meet the specified criteria. Developers can further refine the query using additional parameters like select to specify columns or limit to control the number of results.

The Update operation is handled via HTTP PATCH requests. This method enables partial updates to existing records by specifying only the fields that require modification. It is essential to include appropriate filters in the URL or within the SQL function binding to ensure that only the targeted records are updated. For example, modifying the price of a specific item can be accomplished with a PATCH request. The following example demonstrates updating the price of an item with a particular identifier:

```
curl -X PATCH -H "apikey: YOUR_SUPABASE_KEY" \
     -H "Authorization: Bearer YOUR_JWT_TOKEN" \
     -H "Content-Type: application/json" \
     -d '{"price": 59.99}' \
     "https://your-project.supabase.co/rest/v1/items?id=eq.123"
```

Here, the JSON payload specifies the new price, while the URL parameter id=eq.123 filters the update to the record with an identifier of 123. Utilizing precise filters in the request is crucial for ensuring that updates do not inadvertently affect multiple records. This mechanism aligns with best practices for database operations by emphasizing minimal data change and clear intent.

The Delete operation utilizes the HTTP DELETE method and allows developers to remove records from the database. As with updating, it is paramount to apply proper filtering to target the precise record or

321

set of records intended for deletion. A Delete request must always be constructed with caution, particularly in production environments, to avoid unintentional cascades. The following example shows a DELETE request for an item with a specific identifier:

```
curl -X DELETE -H "apikey: YOUR_SUPABASE_KEY" \
    -H "Authorization: Bearer YOUR_JWT_TOKEN" \
    "https://your-project.supabase.co/rest/v1/items?id=eq.123"
```

In this illustrative command, the identifier filter id=eq.123 specifies exactly which record should be removed from the items table. Supabase's API returns appropriate HTTP status codes to indicate whether the deletion was successful, thereby providing feedback for error handling and logging.

Supabase's adherence to the RESTful architecture enables developers to seamlessly manage CRUD operations within a unified framework. Each operation is executed in a consistent manner that leverages HTTP methods and query parameters to directly interact with the underlying PostgreSQL database. This approach not only simplifies development but also encourages the use of standard web protocols for data management.

Integrating these operations into a web application involves thoughtful consideration of client-side interactions. For example, single-page applications (SPAs) benefit from asynchronous data fetching methods that implement these API calls on demand. Most modern front-end frameworks such as React, Angular, and Vue can interact with RESTful APIs using libraries such as Axios or the native Fetch API. Consider a simplified example using JavaScript and the Fetch API for performing a GET request:

```
fetch("https://your-project.supabase.co/rest/v1/items?price=gt.25&
    order=name.asc", {
    headers: {
        "apikey": "YOUR_SUPABASE_KEY",
        "Authorization": "Bearer YOUR_JWT_TOKEN"
    }
```

322

```
})
.then(response => response.json())
.then(data => console.log(data))
.catch(error => console.error('Error:', error));
```

This snippet demonstrates an asynchronous GET request to retrieve items that satisfy specific criteria. Error handling is incorporated using the `catch` statement, ensuring that network or application errors are appropriately managed. The approach highlights how CRUD operations can be embedded within client-side code, thereby enabling dynamic user interfaces that reflect real-time data.

Developers must also consider security best practices when handling CRUD operations. Supabase supports JSON Web Tokens (JWT) which form the backbone of its authentication strategy. Each CRUD operation should be guarded by proper authentication and authorization checks. Additionally, Row-Level Security (RLS) policies implemented on the PostgreSQL database ensure that each operation conforms to the permissions structure defined for different user roles. These security measures protect endpoints against unauthorized access and mitigate the risk of data breaches.

Rate limiting and monitoring are other integral parts of managing CRUD operations. When handling high volumes of requests, especially in production environments, implementing rate limiting strategies helps to prevent abuse and ensure that the API remains responsive. Tools integrated within the Supabase ecosystem, such as logging dashboards and performance monitoring, allow developers to track API usage and adjust configurations as needed. These practices, combined with thorough testing of CRUD operations, lead to more resilient and scalable applications.

Testing CRUD operations involves both unit and integration testing processes. Automated tests can simulate API calls and verify the correctness of the data manipulations. For instance, unit tests can assert that a Create operation correctly inserts a new record, while integration tests verify the flow from the client-side request to the final response from the database. Utilizing testing frameworks alongside Supabase's API documentation provides a clear path for validating functionality before deployment.

Beyond direct data operations, CRUD processes might involve additional considerations such as transaction management in cases where multiple related operations need to be executed atomically. Supabase's integration with PostgreSQL opens the door for using transactions to bundle several CRUD operations into a single operation. Although the backend API automatically handles many cases, developers have the flexibility to incorporate SQL transactions when necessary to enforce data consistency and integrity.

The practical application of CRUD operations extends to various use cases in web development. Whether it is creating user profiles, updating transactional data, reading lists of products, or deleting obsolete records, the principles remain consistent. The design of Supabase's API encourages a standardized approach that minimizes boilerplate code and maximizes reliability. The API endpoints are designed to be intuitive, with semantics that clearly reflect the action performed, thereby reducing the cognitive load on developers.

By maintaining a clear mapping between HTTP methods and database operations, Supabase ensures that CRUD operations are both predictable and efficient. The consistency in how resources are manipulated leads to increased productivity and simplifies debugging. Each operation validates the input data, checks for proper authorization, and returns a response that can be directly integrated into client-side workflows.

The detailed handling of CRUD operations ultimately contributes to a robust backend system that can quickly adapt to the evolving requirements of modern web applications. The uniformity across operations facilitates easier maintenance and enhances the overall developer experience. Real-time feedback from the database, combined with effective error management and security practices, produces an environment in which data integrity and application performance can thrive.

Integrating these well-defined CRUD operations into the broader development workflow results in systems that are not only scalable and reliable but also aligned with contemporary standards in API design and web development practices. The careful consideration of how data is created, read, updated, and deleted sets the foundation for applications that can handle complex interactions while maintaining an emphasis on security and performance.

8.4. Securing API Access

Ensuring proper security measures is paramount when exposing APIs in any backend solution. Supabase integrates several strategies that protect the integrity of data and restrict access to authorized users. The approach taken encompasses robust authentication mechanisms, precise authorization rules based on Row-Level Security (RLS), and techniques such as rate limiting to prevent abuse.

Authentication is the first line of defense in securing API access. Supabase relies on JSON Web Tokens (JWT) to confirm the identity of users making API requests. When a user logs in, they receive a JWT that must be included in subsequent HTTP headers. The inclusion of this token not only validates the user's identity but also attaches their associated claims which can be used to enforce further authorization rules. A typical API call that uses authentication headers is presented below:

```
curl -H "apikey: YOUR_SUPABASE_KEY" \
    -H "Authorization: Bearer YOUR_JWT_TOKEN" \
```

```
"https://your-project.supabase.co/rest/v1/your_table"
```

In this example, the headers ensure that the API endpoint processes only those requests that include valid tokens. The use of JWTs minimizes overhead while maintaining security during stateless transactions and scales well as the number of users increases.

Authorization in Supabase is implemented using Row-Level Security (RLS) policies, which are defined directly within the PostgreSQL database. RLS enables the creation of rules that determine which records can be accessed or modified by a given user. This fine-grained control ensures that even valid users are only able to interact with data permitted by their roles. For instance, consider a policy that restricts access so users can only update their own records in a `profiles` table. This is achieved with the following SQL command:

```
ALTER TABLE profiles ENABLE ROW LEVEL SECURITY;

CREATE POLICY "Allow only owner to update profile"
  ON profiles
  FOR UPDATE
  USING (auth.uid() = id);
```

Enabling RLS and configuring such policies serve to enforce data segregation without the need for custom middleware on each endpoint. The policy leverages the `auth.uid()` function to compare the authenticated user's identifier with the record's identifier, ensuring that every update is host-specific and reducing potential attack vectors associated with data exposure.

It is essential to integrate both authentication and authorization seamlessly. When a user sends a request with a token, the JWT is decoded to extract user information, which is then evaluated against the RLS policies. The combination of these checks ensures that the API is secure both at the entry point and during data manipulation. The architecture benefits from centralized security checks at the database level that reduce the risk of misconfiguration and potential backdoor hazards.

Beyond authentication and authorization, rate limiting represents a crucial aspect of API security. Rate limiting helps prevent abuse and protects server resources by restricting the number of requests a client can make in a specified time frame. Although Supabase does not enforce rate limiting directly at the API gateway level, developers can integrate external solutions and reverse proxies, such as NGINX or cloud-based API management systems, to impose such controls. An example of an NGINX configuration snippet that implements rate limiting is as follows:

```
http {
    limit_req_zone $binary_remote_addr zone=api_limit:10m rate=10r/s;

    server {
        location /rest/v1/ {
            limit_req zone=api_limit burst=20;
            proxy_pass http://backend;
        }
    }
}
```

In this configuration, the directive `limit_req_zone` sets a rate limit of 10 requests per second with a burst capacity of 20. Such controls ensure that even if an attacker attempts to overload the API with requests, the system will effectively throttle the traffic and maintain service availability.

Another security aspect that needs attention is the proper configuration of Cross-Origin Resource Sharing (CORS). Supabase allows you to specify which domains are permitted to interact with your API. By restricting CORS to trusted origins, you can prevent unauthorized access from unverified domains. This configuration is typically managed via the Supabase dashboard or through SQL commands that interact with the security configuration. For example, a simplified CORS directive might look like:

```
ALTER SYSTEM SET cors.allowed_origins = 'https://trusted-domain.com';
SELECT pg_reload_conf();
```

This command ensures that only requests originating from the trusted domain are processed, thus reducing the surface for cross-site scripting (XSS) or cross-site request forgery (CSRF) attacks.

Securing API endpoints further involves the implementation of comprehensive logging and auditing mechanisms. Logging every request and associated metadata, such as user identifiers, endpoint accessed, and request timestamps, is critical for detecting abnormal patterns and investigating security incidents. Developers are advised to integrate monitoring tools that capture both successful and failed authentication attempts, flagging any anomalies. These logs can then be used in conjunction with automated alerting systems to ensure that any suspicious activity is addressed promptly.

Practicing the principle of least privilege is another fundamental strategy. This approach requires that users and applications are granted the minimum level of access necessary to perform their tasks. In Supabase, this can be managed by carefully constructing RLS policies and by defining roles with restricted permissions. For example, a user role that is only granted read permissions on a table might be defined as:

```
CREATE ROLE readonly_user;
GRANT SELECT ON TABLE your_table TO readonly_user;
```

Assigning such roles minimizes the risk of data modification or deletion by unauthorized users. It also simplifies auditing since each role's access rights are clearly defined and limited, reducing complexity in the security model.

More advanced security techniques involve establishing a robust process for token lifecycle management. JWTs have an expiration time, and mechanisms must exist to refresh tokens securely without exposing long-lived credentials. The implementation of token refresh endpoints should be handled with strict validation procedures. In a typical setup, an expired token can be exchanged for a new one after validating the refresh token stored securely by the client. This workflow minimizes the risk of token reuse by malicious entities.

Encryption also plays a vital role in securing API access. Transport Layer Security (TLS) is used to encrypt data transmitted between clients and the API server, preventing eavesdropping and man-in-the-middle attacks. Supabase enforces HTTPS, and developers must ensure that their applications adhere to best practices for certificate management. In addition to transport encryption, sensitive data stored within the database should be encrypted at rest, adding another layer of protection in the event of a server breach.

Further, regular security reviews and penetration testing are recommended to identify and mitigate vulnerabilities. As Supabase continues to evolve, staying informed of platform updates and emerging security threats is essential. Developers should subscribe to security bulletins and leverage community and professional resources to ensure that their API implementations comply with the latest standards and security practices.

Achieving a balance between usability and security is vital in API design. While restrictions such as strict rate limiting and comprehensive RLS policies enhance security, they should be implemented in a way that does not inhibit legitimate user activity. Performance testing and iterative tuning of security configurations help achieve this balance, ensuring that security controls are robust yet flexible enough to accommodate changing usage patterns.

It is important to document each security strategy in detail. Clear documentation of authentication flows, authorization policies, rate limiting rules, and incident response protocols serves as a vital resource for both current developers and future maintainers of the system. This practice not only enhances transparency but also expedites troubleshooting and compliance audits. Including code documentation and inline comments in SQL procedures and middleware further aids in understanding the security architecture.

In environments where multiple applications interact with Supabase APIs, it is advisable to implement logging of user actions for audit purposes. This is particularly relevant in scenarios where multiple roles interact with sensitive data. Such logs should be stored securely and periodically reviewed to detect any deviations from normal operational patterns. The aggregation of audit trails further assists in compliance with data protection regulations and internal governance policies.

In summary, securing API access necessitates a multi-layered approach that combines authentication, authorization, rate limiting, and encryption. The integration of JWT-based authentication with comprehensive RLS policies forms the cornerstone of user-specific access control. Alongside these, implementing rate limiting through external proxies and careful CORS configuration further reinforces the security posture of the API. Combining these strategies with rigorous logging, encryption protocols, and regular security reviews creates a high-assurance environment for handling sensitive data. Organizations that employ these practices can confidently expose their APIs to a broad audience while maintaining robust protection against unauthorized access and potential attacks.

8.5. Integrating APIs with Web Applications

Integrating Supabase APIs with frontend applications is a critical step in developing responsive and dynamic web applications. This integration involves establishing communication between client-side components and the Supabase backend, enabling real-time data interactions and smooth user interfaces. The process leverages RESTful endpoints, real-time subscriptions, and remote procedure calls to create an effective data flow that adheres to modern web development standards.

A common approach for integrating Supabase APIs into web applications is through client-side libraries, such as supabase-js. This library abstracts the complexities of HTTP requests, authorization headers, and real-time updates, allowing developers to focus on building user interfaces. To use supabase-js, start by installing the package via npm or yarn. An example of initializing a Supabase client in a frontend project is provided below:

```
import { createClient } from '@supabase/supabase-js';

const SUPABASE_URL = 'https://your-project.supabase.co';
const SUPABASE_ANON_KEY = 'YOUR_SUPABASE_ANON_KEY';

const supabase = createClient(SUPABASE_URL, SUPABASE_ANON_KEY);
```

Once the client is initialized, developers can perform CRUD operations with concise function calls. For instance, retrieving data from a products table can be done as follows:

```
async function fetchProducts() {
  const { data, error } = await supabase
    .from('products')
    .select('*')
    .gt('price', 25)
    .order('name', { ascending: true });

  if (error) console.error('Error fetching products:', error);
  else console.log('Products:', data);
}
```

The example above demonstrates the combination of filtering and ordering directly within the Supabase query call. The asynchronous nature of the request aligns with modern JavaScript practices, ensuring that the user interface remains responsive while waiting for the data.

Real-time functionalities offered by Supabase further enhance the interactivity of web applications. By subscribing to changes in the

331

database, developers can update the UI as data is inserted, updated, or deleted. This approach is particularly useful in applications like dashboards, chats, or collaborative platforms. Integration of real-time capabilities is straightforward with the client library. The following code snippet illustrates how to subscribe to changes in a specific table:

```
const subscription = supabase
  .from('products')
  .on('*', payload => {
    console.log('Change received!', payload);
    // Update UI accordingly
  })
  .subscribe();
```

In this example, any change occurring in the products table triggers the on event, allowing the frontend to seamlessly reflect real-time changes. It is important to manage subscriptions carefully, unsubscribing when components unmount or when updates are no longer required.

Integrating Supabase APIs with frameworks such as React can further streamline data management processes. In a React application, hooks such as useEffect and state management via useState can be used to fetch and update data on component mount or upon specific user interactions. Consider the following example of a React component that fetches data from Supabase and updates a list of products:

```
import React, { useState, useEffect } from 'react';
import { createClient } from '@supabase/supabase-js';

const supabase = createClient('https://your-project.supabase.co', '
    YOUR_SUPABASE_ANON_KEY');

const ProductList = () => {
  const [products, setProducts] = useState([]);
  const [loading, setLoading] = useState(true);

  useEffect(() => {
    async function getProducts() {
      const { data, error } = await supabase
        .from('products')
        .select('*')
```

```
        .order('name', { ascending: true });

    if (error) {
      console.error('Error fetching products:', error);
    } else {
      setProducts(data);
    }
    setLoading(false);
  }
  getProducts();
}, []);

if (loading) return <div>Loading...</div>;

return (
  <ul>
    {products.map(product => (
      <li key={product.id}>
        {product.name} - ${product.price}
      </li>
    ))}
  </ul>
);
};

export default ProductList;
```

This component fetches data upon mounting and updates the state accordingly. The integration with Supabase is encapsulated within the asynchronous function, separating business logic from the presentation layer. React's component lifecycle management further simplifies integrating real-time subscriptions, where an additional useEffect hook can manage subscriptions and clean them up on component unmount.

For applications that require more complex data flows, state management libraries like Redux or React Query can be integrated with Supabase APIs. React Query, for example, offers features such as caching and automatic refetching, which reduce the need for explicit state management when dealing with asynchronous data. A sample integration using React Query might look as follows:

```
import { useQuery } from 'react-query';

const fetchProducts = async () => {
  const { data, error } = await supabase
    .from('products')
    .select('*')
    .order('name', { ascending: true });

  if (error) throw new Error(error.message);
  return data;
};

function Products() {
  const { data, error, isLoading } = useQuery('products',
    fetchProducts);

  if (isLoading) return <div>Loading...</div>;
  if (error) return <div>Error fetching products</div>;

  return (
    <ul>
      {data.map(product => (
        <li key={product.id}>
          {product.name} - ${product.price}
        </li>
      ))}
    </ul>
  );
}

export default Products;
```

Such integration abstracts much of the boilerplate code associated with data fetching and mutation, allowing developers to concentrate on creating responsive and dynamic user interfaces. Additionally, incorporating error boundaries ensures that the UI remains robust, even when network issues or API errors occur.

Integrating Supabase APIs also involves managing authentication sessions on the frontend. Since Supabase supports JWTs, a typical web application must store and manage these tokens to ensure secure API access. Libraries such as `js-cookie` or built-in browser storage mechanisms like `localStorage` can manage tokens between sessions. An

334

example of storing a token after a user logs in is shown below:

```
async function signIn(email, password) {
  const { user, session, error } = await supabase.auth.signIn({
    email: email,
    password: password
  });

  if (error) {
    console.error('Login error:', error);
    return;
  }

  localStorage.setItem('supabase.auth.token', session.access_token);
  console.log('User logged in:', user);
}
```

Managing authentication tokens on the client side is critical for maintaining session persistence and ensuring that subsequent API requests are authenticated securely. Taking care to prevent unauthorized access to tokens, such as implementing secure storage practices and refreshing tokens appropriately, is essential for built-in application security.

Moreover, integrating APIs with web applications often requires consideration of offline capabilities and data synchronization. Progressive Web Applications (PWAs) benefit from caching strategies and service workers, which can locally store data retrieved from Supabase and synchronize updates when connectivity is restored. While native support for offline mode may vary, designing the frontend in a way that accommodates transient connectivity issues contributes to a more resilient application. Developers can integrate caching strategies by utilizing libraries like Workbox, ensuring that critical API calls are cached and updated when possible.

Another important aspect is error handling and feedback. When interacting with Supabase APIs, user interfaces must gracefully handle errors such as network failures, API rate limiting, or authorization issues. Clear error messages, retry mechanisms, and loading indicators improve the user experience by providing transparent feedback. A uni-

335

fied error handling strategy might include global request interceptors that log errors and display notifications to users. For instance, the following pseudocode outlines a typical error handling flow when using fetch:

```
async function fetchData(url) {
  try {
    const response = await fetch(url, { headers: { Authorization: '
    Bearer ' + token } });
    if (!response.ok) throw new Error('Network response was not ok');
    return await response.json();
  } catch (error) {
    console.error('Fetching data failed:', error);
    // Notify user via UI component
  }
}
```

Implementing comprehensive error handling ensures that application stability remains high even when encountering issues with the backend API.

Integration also extends to the design of user interfaces that intuitively display data retrieved from Supabase. Utilizing data visualization libraries such as Chart.js or D3.js alongside real-time data updates can create interactive dashboards and analytical tools. For example, a live-updating chart that reflects sales data can be implemented by subscribing to changes in the underlying data and updating a chart component accordingly. This seamless integration of visualization components and API data creates a more engaging and informative user experience.

The modular architecture of Supabase, coupled with its straightforward API design, allows frontend developers to adopt a component-based approach to data interaction. Components can be designed to handle specific API calls, manage local state, and update as necessary without conditional rerenders or redundant code. This modularity fosters code reusability and maintainability across larger applications, making it simpler to scale projects over time.

Incorporating Supabase APIs into web applications ultimately results in a cohesive ecosystem where the frontend and backend communicate efficiently and securely. The robust client libraries, advanced real-time capabilities, and standardized API endpoints facilitate the creation of applications that are both performant and scalable. Developers benefit from reduced development overhead, streamlined data flows, and enhanced user experiences. The techniques discussed in this section provide a foundation for integrating Supabase APIs, ensuring that web applications are capable of handling dynamic data interactions while maintaining simplicity and clarity in their codebases.

8.6. Testing and Debugging APIs

Rigorous testing and debugging are essential components in API development to ensure reliability, performance, and security in production environments. Testing APIs systematically not only validates endpoint functionality but also identifies potential bottlenecks and security loopholes. Supabase APIs, conforming to RESTful standards, can be tested using a combination of automated test suites, manual tools, and integrated logging mechanisms. This section details various tools and methods for testing and debugging API endpoints, emphasizing strategies that lead to robust and efficient applications.

One common approach for testing an API is the use of automated testing frameworks. Frameworks such as `Jest` for JavaScript and `Mocha` for Node.js provide a structure for writing unit tests, integration tests, and end-to-end tests. These tests simulate API calls, evaluate responses, and assert that the results match expected outcomes. For example, using `Jest` in conjunction with the `supertest` library allows developers to create comprehensive tests for Supabase endpoints. An illustrative example of testing a GET endpoint might be structured as follows:

```
const request = require('supertest');
const app = require('../app'); // Your Express or similar server

describe('GET /rest/v1/products', () => {
  it('should return a list of products with status code 200', async
    () => {
    const res = await request(app)
      .get('/rest/v1/products')
      .set('apikey', 'YOUR_SUPABASE_KEY')
      .set('Authorization', 'Bearer YOUR_JWT_TOKEN');

    expect(res.statusCode).toEqual(200);
    expect(res.body).toBeInstanceOf(Array);
  });
});
```

Automated tests not only verify that endpoints behave as expected but also help prevent regressions when changes are introduced to the codebase. Continuous integration pipelines can execute these tests on every commit, ensuring that new updates do not degrade API performance or cause unexpected errors.

In addition to automated testing frameworks, API-specific tools such as Postman and Insomnia offer interactive environments for manual testing and debugging. These tools enable developers to send complex requests, inspect responses, and modify requests on the fly. Development teams benefit from the ability to simulate different request scenarios including edge cases. Postman, for instance, provides a user-friendly interface where queries, headers, and payloads can be set explicitly. A typical request configuration in Postman includes setting the HTTP method to GET, adding the required authentication headers, and appending query parameters to filter results. Once executed, Postman displays the full response, including status codes, response times, and returned JSON payloads, which can then be analyzed to identify issues.

Supabase APIs return structured error messages that conform to standard HTTP status codes. Debugging these responses effectively requires an understanding of different status codes and their meanings. For example, HTTP 400 indicates a bad request, while 401 points to unauthorized access. Developers can establish mappings between status codes and potential issues, streamlining the debugging process. A common practice is to log error details both on the server and the client side. Using tools like Sentry or LogRocket to capture and analyze these errors in real time can prove invaluable. The debugging process is further enhanced by enabling verbose logging on the server, where each API request, along with its headers, payloads, and eventual responses, is recorded.

Integrated logging within Supabase itself provides traceability for each API transaction. Leveraging PostgreSQL's logging capabilities along with Supabase's internal tracking systems, developers can monitor real-time operations and capture anomalies such as failed authentication attempts or unusually long query times. A typical logging configuration might include the following SQL commands:

```
ALTER SYSTEM SET log_statement = 'all';
SELECT pg_reload_conf();
```

Such configurations, though useful during development and debugging, should be tuned properly when moving to production environments to avoid performance overhead and potential exposure of sensitive information.

Debugging also involves analyzing the performance of individual endpoints. Performance issues such as latency or inefficient query execution can be diagnosed using tools like pgAdmin for PostgreSQL, which illustrates query plans and identifies slow operations. Profiling API endpoints in this manner allows developers to optimize queries, add indexes, or refactor endpoints to reduce response times. Additionally, employing monitoring tools such as Prometheus or Grafana to keep track of API response times and request rates can provide insights into performance trends and enable proactive tuning of the system.

The establishment of a testing environment that mirrors the production configuration is critical to effective debugging. Developers often use containerization platforms such as Docker to simulate the API server, database, and client environments in a controlled setting. Docker Compose scripts can be used to spin up these integrated environments quickly, enabling repeated testing cycles and ensuring consistency between development, staging, and production environments. An example Docker Compose snippet for a Supabase-like environment might look as follows:

```
version: '3.8'
services:
  db:
    image: postgres:13
    environment:
      POSTGRES_USER: supabase_user
      POSTGRES_PASSWORD: supersecret
      POSTGRES_DB: supabase_db
    ports:
      - "5432:5432"
  api:
    image: your-supabase-api-image
    environment:
      DATABASE_URL: postgres://supabase_user:supersecret@db:5432/
    supabase_db
      SUPABASE_KEY: YOUR_SUPABASE_KEY
    ports:
      - "8000:8000"
    depends_on:
      - db
```

This environment allows developers to conduct integration tests that cover scenarios from data creation to real-time subscription handling, ensuring that each API component performs reliably under load.

Another effective testing method is contract testing, which focuses on the interface between the API and its consumers. Tools like Pact and Dredd help ensure that API contracts are respected, meaning that the endpoints respond with expected formats, structures, and data types. These tools simulate calls from a consumer service and verify that the

340

provider (the API) adheres to the established contract. Contract testing is particularly useful in microservices architectures where different services interact through defined APIs. By validating these interactions, developers reduce the risk of integration failures when multiple teams work on different components of the system.

Simulation of error conditions is another valuable testing technique. By intentionally causing errors—such as sending malformed requests, simulating network delays, or exceeding rate limits—developers can observe how the API handles such scenarios. For instance, testing for rate limiting might involve using scripts to send a high volume of requests in a short time frame, ensuring that the API throttles requests appropriately. An exemplary script using `curl` in a loop might be constructed as follows:

```
for i in {1..50}
do
  curl -X GET -H "apikey: YOUR_SUPABASE_KEY" -H "Authorization:
    Bearer YOUR_JWT_TOKEN" "https://your-project.supabase.co/rest/v1/
    products"
  echo "Request $i"
done
```

Observing the responses for status codes like 429 (Too Many Requests) confirms that rate limiting mechanisms are in place and functioning as expected. Such simulation tests reveal how the API behaves under stress and ensure it remains secure and responsive even in adverse conditions.

Debugging complex API issues often necessitates a step-by-step approach wherein the problem is isolated to a specific component or layer—be it the network, API gateway, or database. Using network diagnostic tools such as `curl` for command-line testing, `Wireshark` for packet analysis, or browser developer tools for inspecting network calls can pinpoint the source of issues. Analyzing HTTP headers and payloads in these tools provides insight into problems such as misconfigured authentication tokens, incorrect query parameters, or unexpected data formats.

When an issue is identified, replicating the problem in a controlled testing scenario is critical. This method aids in understanding the failure modes and in crafting corresponding fixes. For example, if a specific query parameter leads to a malformed SQL query, reproducing the query in the database directly can reveal the syntax error. Once isolated, the developer can refactor the API logic to handle such edge cases more gracefully.

Furthermore, debugging is enhanced by maintaining detailed documentation of test cases and known issues. This documentation, integrated into the project knowledge base, helps developers to avoid repeating past mistakes and provides a quick reference during troubleshooting. Version control systems also play an important role in debugging by allowing developers to revert to previously stable states when new changes introduce bugs.

The combination of automated tests, manual inspection tools, integrated logging, and performance monitoring forms a comprehensive ecosystem for testing and debugging. Supabase APIs benefit from this multi-layered approach to quality assurance, ensuring that endpoints remain robust across various deployment scenarios. The collective insights gained from these methods guide developers in optimizing response times, enforcing security policies, and improving overall reliability.

By systematically applying these testing and debugging strategies, developers can create APIs that not only meet functional requirements but also perform reliably under load and against malicious attacks. Continuous refinement through testing cycles, coupled with proactive performance monitoring, establishes a strong foundation for scalable, secure, and efficient API systems.

8.7. API Documentation and Maintenance

Maintaining clear and comprehensive API documentation is critical to ensuring that both current developers and future maintainers can understand the intended functionality, usage patterns, and limitations of the API endpoints. Supabase APIs, with their automatically generated endpoints and rich functionality, require documentation that elucidates endpoint behavior, expected payloads, authentication requirements, and error responses. Documenting these elements aids in onboarding new team members, facilitates debugging, and ensures that the system remains consistent over time.

One effective way to document API endpoints is to adopt structured documentation formats such as OpenAPI (formerly known as Swagger). OpenAPI specifications provide a machine-readable description of the API, including details on endpoints, parameters, responses, and security schemes. A sample OpenAPI specification snippet for a Supabase endpoint might appear as follows:

```
openapi: 3.0.0
info:
  title: Supabase API Documentation
  version: 1.0.0
paths:
  /rest/v1/products:
    get:
      summary: Retrieve a list of products
      parameters:
        - in: query
          name: price
          schema:
            type: number
          description: Filter products with price greater than the
  specified value, using 'gt.50'
        - in: query
          name: order
          schema:
            type: string
          description: Order the results (e.g., 'price.desc' for
  descending order)
      responses:
```

343

```
        '200':
          description: A JSON array of product objects
          content:
            application/json:
              schema:
                type: array
                items:
                  type: object
                  properties:
                    id:
                      type: integer
                    name:
                      type: string
                    price:
                      type: number
        '401':
          description: Unauthorized access
components:
  securitySchemes:
    bearerAuth:
      type: http
      scheme: bearer
security:
  - bearerAuth: []
```

Such documentation not only serves as a guide to developers but also can be imported into API management platforms and interactive tools like Swagger UI, providing a live interface for testing and validation. Integrating OpenAPI documentation into the project repository ensures that it is updated alongside code changes, minimizing discrepancies between implementation and documentation.

Maintaining API documentation requires establishing a disciplined process where changes to the API endpoints are reflected promptly within the documentation. Automated tools can facilitate this process by generating documentation from source code annotations or database schemas. For example, using tools like PostgREST in conjunction with Supabase can automatically produce documentation for each table-based endpoint. Embedding inline comments in SQL scripts when defining functions, views, and RLS policies ensures that the rationale behind design decisions is preserved in the documenta-

344

tion.

Version control is another critical aspect of API maintenance. With evolving applications, endpoints might undergo modifications, enhancements, or deprecations. It is essential to version the API appropriately, documenting changes in a version history. One recommended practice is to include version numbers in the API URL (e.g., /rest/v1/ or /rest/v2/). This strategy allows developers to support legacy versions while rolling out new functionality. A versioning management section in the documentation should detail any breaking changes, migration guides, and backward compatibility considerations.

A well-maintained API documentation also encompasses clear guidelines on authentication, usage limits, and error handling. Documenting the authentication flow, for example, clarifies how JSON Web Tokens (JWT) must be integrated into API requests. Including examples with detailed header configurations can reduce misconfiguration errors. An example snippet demonstrating the correct use of authentication headers might be:

```
curl -H "apikey: YOUR_SUPABASE_KEY" \
    -H "Authorization: Bearer YOUR_JWT_TOKEN" \
    "https://your-project.supabase.co/rest/v1/products"
```

Error codes and messages should be clearly described, specifying the conditions under which errors occur, and providing suggestions for troubleshooting. For instance, a 429 response should be accompanied by recommendations on rate limiting or retry logic. Incorporating these details into the documentation aids developers in designing client-side code that gracefully handles unexpected responses.

In addition to static documentation, interactive documentation platforms enhance the developer experience. Tools that offer "try-it-out" features, such as Swagger UI or Redoc, enable users to simulate API calls directly from the documentation page. This interactivity accelerates debugging, allows developers to validate endpoint behaviors, and fosters a better understanding of the API's capabilities. Maintaining a dedicated documentation portal that is synchronized with the API version lifecycle ensures that the latest guidelines and updates are readily available.

Long-term maintenance of API documentation involves regular audits and reviews. As the application evolves, periodic reviews should identify outdated components, deprecated endpoints, or inconsistencies between implemented features and documented behaviors. A common best practice is to integrate documentation audits into the release cycle. Before deploying updates, teams can run automated checks to ensure that all new endpoints are documented and that modifications to existing endpoints are reflected in the documentation repository. Continuous integration (CI) pipelines can be configured to flag discrepancies, ensuring that documentation remains current with the codebase.

Adopting a feedback loop is equally important in the maintenance phase. Encouraging developers and users to report issues or ambiguities in the documentation fosters an environment of continuous improvement. A dedicated issue tracker or feedback form integrated into the documentation portal can collect user experiences and suggestions. This collaborative approach not only improves the clarity of the documentation but also enhances overall API usability and reduces support queries.

Beyond technical documentation, maintaining API documentation requires attention to organizational guidelines and style consistency. Establishing a style guide for API documentation sets a consistent tone and format that makes the documentation easily navigable. Elements such as code examples, response schemas, and usage guidelines should adhere to predefined formatting rules. This consistency ensures that all sections of the documentation are coherent, facilitating easier comprehension and reference. Using Markdown or reStructuredText, combined with version control systems like Git, supports collaborative editing and seamless integration with continuous deployment pipelines.

Documentation should also detail the maintenance procedures for the API. This includes instructions for troubleshooting, escalation paths for critical issues, and backup strategies for restoring previous API versions if necessary. A section dedicated to maintenance procedures within the documentation can outline routine operations such as database backups, log rotation, and incremental updates. Such detailed procedures are invaluable during incidents, providing a clear roadmap for resolving issues without extensive downtime.

The documentation process for APIs also benefits from automated documentation generation. Integration with documentation generators, such as Docusaurus or MkDocs, enables the creation of static sites that host the API documentation. These platforms support automated rebuilds whenever the underlying source files, such as OpenAPI specifications or inline code comments, are updated. Automation reduces the overhead of manual updates and ensures that documentation is an accurate reflection of the current API state.

Another aspect that contributes to comprehensive API documentation and maintenance is the inclusion of migration guides and change logs. A migration guide communicates the steps required when upgrading from one version of the API to another, highlighting potential pitfalls and offering practical solutions to accommodate changes. Detailed change logs serve as a historical record of modifications, providing context and reasoning behind updates or deprecations. Including these elements not only supports current users in managing transitions but also serves as a reference for future development and design decisions.

Ultimately, maintaining high-quality API documentation enhances the overall stability and reliability of the Supabase backend. When documentation is clear, comprehensive, and kept up to date, developers can quickly diagnose issues, integrate new features with confidence, and reduce time-to-market for new releases. Moreover, robust documentation instills confidence in both internal and external stakeholders, reinforcing trust in the system's capabilities and its long-term maintainability.

By adhering to best practices in API documentation and establishing a culture of continuous review and improvement, development teams can ensure that their API ecosystem remains transparent, secure, and robust. This methodology not only contributes to the successful operation of current applications but also lays the groundwork for scalable growth and future enhancements with minimized technical debt and operational risks.

Chapter 9

Performance Optimization and Scaling

This chapter examines techniques for optimizing performance and scaling Supabase applications. It addresses identifying bottlenecks, optimizing database queries, and improving API response times. It includes strategies for scaling projects, implementing caching, and effective monitoring. By focusing on performance and cost management, developers are equipped with actionable insights to enhance application efficiency and scalability with Supabase.

9.1. Understanding Performance Bottlenecks

Performance issues in Supabase applications frequently originate from inefficient database operations, suboptimal query designs, and network-induced delays. A careful analysis of these bottlenecks begins by evaluating the specific interactions between your application logic and Supabase services. The first step in diagnosing performance problems is to profile the application, identify slow queries, and determine if the latency is caused by database processing, network conditions, or inefficient use of APIs.

When examining the database layer, common bottlenecks include unoptimized query structures, missing indexes, and excessive data retrieval that leads to high input/output operations. For instance, queries that perform full table scans due to the absence of an appropriate index can considerably slow down operations. Developers should employ the EXPLAIN command provided by PostgreSQL to investigate query plans. This tool details the execution strategy adopted by the database, revealing potential inefficiencies. Consider the following example that demonstrates how to use the EXPLAIN command to analyze query performance:

```
EXPLAIN SELECT * FROM orders WHERE customer_id = 12345;
```

The output of the above command may indicate whether the query is leveraging an index or performing a sequential scan, as shown below:

```
Seq Scan on orders  (cost=0.00..35.50 rows=5 width=128)
  Filter: (customer_id = 12345)
```

If an index on customer_id exists, the execution plan should reflect an indexed scan rather than a sequential scan. That detail directs the developer to either create or reconfigure indexes effectively. An example of creating an index is provided below:

```
CREATE INDEX idx_orders_customer ON orders(customer_id);
```

After the creation of the index, re-running the EXPLAIN command should display a more efficient plan, such as an Index Scan:

```
Index Scan using idx_orders_customer on orders  (cost=0.28..8.50 rows=5 width
=128)
   Index Cond: (customer_id = 12345)
```

Another typical bottleneck arises from the use of complex joins and subqueries that are not adequately optimized. When performing multiple joins across tables, ensure that the underlying columns used for the join conditions are indexed. In addition, restructuring queries to simplify join operations or dividing them into smaller, more manageable subqueries can minimize processing time. The following snippet illustrates a common scenario of optimizing join operations:

```
SELECT o.order_id, c.name, o.total
FROM orders o
JOIN customers c ON o.customer_id = c.id
WHERE o.order_date >= '2023-01-01';
```

In this example, ensuring that `orders.customer_id` and `customers.id` are indexed is vital for performance improvement. The application layer should also be designed to retrieve only the necessary data fields rather than entire records. Over-fetching results in additional data transfer between the database and the client, increasing latency.

Network latency often compounds the perceived performance lag in Supabase applications. This issue becomes pronounced when the application logic makes multiple round-trip calls to the Supabase backend or when large data payloads are transmitted. To mitigate such delays, consolidate multiple data requests into a single batch operation where feasible. Additionally, enable data compression on network requests if supported by the client libraries. For example, if you are using a Supabase client in JavaScript, consider structuring your requests to minimize redundant calls and optimizing the data payload size:

```
// Initialize Supabase client
const { createClient } = require('@supabase/supabase-js');
const supabase = createClient('https://your-project-ref.supabase.co',
    'public-anon-key');
```

```
// Batch data retrieval to reduce network latency
async function fetchData() {
    const { data, error } = await supabase
        .from('orders')
        .select('order_id, total, order_date')
        .gte('order_date', '2023-01-01');
    if (error) {
        console.error('Error fetching data:', error);
    } else {
        console.log('Retrieved orders:', data);
    }
}
fetchData();
```

In diagnosing performance bottlenecks, it is essential to combine both application-level logging and database profiling. Integrating logging mechanisms into the application code helps record execution times for critical functions. For a Supabase application, consider embedding timers around database calls to capture latency metrics. The output from these logs can then be analyzed to identify slow operations. The following JavaScript snippet demonstrates a simple approach:

```
async function timedQuery() {
    const startTime = Date.now();

    const { data, error } = await supabase
        .from('orders')
        .select('*')
        .eq('customer_id', 12345);

    const elapsedTime = Date.now() - startTime;
    console.log('Query executed in', elapsedTime, 'ms');

    if (error) {
        console.error('Query error:', error);
    } else {
        console.log('Query data:', data);
    }
}
timedQuery();
```

Analysis of these logs should reveal if certain queries or functions consistently exceed expected execution times. If patterns emerge, focus on re-evaluating query structures, ensuring that indexes are being used, or consider refactoring the application logic to defer or batch resource-intensive tasks.

A further dimension to consider is the impact of concurrent loads on your Supabase application. When multiple users access the system simultaneously, the database may eventually become a bottleneck due to resource contention. Utilize PostgreSQL's built-in statistics views such as `pg_stat_activity` and `pg_stat_statement` to monitor active processes and query execution statistics. Database-level connection pooling is also a critical area of consideration. Supabase typically handles connection pooling internally; however, misconfigured settings can lead to saturation points. To address this, adjust parameters such as pool size or timeouts, and assess the performance differences after each adjustment.

Monitoring tools that interface directly with PostgreSQL, like pgAdmin or custom dashboard solutions, provide insights into the distribution of query execution times, memory usage, and CPU consumption. These tools facilitate a comprehensive diagnostic approach by pairing real-time data with historical trends, thereby enabling precise identification of stress points. Additionally, it may be worthwhile to integrate application performance monitoring (APM) services. They offer detailed insights, from the time a query is initiated to the moment its result is returned, thereby highlighting the exact phases where bottlenecks occur.

Iterative testing constitutes a key strategy in diagnosing performance bottlenecks. Developers should progressively implement changes and monitor the impact on execution times and resource usage across different components of the system. Consider the following structured approach when diagnosing performance issues:

1. Identify slow queries or functions using logging and profiling

tools.

2. Analyze the execution plans of these queries, both before and after any modifications.

3. If a query is identified as slow due to missing indexes, create the necessary indexes and compare performance.

4. Refactor complex joins or subqueries into simpler or partitioned queries, and benchmark the results.

5. Adjust network configurations by batching requests, compressing data, or reducing redundant communications.

Each step should be documented with metrics to track improvements and understand which modifications yield the most significant benefits. Attention to detail, such as precise measurement of execution times before and after changes, is essential for quantifying improvements accurately.

Beyond these technical diagnostics, application architecture plays a critical role in determining the overall performance. Supabase services rely on efficient synchronization between the application's client-side and server-side components. Poorly structured client code, such as frequent re-renders or unnecessary polling, can exacerbate the performance challenges identified at the database level. Refactoring application logic to cache frequent, unchanged queries or employing data prefetching where appropriate can offload some of the burdens on the server.

Fault tolerance in high-demand scenarios is also linked to how performance diagnostics are embedded within an application's update cycle. Regularly reviewing and refining performance aspects—including reviewing logs, query plans, and monitoring metrics—ensures that performance bottlenecks are quickly identified and mitigated. Automated alerting mechanisms, tied to key performance indicators (KPIs), can prompt immediate attention if certain thresholds are exceeded.

Attention to these details, combined with methodical diagnosis procedures, guides developers to identify the underlying causes of performance bottlenecks. This structured approach does not merely address immediate slowdowns but lays the groundwork for scalable, sustainable application enhancements. Both mitigation and proactive monitoring strategies become indispensable tools in ensuring that Supabase-powered systems remain responsive under varying load conditions.

9.2. Optimizing Database Queries

Optimizing database queries is a critical component in enhancing overall application performance. In Supabase applications, query optimization primarily involves designing efficient SQL statements, proper usage of indexes, and restructuring complex query operations. Building on previous discussions on performance bottlenecks, this section delves into techniques that can reduce execution time, lessen server load, and improve data retrieval efficiency.

One of the primary strategies for query optimization is the creation and maintenance of indexes. Indexes enable rapid lookup of rows based on indexed columns, significantly reducing the time required for query execution, especially on large datasets. When constructing indexes, understanding the specific query patterns is essential. For instance, if a query frequently retrieves records based on a foreign key column, a B-tree index could be appropriate. The following SQL snippet illustrates how to create an index on a column commonly used in a WHERE clause:

```
CREATE INDEX idx_orders_customer ON orders(customer_id);
```

Indexes come with trade-offs, however. While they accelerate read operations, they may slow down write operations due to the overhead of updating index structures. It is important to balance these trade-offs by analyzing query performance and workload characteristics through tools such as PostgreSQL's EXPLAIN or EXPLAIN ANALYZE. The execution plan obtained from these commands provides insights into whether an index is properly exploited during query execution. For example:

```
EXPLAIN ANALYZE
SELECT *
FROM orders
WHERE customer_id = 12345;
```

The output can reveal if the query engine performs an Index Scan rather than a full table scan, highlighting the effectiveness of the index. By examining execution costs and row estimates, developers can fine-tune indexes and adjust query structures accordingly.

Query restructuring is another essential technique. Complex queries involving multiple joins, nested subqueries, or aggregate functions can often be rewritten for improved performance. Breaking down a complicated query into simpler parts or replacing subqueries with joins or Common Table Expressions (CTEs) can reduce the computational burden on the database. Consider a complex query that retrieves order details along with customer information:

```
SELECT o.order_id, o.order_date, c.name, c.email
FROM orders o
JOIN (
    SELECT id, name, email
    FROM customers
    WHERE status = 'active'
) c ON o.customer_id = c.id
WHERE o.order_date >= '2023-01-01';
```

In this instance, restructuring the query to use a CTE may enhance readability and maintainability, while possibly allowing the query planner to optimize execution paths more effectively. The equivalent formulation using a CTE is as follows:

```
WITH active_customers AS (
    SELECT id, name, email
    FROM customers
    WHERE status = 'active'
)
SELECT o.order_id, o.order_date, ac.name, ac.email
FROM orders o
JOIN active_customers ac ON o.customer_id = ac.id
WHERE o.order_date >= '2023-01-01';
```

CTEs can be especially beneficial when similar subqueries are reused multiple times within a query. Although CTEs were originally designed for clarity, modern PostgreSQL versions allow the planner to inline them if beneficial.

Another angle to consider is the optimization of JOIN operations. When joining multiple tables, ensure that join predicates match indexed columns. For instance, joining tables on non-indexed columns forces the database to perform a full scan, which can severely impact performance with large data sets. Besides creating indexes, careful restructuring of JOIN operations by filtering rows before joining can also reduce the intermediate dataset size. For example, applying a WHERE clause within a subquery can limit the data set before it is joined with another table:

```
SELECT o.order_id, o.order_date, c.name
FROM orders o
JOIN (
    SELECT id, name
    FROM customers
    WHERE region = 'North America'
) c ON o.customer_id = c.id
WHERE o.order_date >= '2023-01-01';
```

This approach minimizes the number of records that need to be processed during the join operation.

Optimizing the use of aggregate functions and groupings is also vi-

357

tal. Queries with GROUP BY clauses and aggregate computations can often be restructured to minimize processing overhead. Partitioning data logically and pre-aggregating values during periods of lower load can reduce the frequency and complexity of heavy queries during peak times. For example, creating materialized views that store precomputed aggregates may offload the runtime burden, serving as a caching mechanism. Consider the following materialized view creation:

```
CREATE MATERIALIZED VIEW order_summary AS
SELECT customer_id, COUNT(*) AS order_count, SUM(total) AS
    total_spent
FROM orders
GROUP BY customer_id;
```

Periodic refreshment of this materialized view allows the application to retrieve summary data quickly, mitigating the need to perform intensive grouping operations repeatedly.

Parameterizing queries is a further optimization technique, particularly for applications facing high query volumes. Parameterized queries allow the database to create and cache an execution plan that can be reused, reducing the overhead of query planning and parsing for repetitive statements. For example, a parameterized query for retrieving orders by customer ID might look like this in a Supabase client integration:

```
// Using a prepared statement in a Supabase client
const { data, error } = await supabase
    .from('orders')
    .select('*')
    .eq('customer_id', $1)
    .execute([12345]);
```

Using parameterized queries not only improves performance but also enhances the security of the application by mitigating SQL injection risks.

Developers should also consider query caching mechanisms. Frequently executed queries that retrieve data unlikely to change can benefit significantly from caching at the database or application level. Post-greSQL caching strategies involve both in-memory caching and the use of external caching solutions like Redis. The selection of caching strategy depends on the data access pattern and the volatility of the dataset.

To systematically approach query optimization, a cyclical process of benchmarking, analyzing, restructuring, and validating changes is recommended. Iterative testing using controlled workloads can highlight bottlenecks and measure the impact of adjustments. Document metrics such as execution time, CPU usage, and memory consumption to arrive at quantifiable improvements. Tools like `pg_stat_statements` can further assist in identifying long-running queries that require attention.

Efficient query design is not solely dependent on indexing and restructuring but also on an overall understanding of the underlying relational database model. Consider the normalization of data to reduce redundancy while also balancing the need for denormalization in read-heavy applications to avoid excessive JOIN operations. In some cases, a slight relaxation of normalization rules, accompanied by carefully engineered redundancy, can result in more efficient queries.

Attention to these query optimization techniques leads to more robust and scalable applications, reducing latency and ensuring a responsive user experience. Such optimizations are critical in maintaining the balance between rapid data access and system resource management, ensuring that Supabase-powered applications continue to perform well under varying load conditions while remaining maintainable over time.

9.3. Improving API Response Times

Enhancing API response times in Supabase applications is paramount to ensuring a seamless user experience. Efficient data retrieval combined with minimized latency plays a central role in achieving responsive endpoints. This section examines methods for reducing API response times through optimized data access patterns, intelligent request handling, and network-level enhancements.

Efficient data retrieval begins with reducing the amount of data transmitted over the network. One common technique is to fetch only the necessary fields in a query instead of retrieving entire records. This practice decreases payload size, reducing both serialization time on the server side and deserialization time on the client side. For example, consider retrieving only the `order_id` and `total` from the `orders` table instead of all columns:

```
SELECT order_id, total FROM orders WHERE customer_id = 12345;
```

By explicitly selecting only the essential columns, the query reduces the amount of data processed and transferred, thereby improving API response times.

Techniques such as pagination and limiting the amount of data returned are also crucial. When an endpoint potentially returns a large dataset, implementing pagination ensures that only a fraction of the data is loaded per request. The following SQL snippet demonstrates how to use LIMIT and OFFSET to implement pagination:

```
SELECT order_id, total FROM orders
WHERE customer_id = 12345
ORDER BY order_date DESC
LIMIT 20 OFFSET 0;
```

Pagination not only prevents the overloading of the API response but also enables the client to request additional data as needed, further

360

contributing to a more efficient data retrieval process.

At the API layer, managing multiple asynchronous requests in parallel or batching them together can significantly reduce perceived latency. In a Supabase-powered application, asynchronous programming enables non-blocking operations that allow the API to initiate multiple data retrieval tasks concurrently. The JavaScript example below illustrates how to batch API calls:

```javascript
async function fetchOrdersAndCustomers(customerId) {
    const ordersPromise = supabase
        .from('orders')
        .select('order_id, total, customer_id')
        .eq('customer_id', customerId);

    const customerPromise = supabase
        .from('customers')
        .select('id, name, email')
        .eq('id', customerId);

    const [ordersResult, customerResult] = await Promise.all([
    ordersPromise, customerPromise]);

    if (ordersResult.error || customerResult.error) {
        console.error('Error retrieving data:', ordersResult.error ||
      customerResult.error);
        return;
    }

    return {
        orders: ordersResult.data,
        customer: customerResult.data[0]
    };
}
```

In this example, the two API calls execute concurrently rather than sequentially. Batching requests reduces overall wait time and ensures that the most time-sensitive operations are prioritized, which directly impacts API response times.

Minimizing network latency is an essential consideration in API performance optimization. Reducing round-trip times can be achieved by consolidating endpoint calls and avoiding redundant requests in the client application. When multiple small requests are sent over the network, protocol overhead multiplies, leading to increased latency. Combining these calls into a single, more comprehensive request or using bulk endpoints where applicable helps to reduce the cumulative delay. Moreover, configuring the Supabase client to use HTTP/2 or other optimized protocols where network conditions allow further minimizes overhead and supports concurrent streams within the same connection.

Implementing data compression is another effective means of minimizing latency, especially when dealing with large responses. Both the client and server should be capable of handling compressed content. Many modern web frameworks support gzip or brotli compression, significantly reducing the size of the transmitted response. For APIs served over HTTPS, compression can be configured at the server level, ensuring that payloads are compressed before being sent to the client. This optimization reduces data transfer times, resulting in faster API responses.

Another important aspect involves server-side caching strategies. Caching frequently requested data can prevent the need for repeated, costly computations and database queries. In a Supabase environment, materialized views or database-level caching can be used to store precomputed query results. When the underlying data does not change frequently, returning cached data eliminates unnecessary processing, thereby reducing the time spent on data retrieval. An example of creating a materialized view for order summaries is shown below:

```
CREATE MATERIALIZED VIEW order_summary AS
SELECT customer_id, COUNT(*) AS order_count, SUM(total) AS
    total_spent
FROM orders
GROUP BY customer_id;
```

Recurrence of this materialized view within API endpoints ensures that aggregate computations are executed once, rather than with every request, leading to a consistent reduction in response times.

The proper use of connection pooling also contributes significantly to the efficiency of data retrieval in API endpoints. Connection pooling limits the cost of establishing new connections for every request. By reusing existing connections, the overhead associated with network handshakes and secure session setups is minimized. Although Supabase manages connections internally, awareness of these connections and correct configuration on the client side, such as timer settings and retry strategies, play a key role in minimizing latency.

Inefficient serialization and deserialization routines in the API layer can increase response times noticeably. Optimizing these processes by using efficient data formats, such as JSON with minimal nesting or employing binary formats like Protocol Buffers when feasible, can yield improvements. For instance, when using JSON to transfer data, ensure that the API response is stripped of unnecessary metadata that could inflate the payload:

```
function simplifyOrderData(order) {
    return {
        orderId: order.order_id,
        total: order.total
    };
}

async function getSimplifiedOrders(customerId) {
    const { data, error } = await supabase
        .from('orders')
        .select('order_id, total')
        .eq('customer_id', customerId);

    if (error) {
        console.error('Error fetching orders:', error);
        return [];
    }

    return data.map(simplifyOrderData);
}
```

The above JavaScript function demonstrates how reducing the data structure to its necessary elements before sending it to the client can streamline processing times on both ends of the API.

Reducing the computational overhead on the server is another technique for improving API response times. Employing asynchronous job queues for tasks that are not required to be synchronous with the API response allows the API to return data faster in response to client requests. Time-intensive operations, such as sending emails or updating secondary systems, should be offloaded to background processes. In many scenarios, using a message queue or a dedicated background worker system decouples these longer-running operations from the API endpoint, ensuring that the primary data retrieval remains swift and efficient.

Ensuring that Supabase client libraries are optimally configured also plays an integral role in achieving low latency. Default settings might not always provide the best performance for every application scenario. Developers should consider fine-tuning parameters such as timeout durations, maximum simultaneous connections, and retries. Additionally, in edge deployments or regions far from the Supabase server location, configuring geo-replication or deploying a Content Delivery Network (CDN) for static assets helps in reducing latency by positioning resources closer to the end user.

Load balancing strategies further enhance API response times during high-traffic periods. Distributing incoming requests across multiple servers ensures that no single instance is overwhelmed. Although Supabase abstracts many aspects of load balancing, application-level load distribution—particularly in hybrid architectures involving custom business logic—can prevent bottlenecks. Effective load balancing ensures that response times remain consistent even as the number of concurrent users increases.

Monitoring plays a critical role in maintaining optimal API performance. Logging detailed performance metrics such as request processing time, time spent waiting for data from the database, and overall latency enables developers to identify inefficiencies. The integration of Application Performance Monitoring (APM) tools aids in pinpointing slow API endpoints. For example, developers might monitor API latency with a middleware that measures the duration of each request:

```
app.use(async (req, res, next) => {
    const start = Date.now();
    await next();
    const duration = Date.now() - start;
    console.log(`Request to ${req.path} took ${duration}ms`);
});
```

Analyzing such logs assists in diagnosing whether delays are caused by slow database queries, network latency, or processing overhead in the application logic. Establishing alert thresholds within these monitoring systems provides real-time awareness when response times deviate from acceptable performance levels.

Additionally, optimizing security features without compromising speed is essential. Authentication and authorization mechanisms, when implemented efficiently, contribute minimally to the overall latency. Token-based authentication, such as JSON Web Tokens (JWT), usually incurs only slight overhead. However, ensuring these mechanisms are properly cached and validated quickly—potentially through the use of in-memory stores or well-designed middleware— prevents them from becoming a performance bottleneck.

Techniques such as request debouncing and throttling help protect API endpoints from being overwhelmed by excessive requests. By implementing these controls, applications can maintain consistent performance, even under sporadic bursts of high traffic. These measures, which can be implemented via middleware or proxy configuration, ensure that all incoming requests receive the necessary level of service without resulting in cascading delays.

Overall, improving API response times in a Supabase context necessitates a multi-layered approach that addresses efficient data retrieval, network optimizations, caching, and thoughtful system architecture. Each modification, from reducing the size of the data payload to asynchronous processing and caching frequently accessed data, contributes incrementally to reducing overall latency. The combined effect of these strategies forms a robust foundation for responsive, scalable API endpoints that remain performant under varying load conditions while preserving application integrity and user experience.

9.4. Scaling Your Supabase Project

Scaling Supabase projects involves optimizing both the database layer and the application architecture to handle increased user loads while maintaining performance. As user traffic grows, a comprehensive approach that addresses vertical and horizontal scaling, dynamic resource allocation, connection management, and caching becomes critical. This section focuses on strategies to scale Supabase projects, building on earlier discussions about optimizing queries and improving API response times.

Database scalability is fundamental to handle growing amounts of data and concurrent requests. Supabase, built on PostgreSQL, supports both vertical scaling and horizontal scaling techniques. Vertical scaling involves increasing the computational resources—such as CPU, memory, and storage—of the database server. This approach can offer immediate performance improvements by reducing query latency and speeding up data processing. However, vertical scaling has its limits, and eventually, a more distributed approach is necessary.

Horizontal scaling, by contrast, involves distributing the database load across multiple nodes or instances. PostgreSQL offers several methods for horizontal scaling, including replication and partitioning. Replication allows the creation of read replicas that can handle read-heavy workloads. By directing read queries to replicas, the primary database is freed to handle write operations and critical transactions. For example, configuring a read replica setup in PostgreSQL may involve the following parameters in the configuration file:

```
# Example PostgreSQL replication settings in postgresql.conf
listen_addresses = '*'
max_wal_senders = 10
wal_level = replica
archive_mode = on
archive_command = 'cp %p /var/lib/postgresql/wal_archive/%f'
```

Directing application queries conditionally based on read or write requirements can be implemented in the application logic. Using a load balancing strategy across replicas can significantly reduce response times for read-intensive endpoints.

Partitioning is another effective method for handling large datasets. By splitting a database table into smaller segments, or partitions, based on specific criteria such as date ranges or user IDs, queries can be limited to the relevant partition rather than scanning a monolithic table. Consider a scenario where an orders table is partitioned by month. The SQL code below outlines the creation of a partitioned table and a partition for a specific month:

```
CREATE TABLE orders (
    order_id SERIAL PRIMARY KEY,
    customer_id INTEGER NOT NULL,
    order_date DATE NOT NULL,
    total NUMERIC
) PARTITION BY RANGE(order_date);

CREATE TABLE orders_2023_01 PARTITION OF orders
    FOR VALUES FROM ('2023-01-01') TO ('2023-02-01');
```

Partitioning allows queries that filter based on the order_date column to execute more efficiently by accessing only relevant partitions.

In addition to database partitioning and replication, connection pool management is essential to scaling projects efficiently. As the number of concurrent connections increases, establishing and maintaining individual connections for every user request can lead to performance degradation. Supabase and PostgreSQL typically employ connection pooling to reuse existing connections rather than establishing new ones repeatedly. Fine-tuning pool size and timeout settings can reduce overhead. The following pseudo-code illustrates how an application might handle connection pooling using a Supabase client:

```
const poolConfig = {
    max: 20,            // Maximum number of connections
    idleTimeoutMillis: 30000 // Close idle connections after 30
      seconds
};

const supabase = createClient('https://your-project.supabase.co', '
    public-anon-key', { pool: poolConfig });
```

Proactive connection management ensures that the system remains responsive even under heavy load, preventing saturation and allowing more efficient handling of concurrent requests.

Scaling the application layer involves improvements in architectural design and resource allocation. Implementing load balancing at the API level ensures that incoming requests are distributed evenly across multiple instances of the application server. This not only prevents any single server from becoming overloaded but also minimizes response times by using the closest available resource. Many cloud providers offer load balancing as a service, which can automatically adjust to incoming traffic. Load balancers can route requests based on geographical location, session persistence, or request type, significantly improving the scalability and resilience of the application.

Microservices architecture can also contribute to scaling a Supabase project. Segregating application functionalities into discrete services enables independent scaling of each component. For instance, user authentication, data reporting, and real-time notifications can be managed by separate services that scale based on their specific usage patterns. Employing asynchronous communication between microservices reduces dependencies and provides better fault isolation. An example of invoking an asynchronous microservice call in Node.js is shown below:

```
const axios = require('axios');

async function notifyService(eventData) {
    try {
        await axios.post('https://notification-service.example.com/
    notify', eventData);
    } catch (error) {
        console.error('Notification service error:', error);
    }
}

module.exports = notifyService;
```

This approach alleviates pressure on the primary service handling core business logic by offloading auxiliary responsibilities to independent, scalable services.

Caching remains one of the most effective strategies to scale systems and improve performance under high load. By storing frequently accessed data in a cache, applications can significantly reduce the number of time-consuming database queries. Supabase projects should consider both server-side and client-side caching. Server-side caching involves using in-memory data stores like Redis to store results of common queries. Caching layers reduce the need to access the database repeatedly for data that does not change often. An illustrative Redis caching example in JavaScript might look like this:

```
const redis = require('redis');
const client = redis.createClient();

async function getCachedOrderSummary(customerId) {
```

```
    return new Promise((resolve, reject) => {
        client.get(`order_summary:${customerId}`, (err, data) => {
            if (err) return reject(err);
            if (data) return resolve(JSON.parse(data));
            resolve(null);
        });
    });
}

async function setCachedOrderSummary(customerId, summary) {
    client.set(`order_summary:${customerId}`, JSON.stringify(summary)
    , 'EX', 300);
}
```

On the client side, caching can reduce repeated API calls by storing previously fetched data. In-memory caches on the client or browser-based storage decrease latency and the load on the back-end API.

Monitoring plays a vital role in scaling Supabase projects. Continuously tracking performance metrics such as CPU usage, memory consumption, query execution times, and connection pool statistics enables proactive adjustments to resource allocation. Tools like pgAdmin, Datadog, or custom dashboards provide insights into the evolving needs of the application. Setting up automated alerts when predefined thresholds are exceeded can trigger scaling events, whether by adding more resources or optimizing existing processes dynamically.

A comprehensive scaling strategy also considers security and data consistency. As projects scale horizontally or implement multiple read replicas, ensuring that data remains consistent across all nodes is crucial. Techniques such as eventual consistency, use of consistent hashing for load distribution, and synchronization through transaction logs can help maintain integrity while allowing the system to scale. Supabase benefits from PostgreSQL's robust transaction management, but developers must design applications with an understanding of the trade-offs when operating in distributed environments.

Handling increased user loads also involves preparing the application for sudden surges in traffic. Auto-scaling capabilities provided by cloud platforms enable dynamic resource allocation, adjusting the number of active instances based on real-time demand. Implementing continuous integration and deployment (CI/CD) pipelines that support rapid scaling events minimizes downtime during peak usage periods. A sample configuration for auto-scaling in a cloud environment may appear as follows (this is a conceptual representation):

```
{
    "autoScaling": {
        "minInstances": 2,
        "maxInstances": 20,
        "metrics": {
            "cpuUtilization": 70,
            "requestCount": 1000
        }
    }
}
```

This configuration, or its equivalent in a specific cloud provider's platform, helps maintain service levels by automatically adding or removing resources as necessary.

Additionally, a robust error handling and fallback mechanism is essential when scaling. Under heavy load, some requests may fail, and graceful degradation ensures that the user experience is not completely compromised. Implementing circuit breakers, retry mechanisms, and graceful degradation strategies helps maintain a smooth service. These strategies, often implemented through middleware or external libraries, catch failures and provide alternative paths for service delivery, ensuring that occasional issues do not escalate into systemic failures.

Scaling a Supabase project is an iterative process. It requires a combination of proactive planning, real-time monitoring, and adaptive execution. By embracing both vertical and horizontal scaling strategies, employing proper load balancing, and integrating efficient caching and connection pooling, developers can design systems that thrive under increased user loads. The coordinated orchestration of these techniques allows the project to handle growth without sacrificing performance or reliability. Every component, from database partitioning to asynchronous microservices, contributes to a scalable infrastructure capable of meeting the evolving demands of the user base while maintaining data integrity and delivering consistent performance.

9.5. Implementing Caching Strategies

Caching mechanisms are essential for reducing load times and improving overall application performance in Supabase projects. Effective caching minimizes direct requests to the database by storing frequently accessed data in faster, intermediary storage. Drawing from previous discussions on query optimization and scaling, this section details methods of implementing caching to achieve lower latency and reduced server load.

Efficient caching strategies begin with identifying suitable candidates for caching. Data that is retrieved repeatedly but changes infrequently is ideal for caching. Examples include configuration settings, user session data, and aggregated query results. On the database side, materialized views can serve as a form of caching by storing the results of expensive queries. For instance, precomputed summaries of orders can be created as materialized views, allowing the API to respond rapidly without recalculating aggregates for each request:

```
CREATE MATERIALIZED VIEW order_summary AS
SELECT customer_id, COUNT(*) AS order_count, SUM(total) AS
    total_spent
FROM orders
GROUP BY customer_id;
```

This materialized view can be refreshed periodically, ensuring that the data remains up-to-date while avoiding the overhead of repeated aggregation. When an application predominantly reads such summary data, referencing the materialized view substantially reduces query execution time.

Caching is not limited to the database level. Application-level caching using in-memory data stores like Redis or Memcached is a widely adopted approach. Redis, in particular, is well-suited for caching due to its support for a variety of data structures and its ability to handle high throughput with low latency. In a Supabase project, the API layer can check whether a requested resource exists in the cache before querying the database. The following JavaScript example demonstrates how this can be achieved using Redis:

```javascript
const redis = require('redis');
const client = redis.createClient();

client.on('error', (err) => {
    console.error('Redis error:', err);
});

async function getOrderSummary(customerId) {
    return new Promise((resolve, reject) => {
        client.get(`order_summary:${customerId}`, async (err,
    cachedData) => {
            if (err) return reject(err);
            if (cachedData) {
                return resolve(JSON.parse(cachedData));
            } else {
                // Fallback to the database query if cache miss
    occurs
                const { data, error } = await supabase
                    .from('order_summary')
                    .select('*')
                    .eq('customer_id', customerId);
                if (error) return reject(error);
                // Cache the result for subsequent requests
                client.setex(`order_summary:${customerId}`, 300, JSON
    .stringify(data[0]));
                return resolve(data[0]);
            }
        });
    });
}
```

In this example, the function `getOrderSummary` first checks Redis for a cached version of the order summary. On a cache hit, the data is parsed and returned immediately; on a miss, a database query is executed, and the result is cached for future requests with an expiry time of 300 seconds. This pattern significantly reduces the number of repetitive queries to the database, thereby decreasing load and response times.

Beyond caching entire dataset responses, a granular approach can be implemented by caching parts of the response or even individual query results. This method is particularly beneficial when different components of the response have varying update frequencies. For example, in a scenario where a user's profile information rarely changes compared to their activity feed, caching the profile data separately allows updates to the feed without invalidating the entire response. In such cases, a combined cache strategy using multiple keys may be employed:

```
async function getUserDashboard(userId) {
    const [profileData, activityData] = await Promise.all([
        getCachedData(`user_profile:${userId}`, () =>
            supabase.from('profiles').select('*').eq('id', userId)
        ),
        getCachedData(`user_activity:${userId}`, () =>
            supabase.from('activities').select('*').eq('user_id',
    userId)
        )
    ]);

    return { profile: profileData, activities: activityData };
}

async function getCachedData(cacheKey, dbQuery) {
    return new Promise((resolve, reject) => {
        client.get(cacheKey, async (err, cached) => {
            if (err) return reject(err);
            if (cached) {
                resolve(JSON.parse(cached));
            } else {
                const { data, error } = await dbQuery();
                if (error) return reject(error);
                client.setex(cacheKey, 600, JSON.stringify(data));
```

```
            resolve(data);
        }
    });
    });
}
```

This approach not only improves performance by serving cached data for both user profiles and activity feeds but also offers flexibility regarding cache invalidation strategies. Changing the cache time-to-live (TTL) for each key based on data volatility yields better control over consistency and freshness.

Another critical aspect of caching strategy involves managing cache invalidation. The process ensures that the cache does not become stale with outdated data. Techniques such as time-based expiration, also known as TTL, are commonly used. With a TTL mechanism, cache entries automatically expire after a set period, ensuring that the system eventually fetches fresh data from the persistent store. Event-driven invalidation can also be implemented, whereby the cache is explicitly cleared or updated when changes occur in the underlying data. For example, in an API that updates order details, it is prudent to invalidate the order summary cache for the affected customer:

```
async function updateOrder(orderId, newData) {
    const { data, error } = await supabase
        .from('orders')
        .update(newData)
        .eq('order_id', orderId);
    if (error) {
        throw error;
    }
    // Invalidate cached summary for the customer
    if (data && data.length > 0) {
        const customerId = data[0].customer_id;
        client.del(`order_summary:${customerId}`);
    }
    return data;
}
```

Balancing between automatic expiration and event-driven invalidation is vital to maintaining a consistent state across the cache and the database. For read-heavy systems where data changes infrequently, longer TTL values may be appropriate, while highly dynamic data might require shorter TTL periods or explicit invalidation upon data modifications.

In distributed systems, additional challenges can arise with caching strategies. Ensuring cache coherence across multiple application instances is necessary to prevent race conditions and stale data. Distributed cache systems like Redis support clustering and replication, which can be configured to ensure high availability and load distribution. Careful consideration should be given to cache hot keys—keys that receive an unexpectedly high volume of requests—as they can become a single point of failure. Sharding and consistent hashing are effective techniques to distribute the load evenly across multiple cache nodes, mitigating the risk of overloading a single instance.

A multi-tier caching approach further enhances performance. This technique involves using several cache layers, with the fastest being in-memory caches within the application, followed by external caches like Redis, and finally database caches such as materialized views. Each layer contributes to reducing response times based on the type of data and frequency of access. The combination ensures that the most frequently accessed data is retrieved from the quickest cache layer possible, while less frequently accessed data remains available in secondary caches without burdening the database.

Monitoring and analytics play a crucial role in evaluating the effectiveness of caching strategies. Caching metrics such as hit rate, miss rate, average latency, and eviction counts are key performance indicators that help diagnose and refine cache configurations. Tools that integrate with Redis or other cache systems can provide detailed insights into cache performance, enabling periodic reviews and adjustments. Regular analysis of these metrics ensures that the caching system operates optimally and facilitates early detection of issues such as cache stampedes—situations where large numbers of clients simultaneously attempt to fetch data on a cache miss.

Implementing caching strategies in Supabase applications complements earlier performance optimizations. While query restructuring, indexing, and API improvements reduce load times at various levels, caching provides significant additional performance gains by minimizing direct database access. This layered approach, combining static caching through materialized views, dynamic caching using distributed in-memory stores, and agile invalidation techniques, results in a robust performance enhancement that scales with user demand.

Applying these caching techniques requires careful planning and continuous refinement. Developers must evaluate data characteristics, choose appropriate caching mechanisms, and fine-tune configurations according to user access patterns. The overall goal is to achieve a harmonious balance between data freshness and the speed of access. Each caching strategy contributes to an architecture that delivers quick, reliable responses to client requests while reducing the computational burden on core systems. The precise implementation of these techniques ensures that Supabase applications remain performant and scalable, catering to the demands of an evolving user base and dynamic data streams.

9.6. Monitoring and Analytics

Monitoring and analytics are pivotal in enabling developers to understand the behavior of their Supabase applications under production loads. By employing a combination of tools and best practices, developers can gather actionable insights into performance metrics, diagnose issues proactively, and optimize application components iteratively. The following discussion details the integration of monitoring

377

infrastructures and analytics solutions that inform optimization efforts across multiple layers of a Supabase deployment.

A robust monitoring framework begins with collecting real-time data across the application stack. This includes measuring response times, query performance, CPU utilization, memory usage, and network latency. Instrumentation at both the database and API levels is essential to capture comprehensive performance metrics. PostgreSQL's pg_stat_statements extension is instrumental in profiling query execution by logging execution frequency and the time spent per query. For instance, running a query such as:

```
SELECT query, calls, total_time, mean_time
FROM pg_stat_statements
ORDER BY total_time DESC
LIMIT 10;
```

allows developers to identify the most resource-intensive queries, thereby highlighting areas that could benefit from indexing or query optimization. Monitoring these metrics over time reveals trends and inefficiencies that might not be evident from isolated snapshots.

Beyond database-level monitoring, incorporating Application Performance Monitoring (APM) tools into the API layer provides visibility into the end-to-end performance experienced by users. Solutions such as Prometheus, Grafana, Datadog, or New Relic offer real-time dashboards, alerting systems, and detailed analytics. Integrating Prometheus with a Node.js application, for example, can be achieved by exposing an endpoint for metrics collection. A simplified implementation might resemble:

```
const express = require('express');
const client = require('prom-client');
const app = express();

// Create a Registry which registers the metrics
const register = new client.Registry();

// Define a custom metric for API response time in milliseconds
```

```
const responseTimeHistogram = new client.Histogram({
    name: 'api_response_time_ms',
    help: 'API response times in milliseconds',
    buckets: [50, 100, 200, 300, 500, 1000]
});


register.registerMetric(responseTimeHistogram);

// Middleware to record response times
app.use((req, res, next) => {
    const start = Date.now();
    res.on('finish', () => {
        const duration = Date.now() - start;
        responseTimeHistogram.observe(duration);
    });
    next();
});

// Endpoint to expose metrics
app.get('/metrics', async (req, res) => {
    res.set('Content-Type', register.contentType);
    res.send(await register.metrics());
});

app.listen(3000, () => {
    console.log('Server listening on port 3000');
});
```

This code segment demonstrates how response times, one of the crucial performance metrics, can be captured and exposed via a dedicated endpoint. Such instrumentation enables monitoring systems to scrape metrics, generate alerts based on configurable thresholds, and produce visualizations that pinpoint performance degradation.

Effective analytics extend beyond raw metrics; they encompass a comprehensive understanding of user behavior and system utilization. By logging detailed transactional data and analyzing access patterns, developers can identify changes in application load, predict scaling needs, and adjust resources accordingly. Logging middleware integrated within API endpoints can capture critical events such as request duration, error rates, and user authentication attempts. These logs, when aggregated and correlated with system events, facilitate rapid anomaly

379

detection. A simple logging implementation in an Express.js application may look like:

```
app.use(async (req, res, next) => {
    const start = Date.now();
    res.on('finish', () => {
        const duration = Date.now() - start;
        console.log(`Path: ${req.originalUrl}, Status: ${res.
    statusCode}, Duration: ${duration}ms`);
    });
    next();
});
```

Such logs provide a granular view of the system's operational state and help in correlating specific performance issues with user actions or backend processes.

Analytics platforms can further assist by aggregating logs and metrics into long-term storage for historical analysis. Tools like Elasticsearch, Logstash, and Kibana (the ELK stack) are popular choices for parsing and visualizing logs. Integrating these systems facilitates trend analysis over time, allowing developers to project performance implications of growing user loads and evolving application features. For instance, visualizing a time series of API response times can reveal patterns—such as periodic spikes during peak usage—enabling adjustments in resource allocation or query optimization.

Another key aspect of monitoring is the implementation of automated alerting mechanisms. An effective alerting strategy involves setting thresholds for vital metrics such as CPU usage above 80%, unexpected increases in error rates, or prolonged query execution times. Alerts, when integrated with communication channels like email, Slack, or SMS, ensure a rapid response to anomalies. For example, configuring an alert in Grafana might involve specifying a query against time-series data, and setting email notifications when the query value exceeds a pre-defined threshold.

Beyond system performance, monitoring also includes auditing data

380

integrity and security events. Supabase applications benefit from auditing tools that log access patterns, changes to sensitive data, and user authentications. These audit logs not only support security incident responses but also provide insights into usage patterns that might inform future optimizations. Integrating such audit logs with a centralized monitoring solution ensures that alerts can be generated not just for performance issues but also for security events, thus fostering a secure and stable environment.

Emerging trends in monitoring also revolve around distributed tracing. In complex architectures involving microservices, distributed tracing provides the ability to follow a request as it traverses multiple services and databases. Tools like Jaeger or Zipkin help in visualizing dependencies and pinpointing where latency accumulates. The implementation of distributed tracing involves inserting unique trace identifiers into HTTP headers on each incoming request, and propagating these identifiers across downstream services. An example of setting a trace identifier in an Express middleware might be:

```
app.use((req, res, next) => {
    const traceId = req.headers['x-trace-id'] ||
    generateUniqueTraceId();
    req.traceId = traceId;
    res.set('X-Trace-Id', traceId);
    next();
});
```

Distributed tracing provides critical insights into inter-service communication delays and helps to identify bottlenecks across the distributed system. By correlating traces with the metrics collected by Prometheus or logs stored in the ELK stack, a comprehensive picture of system health emerges, facilitating targeted optimizations.

In addition to technical monitoring, gathering analytics on user interactions and application usage is important for guiding product improvements and performance enhancements. User analytics, which

381

track user sessions, feature usage, and behavioral trends, serve as a feedback loop for prioritizing performance optimization efforts. Embedding analytics events within the client-side code and collecting them via a central telemetry service creates a valuable dataset. Such data can inform decisions on caching strategies, query restructuring, and load balancing configurations by revealing which parts of the application encounter the highest demand.

Collecting end-to-end performance data, from the user's device to the database, helps to close the loop on performance optimization. Client-side monitoring tools, including browser performance APIs or third-party libraries, can capture metrics like page load times, resource download durations, and user interaction delays. Aggregate analysis of this data, when combined with server-side metrics, provides a holistic view of the application's performance. This information is especially valuable when guiding architectural changes—such as adopting asynchronous processing or refining API endpoints—to ensure a consistent and responsive user experience.

Best practices for monitoring include establishing a baseline of system performance under normal conditions and continuously comparing real-time data against these baselines. It is essential to document typical performance metrics, and use them as benchmarks for detecting anomalies. Regular performance reviews, incorporating both automated alerting and manual examination of log files and dashboards, are necessary to maintain a steady performance as the system evolves.

Furthermore, setting up anomaly detection using machine learning techniques can augment traditional threshold-based alerts. These advanced analytics approaches can identify subtle shifts in performance patterns that may precede a larger issue. By integrating anomaly detection systems with monitoring tools, applications can gain an additional layer of protection against performance degradation.

Effective monitoring and analytics require an iterative approach built on continuous feedback. Developers and operations teams must collaborate to fine-tune dashboards, adjust alert thresholds, and implement system changes based on the analytics gathered. The iterative process of measurement, analysis, and optimization forms the cornerstone of a resilient and high-performing Supabase application.

Through the systematic application of these monitoring tools and the rigorous collection of performance analytics, developers can ensure that optimization efforts are informed by accurate and current data. This proactive approach not only mitigates performance issues before they impact end users but also guides future enhancements, ensuring that the Supabase application scales gracefully and remains robust as usage grows.

9.7. Budgeting for Performance and Scale

Effective performance optimization and scalable design in Supabase applications require careful budgeting and cost management. As performance enhancements and scale improvements often involve trade-offs, it is important to balance the cost of additional resources, advanced optimizations, and infrastructure modifications with the benefits they deliver. Strategic budgeting encompasses both direct operational expenditures, such as database compute and storage costs, and indirect costs like developer time and maintenance overhead.

A central consideration is the cost associated with scaling the database. Vertical scaling, which involves upgrading the specifications of a single machine (e.g., adding more CPU, memory, or faster storage), can provide immediate performance improvements. However, this approach has diminishing returns and is limited by the maximum capacity of the hardware. Horizontal scaling through read replicas and partitioning distributes load across multiple nodes. Although this method may involve higher costs for additional instances and increased network traffic, it can offer a more sustainable long-term solution for handling increased user loads. Evaluating the cost implications of these scaling strategies is critical in the budgeting process. For example, a cost analysis might involve comparing the expense of upgrading a single instance versus deploying multiple read replicas.

Integration of caching mechanisms, as described in previous sections, also affects budgeting. While employing caching solutions—such as Redis or Memcached—can significantly reduce database load and improve response times, the additional infrastructure incurs extra costs. In many cases, caching infrastructure is priced based on memory allocation and uptime. A well-designed caching strategy must consider the frequency of cache invalidation, the volume of data stored, and the expected hit rate. Running simulations or analyzing historical data can provide estimates regarding cache efficiency, which in turn help anticipate cost savings. The following code snippet shows the integration of Redis in a Node.js environment, serving as part of a cost-benefit analysis plan:

```
const redis = require('redis');
const client = redis.createClient({ host: 'cache-server.example.com',
    port: 6379 });

// Record cache metrics to estimate cache hit rate and performance
    gains
client.on('connect', () => {
    console.log('Connected to Redis for caching analysis.');
});
```

In this context, the cost of running a Redis instance is weighed against the reduction in database query costs and improved application performance.

Another significant component in budgeting for performance and scale is the allocation of resources for monitoring and analytics. Comprehensive monitoring of system metrics, user behavior, and performance

384

trends is vital for timely optimizations. Tools such as Prometheus, Grafana, or commercial platforms like Datadog come with licensing or subscription fees. However, the investment in monitoring is often justified by the increased insight provided, which can preempt costly system outages and performance bottlenecks. The budget should factor in both the upfront implementation costs and ongoing operational expenses related to monitoring. A simple metrics collection endpoint, as shown previously in the Prometheus integration example, typically incurs minimal cost compared to the potential savings in operational stability.

The use of auto-scaling and load balancing services offered by cloud providers introduces another layer of cost considerations. Auto-scaling policies dynamically allocate computing resources based on real-time demand. While auto-scaling improves responsiveness and ensures that the application can handle traffic surges, it can lead to unexpected expenses if not properly configured. Setting appropriate thresholds for scaling events and monitoring auto-scaling behavior helps in avoiding over-provisioning. Cloud budgeting tools provided by services such as AWS, Google Cloud, or Azure can be integrated with Supabase deployments to continuously analyze usage patterns and predict future expenditures. A sample JSON configuration for an auto-scaling policy might look as follows:

```
{
    "autoScaling": {
        "minInstances": 2,
        "maxInstances": 10,
        "metrics": {
            "cpuUtilization": 70,
            "requestCount": 1000
        }
    }
}
```

Such configurations serve as a reference point for implementing cost controls that align with expected traffic patterns and resource usage.

Developer time and maintenance overhead also play an important role in budgeting for performance and scale. Optimizing queries, reconfiguring indexes, implementing caching strategies, and setting up monitoring systems require dedicated development and operations efforts. While these improvements often lead to significant performance gains and cost savings in the long term, they need to be planned within project timelines and budgets. Time spent on performance tuning must be balanced against other feature developments. Investing in automation can reduce manual overhead; for instance, setting up automated performance regression testing or periodic cache invalidation routines lessens the need for constant manual oversight. Code automation for performance monitoring might be implemented as follows:

```
const schedule = require('node-schedule');

// Schedule a periodic task to analyze and log performance metrics
schedule.scheduleJob('0 * * * *', () => {
    // Automated performance analytics
    console.log('Running automated performance analysis tasks...');
    // Insert logic to query monitoring metrics and generate reports
});
```

This proactive approach not only aids in performance tuning but also streamlines cost management by reducing repetitive manual interventions.

Budgeting for performance and scale necessitates the development of a cost-model that continually evaluates the impact of optimization efforts. Utilizing historical data from monitoring tools, developers can predict the financial benefits of implementing specific performance improvements. Key performance indicators (KPIs) such as reduced query times, higher cache hit rates, and lower error incidences can be translated into cost savings. For example, decreasing the average API response time by optimizing database queries might lead to lower infrastructure consumption, thus reducing monthly cloud expenses. Cost models should therefore be iterative and data-driven, adjusting estimates as system usage evolves and providing a basis for informed decision-making.

In addition, the potential return on investment (ROI) of performance-related enhancements should be quantified. The cost of scaling can be justified if the improvements result in increased user satisfaction, higher retention rates, and overall application stability. A quantifiable ROI analysis might compare the additional revenue generated through improved user experiences against the incremental cost of scaling resources. This analysis aids in prioritizing certain optimizations that, although initially resource intensive, will contribute significantly to long-term success. Gathering data on user engagement and correlating it with performance metrics supports a business case that promotes judicious spending on infrastructure enhancements.

It is also important to consider the potential cost implications of unforeseen traffic spikes or system failures. Budgeting for a buffer, such as additional reserved instances or emergency support resources, ensures that the system remains resilient under unexpected loads. This contingency planning may involve negotiating flexible cloud service agreements or setting aside funds specifically for emergency scaling events. The overall budgeting process should include regular reviews to reassess resource needs based on emerging trends and performance analytics. This iterative financial planning approach aligns operational expenditure with real-world usage patterns and guarantees that cost control measures remain effective over time.

Lastly, consideration must be given to the lifecycle of the application. At various stages of the application's evolution—be it early-stage development, rapid growth, or mature operation—the cost structure and performance priorities may shift. Early in the development process, cost-effective solutions and minimal infrastructure may be sufficient; however, as adoption grows, a more sophisticated approach that balances high performance with cost efficiency becomes necessary. Periodic strategic reviews, informed by monitoring and analytics, enable teams to adjust their budgeting strategies and scale their infrastructure in line with evolving business needs.

In summary, budgeting for performance and scale in Supabase applications involves a multi-faceted approach that integrates direct infrastructure costs, the expense of additional caching and monitoring solutions, developer and maintenance overhead, and a data-driven cost model. This strategic process requires continuous evaluation of resource usage, predictive analysis of future demand, and iterative adjustments to ensure that the application remains both performant and cost effective. By applying these cost management principles, developers can achieve sustainable growth while optimizing both performance and financial efficiency.

Chapter 10

Case Studies and Practical Applications

This chapter presents real-world applications of Supabase through detailed case studies across various industries. It examines the development of e-commerce platforms, real-time chat apps, and educational systems, highlighting architectural choices and implementation strategies. The chapter concludes with lessons learned and best practices, offering valuable insights for leveraging Supabase to create effective, scalable solutions.

10.1. Overview of Supabase in Real-World Applications

Supabase has rapidly emerged as a versatile and effective backend solution for various industries, providing an open source alternative to proprietary database platforms while delivering robust capabilities in real-time data management, authentication, and API generation. This section examines the application of Supabase in diverse sectors, showcasing how its modular architecture and extensible features enable developers to construct scalable, secure, and performance-optimized systems across different domains.

Supabase's architecture is built upon PostgreSQL, which is extended through real-time listeners, serverless functions, and an authentication layer. In industries where data consistency, security, and scalability are critical, such as finance and healthcare, Supabase offers a solid foundation. The SQL capabilities inherited from PostgreSQL combined with modern development paradigms enable rapid prototyping and iterative development, as well as comprehensive audit trails — a feature demanded by most regulated industries.

In the financial technology sector, where low latency and accurate data processing are paramount, Supabase's capability for real-time updates and transactional integrity enhances both the user experience and backend responsiveness. Financial applications require rigorous data validation, fraud detection, and compliance with strict regulatory frameworks. By leveraging PostgreSQL's native features and integrating real-time subscriptions, systems can reflect financial transactions and account status changes immediately. A typical implementation in this context might involve listening for incoming transactions and triggering a series of automated compliance checks. The following code snippet illustrates how a client might subscribe to database changes in a financial application:

```
import { createClient } from '@supabase/supabase-js';

const supabaseUrl = 'https://your-project.supabase.co';
const supabaseKey = 'public-anon-key';
const supabase = createClient(supabaseUrl, supabaseKey);

const transactionSubscription = supabase
  .from('transactions')
  .on('INSERT', payload => {
```

```
console.log('New transaction:', payload.new);
// Trigger compliance function or notification service here
})
.subscribe();
```

In healthcare systems, the immediate availability of patient data and real-time collaboration among healthcare professionals is essential. Supabase enables secure handling of sensitive data through its robust authentication system and row-level security policies. Moreover, the real-time data synchronization capabilities assist in clinical monitoring and emergency response scenarios. Hospitals and clinics use such systems to monitor vital signs from various devices, ensuring that alerts are generated promptly if any anomalous readings are detected.

Within the domain of educational technology, the ability to manage dynamic content and interactive user interfaces is crucial. Supabase supports educational platforms by offering serverless functions for processing user inputs, managing course content, and tracking student progress through integrated analytics. By centralizing data within a scalable PostgreSQL database, institutions can run complex queries to monitor performance and provide personalized feedback. The combination of authentication services and real-time subscriptions allows educators to conduct live assessments and collaborative sessions while ensuring that user data remains secure and consistent across devices.

Supabase also excels in enabling rapid development of content management systems (CMS), particularly for organizations that require flexible workflows and a user-friendly interface. Developers can integrate Supabase to handle authentication, file storage, and user permissions seamlessly, ensuring that non-technical users are able to manage content without compromising system security. An example implementation might include a function for updating content after verifying the user's permissions:

```
CREATE OR REPLACE FUNCTION log_content_update()
RETURNS TRIGGER AS $$
```

```
BEGIN
    INSERT INTO content_audit_log(content_id, updated_by,
    update_timestamp)
    VALUES (NEW.id, CURRENT_USER, NOW());
    RETURN NEW;
END;
$$ LANGUAGE plpgsql;

CREATE TRIGGER trigger_content_update
AFTER UPDATE ON cms_content
FOR EACH ROW
EXECUTE FUNCTION log_content_update();
```

This integration demonstrates the seamless blend of SQL functionalities with automated business logic to maintain data integrity and audit compliance — a requirement prevalent in industries managing large volumes of content.

Another area of significant impact is the development of event-driven applications. Industries that rely on real-time data processing, such as logistics and transportation, benefit from Supabase's event subscriptions and webhooks. By automatically triggering processing functions in response to data changes, companies can monitor fleet information, schedule maintenance, or manage supply chain disruptions efficiently. Additionally, the flexibility of PostgreSQL allows for complex, event-specific queries that drive business decisions in near real-time. The following pseudo-code outlines how an event-driven function might be initiated upon new sensor data arriving in a transportation management system:

```
def process_sensor_data(event):
    sensor_id = event['sensor_id']
    reading = event['reading']
    if reading > THRESHOLD:
        trigger_alert(sensor_id, reading)
    record_event(sensor_id, reading)

# Functionized integration with Supabase events would follow a
    similar structured approach
```

In each case presented, the architecture of Supabase supports modularity and decoupled service design. Developers deploy serverless functions, write SQL triggers, and integrate third-party services without being tied to a monolithic backend, thereby enabling rapid adaptation to new business requirements. This inherent flexibility is why Supabase is not limited to specific industries; it is equally applicable in sectors such as retail, where the personalization of marketing campaigns and inventory management demand seamless synchronization between front-end interfaces and backend databases.

The versatility of Supabase extends to its deployment model. Organizations can self-host Supabase, mitigating concerns over vendor lock-in and enabling tailored customizations that meet specific performance or security requirements. The open source nature provides transparency into its internal mechanisms, which is particularly appealing for academic and research institutions. Researchers benefit from a system where experimental changes and optimizations can be directly applied and evaluated in a production-like environment.

Supabase's ecosystem further enriches its real-world applications by supporting a wide range of client libraries, enabling effortless integration with web, mobile, and desktop platforms. These libraries provide advanced functionalities such as offline data persistence and conflict resolution to manage scenarios where network connectivity is intermittent. This is essential in regions where uninterrupted connectivity cannot be guaranteed, yet data consistency remains a critical consideration in sectors such as education, public safety, or fieldwork.

Security and regulatory compliance are fundamental concerns in real-world applications, and Supabase addresses these by allowing the implementation of granular security policies directly at the database level. This approach ensures that data is accessed and modified only by authorized users, a mechanism vital for industries handling confidential or sensitive information. By adopting row-level security, developers can define policies that limit data access based on user roles, time, or contextual parameters. The following SQL example demonstrates the definition of such a policy:

```
ALTER TABLE patient_records ENABLE ROW LEVEL SECURITY;

CREATE POLICY patient_policy ON patient_records
FOR SELECT
USING (auth.uid() = user_id);
```

The ability to implement precise access control without extensive middleware logic not only simplifies backend architecture but also enhances system performance by offloading security verifications to the database engine. In turn, this ensures that applications scale effectively even under high concurrent usage conditions.

In summary, Supabase's comprehensive feature set addresses the multifaceted requirements encountered in modern application development across diverse industries. Its integration of PostgreSQL's proven relational database capabilities with real-time functionalities, robust security measures, and modular deployment options underscores its effectiveness and adaptability. Industrial applications ranging from dynamic financial systems to responsive healthcare monitoring illustrate the platform's capacity to support mission-critical tasks with reliability and low latency. The examples and code snippets provided herein underscore the value proposition of Supabase as a scalable backend solution, affirming its role as a strategic technology choice for developers and organizations seeking to innovate without compromising on performance or security.

10.2.   Building an E-commerce Platform

Designing a scalable e-commerce platform requires a careful orchestration of various components, ranging from user authentication and product management to order processing and real-time inventory updates. Supabase, built on PostgreSQL, provides a unified platform that simplifies backend complexities while ensuring performance and security. The integration of Supabase's real-time subscriptions, serverless functions, and native SQL capabilities offers a robust solution for managing the diverse requirements of an e-commerce application.

The core architecture of an e-commerce platform involves multiple layers. At the foundation is the relational database managed by Supabase, which stores product details, user accounts, orders, and transactional histories. Supabase's real-time features enable immediate synchronization of changes, such as inventory adjustments or order status updates, across the application interface. Using row-level security and authentication, sensitive user data, including personal details and payment information, are protected from unauthorized access.

The first stage in building the system involves defining the database schema. This schema should encapsulate product information (e.g., product names, descriptions, prices, and stock quantities), user profiles, shopping carts, orders, and payment statuses. The relational model supports complex queries, facilitating features such as filtering products by category or tracking order history. A representative schema design might include tables such as `products`, `users`, `orders`, and `order_items`, with foreign key constraints enforcing data integrity.

To support dynamic content updates, Supabase's real-time subscriptions allow the frontend to react to changes in product availability. For instance, when a user completes a purchase, the corresponding product's stock level should be updated immediately, and such changes should propagate to all clients currently viewing the product catalog. An example client-side subscription using Supabase's JavaScript library is provided below:

```
import { createClient } from '@supabase/supabase-js';
```

```
const supabaseUrl = 'https://your-project.supabase.co';
const supabaseKey = 'public-anon-key';
const supabase = createClient(supabaseUrl, supabaseKey);

const inventorySubscription = supabase
  .from('products')
  .on('UPDATE', payload => {
    console.log('Product inventory updated:', payload.new);
    // Refresh the product display or update inventory counter
  })
  .subscribe();
```

User authentication is a pivotal component that underpins secure transactions. Supabase provides built-in authentication that simplifies the process of registration, login, and role management. By integrating this system, the e-commerce platform can protect user accounts and manage sessions effectively. Row-level security policies further restrict access to data so that users can only view or modify their own orders and profiles.

Another critical feature is the shopping cart functionality, which allows users to select products and prepare them for purchase. An effective implementation requires both temporary storage and persistent records of user selections. Serverless functions provide an optimal approach to managing the transition from shopping cart data to confirmed orders. These functions can be triggered upon a checkout event to validate the cart contents, verify inventory levels, and initiate payment processing.

A typical serverless function might perform the following operations:

- Validate and lock selected product quantities.

- Calculate the total order value including taxes and shipping charges.

- Initiate the payment process by interacting with a payment gateway.

- Record the order details in the database and update the stock quantities.

The following pseudo-code outlines a simplified serverless function in a Python-like syntax, demonstrating the integration with Supabase for these operations:

```
def process_checkout(user_id, cart_items):
    total_amount = 0
    for item in cart_items:
        product = fetch_product(item['product_id'])
        if product['stock_quantity'] < item['quantity']:
            raise Exception("Insufficient stock for product:",
    product['name'])
        total_amount += product['price'] * item['quantity']

    payment_response = initiate_payment(user_id, total_amount)
    if not payment_response['success']:
        raise Exception("Payment failed")

    order_id = record_order(user_id, cart_items, total_amount)
    update_stock(cart_items)
    return order_id

def fetch_product(product_id):
    # API call to Supabase to retrieve product information
    pass

def initiate_payment(user_id, amount):
    # Integration with payment gateway
    pass

def record_order(user_id, cart_items, total_amount):
    # Insert order into Supabase orders table
    pass

def update_stock(cart_items):
    # Decrement stock quantities in Supabase products table
    pass
```

Maintaining stock integrity becomes a challenge as the number of concurrent transactions increases. Supabase's support for SQL triggers is helpful in automating the enforcement of business rules. For example, a trigger can be created on the order_items table to automatically decrement the product inventory upon the creation of a new order. The SQL snippet below demonstrates this approach:

```
CREATE OR REPLACE FUNCTION decrement_inventory() RETURNS TRIGGER AS
    $$
BEGIN
    UPDATE products
    SET stock_quantity = stock_quantity - NEW.quantity
    WHERE id = NEW.product_id;
    RETURN NEW;
END;
$$ LANGUAGE plpgsql;

CREATE TRIGGER trg_decrement_inventory
AFTER INSERT ON order_items
FOR EACH ROW
EXECUTE FUNCTION decrement_inventory();
```

The payment process represents another critical area where both security and performance cannot be compromised. Integrating a reliable third-party payment gateway involves securely transmitting payment details and processing responses asynchronously. The e-commerce platform may opt to decouple payment processing from the main checkout flow, using webhooks to synchronize payment status changes. This separation enhances scalability and improves fault tolerance. Moreover, database tables can maintain payment status and audit logs, ensuring that the system accurately reflects the state of each transaction.

Scalability is achieved by designing the e-commerce platform to handle both high throughput and sudden spikes in user activity, such as during promotional events. Supabase's horizontally scalable PostgreSQL setup, combined with serverless functions that auto-scale based on demand, ensures that system performance remains consistent. Developer strategies might include using caching layers, such as Redis, to reduce redundant database queries for frequently accessed data like product listings and customer reviews.

The front-end architecture complements the backend infrastructure by providing a responsive and interactive user experience. Progressive web applications (PWAs) or single-page applications (SPAs) built with frameworks such as React or Vue.js seamlessly integrate with Supabase through its robust client libraries. The asynchronous communication and real-time notifications enrich the user experience, particularly in managing dynamic aspects like shopping cart updates, order confirmations, and inventory alerts.

Error handling is meticulously embedded into each subsystem of the e-commerce platform. Supabase facilitates logging and error notifications through its serverless function ecosystem. Each function, whether handling checkout processes or updating inventory, should be designed with adequate error catching mechanisms. This design not only promotes resilience but also enables developers to recover from partial failures without disrupting the overall user experience. For example, if an order fails during the payment process, the system can automatically revert any temporary reservations or inventory adjustments made during the checkout process.

```
async function submitOrder(cartItems) {
    try {
        let orderResponse = await processCheckout(cartItems);
        console.log('Order submitted successfully:', orderResponse);
    } catch (error) {
        console.error('Order submission failed:', error);
        // Optionally roll back changes or notify the user for
    corrective action
    }
}
```

Furthermore, robust API design principles are adhered to by constructing RESTful endpoints that interact with Supabase's backend. Each endpoint is designed to handle specific functionalities—like retrieving product information, managing user accounts, or processing orders—ensuring that the system remains modular and maintenance-friendly. Versioning of APIs combined with detailed documentation aids in sustaining long-term compatibility as new features are introduced or existing ones are updated.

Strategic use of Supabase's built-in authentication and security measures further reinforces the integrity of the e-commerce platform. Role-based access control ensures that administrative functions, such as catalog management and order auditing, are restricted to authorized personnel. Additionally, encrypting sensitive data during both transit and storage is critical to maintaining compliance with data protection regulations.

The coupling of real-time functionality with robust authentication workflows underlines a design that emphasizes responsiveness and data security. Real-time updates not only improve operational efficiency but also provide an enhanced customer experience—a critical factor in maintaining competitive advantage in the e-commerce space. Developers employ real-time dashboards for tracking order statuses, inventory levels, and sales metrics which empower administrators to make informed decisions promptly.

The systematic integration of these components—database schema design, secure authentication, real-time data handling, serverless processing, and robust API development—results in an e-commerce platform that is both scalable and resilient. The architecture leverages the strengths of Supabase, including its PostgreSQL foundation and open-source extensibility, to deliver a solution that meets the multifaceted demands of modern online commerce.

The described implementation emphasizes modular design principles, ensuring that each component can be developed, tested, and scaled independently. As the platform evolves, additional features such as personalized product recommendations, advanced search capabilities, and multi-vendor support can be incorporated with minimal disruption. Such flexibility highlights Supabase's capability to serve not only as a transaction processing system but also as a comprehensive back-end solution for innovative retail experiences.

10.3. Creating a Real-time Chat Application

Developing a real-time chat application requires a tightly integrated system that can manage user presence, message broadcasting, and conversation persistence with low latency and high reliability. Supabase offers capabilities that streamline the development process by integrating a PostgreSQL database with real-time subscriptions, user authentication, and serverless functions. With these tools, developers can focus on implementing business logic rather than managing infrastructure complexities.

At the heart of the chat application is a robust database schema designed to capture the components of conversation. Core tables typically include `users`, `chat_rooms`, and `messages`. The `users` table handles authentication and profile management, while the `chat_rooms` table defines distinct conversation channels. The `messages` table stores the text content, timestamps, user identifiers, and room identifiers that associate each message with its corresponding chat context. This relational model supports the complex queries needed to retrieve recent messages, search through past conversations, and monitor user activity.

Real-time data synchronization is a fundamental requirement for chat applications. Supabase's subscription functionalities allow the client side to receive immediate notifications when new messages are inserted into the `messages` table. This capability is especially important for maintaining the interactive nature of the chat experience. A typical client-side implementation subscribes to these updates and dynamically updates the chat interface upon detecting new messages. The following code snippet illustrates a practical approach using Supabase's

JavaScript client:

```javascript
import { createClient } from '@supabase/supabase-js';

const supabaseUrl = 'https://your-project.supabase.co';
const supabaseKey = 'public-anon-key';
const supabase = createClient(supabaseUrl, supabaseKey);

const messageSubscription = supabase
  .from('messages')
  .on('INSERT', payload => {
    const newMessage = payload.new;
    displayNewMessage(newMessage);
  })
  .subscribe();

function displayNewMessage(message) {
  // Update the chat UI with the new message
  console.log(`New message in room ${message.room_id}: ${message.
    content}`);
}
```

In addition to real-time updates, user authentication is critical in ensuring that only authorized users can send or receive messages. Supabase's built-in authentication system supports various providers, including email/password and OAuth integrations, which greatly simplifies user management. By leveraging authentication methods and implementing row-level security policies, developers can ensure that each user only accesses messages pertinent to them. A policy might restrict queries on the messages table to only fetch data associated with rooms that a user belongs to:

```sql
ALTER TABLE messages ENABLE ROW LEVEL SECURITY;

CREATE POLICY select_messages_for_user ON messages
FOR SELECT
USING (
    EXISTS (
        SELECT 1 FROM chat_rooms_users
        WHERE chat_rooms_users.room_id = messages.room_id
        AND chat_rooms_users.user_id = auth.uid()
    )
);
```

In this example, a join table `chat_rooms_users` is used to map users to the chat rooms they participate in, thus enforcing fine-grained access control. This approach not only maintains data privacy but also streamlines backend queries, ensuring that users receive only the messages relevant to their conversations.

A typical chat session involves not only the retrieval and broadcasting of messages but also additional features such as message editing, deletion, and delivery acknowledgments. The design of the `messages` table must therefore account for these requirements. Columns to store message statuses, such as `delivered` and `read`, enable the application to track message lifecycle events. Serverless functions can be implemented to update these statuses based on user interactions. For instance, when a user reads a message, a triggered function may update the corresponding record in the database.

To provide further insight into the synchronous handling of such events, consider a serverless function that marks messages as read. The function receives a user identifier and a chat room identifier, then updates all unread messages for that user:

```
def mark_messages_as_read(user_id, room_id):
    query = """
    UPDATE messages
    SET read = TRUE
    WHERE room_id = %s
      AND user_id != %s
      AND read = FALSE;
    """
    connection.execute(query, (room_id, user_id))
    return "Messages marked as read"

# This function would be called via an API endpoint or webhook.
```

Real-time chat applications must also handle network interruptions and synchronization issues gracefully. In scenarios where connectivity is intermittent, Supabase's client libraries can cache messages locally and sync them when the connection is re-established. Optimistic

UI updates ensure that users experience minimal delay, as messages appear immediately in the chat interface while the backend processes them asynchronously. This dual approach minimizes perceived latency and supports a seamless user experience even under suboptimal network conditions.

Privacy and moderation features form another critical aspect of chat applications, especially in large or public channels. Moderation mechanisms often involve serverless functions that scan messages for prohibited content, trigger warnings, or even temporarily suspend users who violate policies. By processing messages in near real-time, these functions support automatic content filtering and aid in maintaining a safe communicative environment. The pseudo-code below demonstrates how a function might analyze the content of incoming messages:

```
def moderate_message(message):
    banned_words = ['spam', 'malicious']
    for word in banned_words:
        if word in message['content'].lower():
            flag_message(message['id'])
            break

def flag_message(message_id):
    query = "UPDATE messages SET flagged = TRUE WHERE id = %s;"
    connection.execute(query, (message_id,))
    return "Message flagged for moderation"
```

Integrating a robust front-end interface is equally important. Single-page applications (SPAs) built with frameworks such as React or Vue.js can leverage Supabase's client libraries to create a dynamic messaging environment that updates in real time. User interface components may include live typing indicators, notification badges, and conversation lists that update automatically through real-time subscriptions. These enhancements lead to a cohesive and interactive user experience that is critical in maintaining ongoing user engagement.

Optimizing the performance and resource utilization of the chat infrastructure is another element to consider. Supabase's serverless functions scale based on demand, ensuring that message processing remains responsive during peak loads. In tandem with efficient query design and indexing strategies for the PostgreSQL database, the system can handle thousands of concurrent users with minimal performance degradation. Strategies such as caching frequently accessed data (e.g., active users list or popular chat rooms) with in-memory data stores further improve read performance while reducing database load.

Error handling and logging are crucial for maintaining operational resilience. Every component within the system, from database triggers to client-side code, should include mechanisms to capture errors and perform graceful recovery. Detailed logging enables the rapid identification and resolution of issues that may arise in production. In client code, for example, errors during message submission can be caught and presented to the user without interrupting the chat service:

```
async function sendMessage(roomId, content) {
  try {
    const { data, error } = await supabase
      .from('messages')
      .insert([
        { room_id: roomId, content: content, user_id: supabase.auth.
      user().id }
      ]);
    if (error) throw error;
    console.log('Message sent:', data);
  } catch (err) {
    console.error('Failed to send message:', err.message);
    // Optionally display error notification to user
  }
}
```

Scalability considerations extend to the handling of large chat rooms and archived conversations. As the volume of messages increases, efficient query strategies and periodic data archival become essential to maintain system responsiveness and manage storage costs. Techniques such as partitioning the messages table by room or time period enable the database to handle queries more efficiently, especially when retrieving historical messages for active rooms.

The integration capabilities of Supabase further allow the chat application to extend its functionality. Third-party services such as push notification engines and analytics platforms can be seamlessly incorporated to monitor user engagement and deliver real-time notifications beyond the chat interface. Such integrations not only enhance user interaction but also provide valuable data-driven insights that can guide further feature development and system improvements.

The case study of building a real-time chat application with Supabase demonstrates the power of combining robust database management with real-time data delivery. Through effective use of Supabase's real-time subscriptions, secure authentication, and serverless functions, developers can construct applications that are both scalable and responsive. This approach minimizes overhead while offering flexibility for adding features such as content moderation and offline messaging, ensuring that the system meets the evolving demands of modern communication platforms.

By leveraging these capabilities, developers create chat applications that maintain high performance and data integrity even under significant load. The systematic design of database schemas, real-time data propagation, authentication measures, and error handling strategies results in a platform that supports dynamic communication in both private and group settings. The cohesive integration of these components underlines the efficiency and adaptability of Supabase in facilitating complex real-time applications.

10.4. Developing a Content Management System

Building a content management system (CMS) using Supabase leverages its robust PostgreSQL foundation along with real-time data synchronization, authentication, and serverless functions. The methodology addresses efficient handling of dynamic content, user-driven modifications, and secure data transactions, which are essential for modern CMS applications. The design philosophy centers on modularity, scalability, and role-based access control to support a multi-user environment where content creation, editing, and publication are handled seamlessly.

A key aspect of the CMS architecture is the underlying database schema. At its core, the schema typically includes tables such as users, posts, categories, tags, and audit_log. The users table manages authentication and profiles whereas the posts table holds the primary content along with metadata such as title, body, publication status, and timestamps. The inclusion of categories and tags facilitates content organization and enables dynamic filtering and searching. An audit log is maintained to track modifications across the system for accountability and versioning purposes.

The following SQL snippet establishes a simplified model for the posts table, demonstrating the expected structure and constraints that ensure data integrity:

```
CREATE TABLE posts (
    id SERIAL PRIMARY KEY,
    title TEXT NOT NULL,
    body TEXT,
    author_id INTEGER REFERENCES users(id) ON DELETE CASCADE,
    status TEXT CHECK (status IN ('draft', 'published', 'archived'))
    DEFAULT 'draft',
    created_at TIMESTAMPTZ DEFAULT NOW(),
    updated_at TIMESTAMPTZ DEFAULT NOW()
);
```

The dynamic nature of a CMS is supported by Supabase's real-time subscriptions. Content editors and viewers can receive updates immediately when changes occur, ensuring that the latest version of the content is always available. For instance, when an article is updated or published, the changes propagate instantly to connected clients, facilitating collaborative editing and live previews. On the frontend, a typical subscription setup using Supabase's JavaScript client integrates these capabilities:

```
import { createClient } from '@supabase/supabase-js';

const supabaseUrl = 'https://your-project.supabase.co';
const supabaseKey = 'public-anon-key';
const supabase = createClient(supabaseUrl, supabaseKey);

const postUpdates = supabase
  .from('posts')
  .on('UPDATE', payload => {
    const updatedPost = payload.new;
    console.log('Post updated:', updatedPost);
    // Refresh post display or update preview interface
  })
  .subscribe();
```

Authentication and authorization are integral to a secure CMS. Supabase simplifies this with its built-in authentication service. By configuring row-level security (RLS), the system ensures that users have access only to content appropriate for their roles. For example, content editors might have permissions to view and edit drafts, while viewers only see published content. The policy enforcement is handled directly at the database level, reducing the need for additional middleware layers. The following example demonstrates a policy that permits content editing only by the author or designated administrators:

```
ALTER TABLE posts ENABLE ROW LEVEL SECURITY;

CREATE POLICY edit_post_policy ON posts
FOR UPDATE
USING (
    auth.uid()::INTEGER = author_id
    OR EXISTS (
        SELECT 1 FROM user_roles
        WHERE user_roles.user_id = auth.uid()::INTEGER
        AND user_roles.role = 'admin'
    )
);
```

An effective CMS must also maintain a detailed history of content changes to support version control and audit trails. By attaching triggers to the posts table, the system can log every significant change such as content updates, publication status modifications, and deletions. This audit trail is crucial not only for monitoring purposes but also for reverting to previous versions if erroneous edits occur. The following SQL snippet shows a trigger function that logs changes to an audit_log table:

```
CREATE TABLE audit_log (
    id SERIAL PRIMARY KEY,
    post_id INTEGER,
    changed_by INTEGER,
    change_time TIMESTAMPTZ DEFAULT NOW(),
    change_type TEXT,
    change_details JSONB
);

CREATE OR REPLACE FUNCTION log_post_update()
RETURNS TRIGGER AS $$
BEGIN
    INSERT INTO audit_log (post_id, changed_by, change_type,
     change_details)
    VALUES (NEW.id, auth.uid()::INTEGER, TG_OP,
            row_to_json(NEW)::JSONB);
    RETURN NEW;
END;
$$ LANGUAGE plpgsql;

CREATE TRIGGER post_update_audit
AFTER UPDATE ON posts
FOR EACH ROW
EXECUTE FUNCTION log_post_update();
```

User interaction design in a CMS often involves a user-friendly interface where content creators can manipulate rich text, upload media, and manage SEO settings. Supabase's file storage integration permits efficient media handling, ensuring that images, videos, and other assets are stored securely and retrieved swiftly. A serverless function can be orchestrated to handle media uploads, linking the uploaded file references into the associated post record. This integration minimizes complexity and avoids the need for external storage services.

Content scheduling and publication workflows provide another layer of functionality in a robust CMS. Editors might schedule posts to be published at a later time or reserve the ability to retract published content. Such functionalities are typically implemented through serverless functions that monitor scheduled timestamps and automatically update the post's status when the time arrives. The automation ensures that content pipelines are managed without constant manual intervention, thereby reducing operational load and potential human error.

The real-time nature of Supabase is particularly valuable when multiple users interact with the CMS simultaneously. Collaborative editing is facilitated by mechanisms that broadcast changes in real time, minimizing data conflicts and latency. Handling concurrent modifications involves strategies such as optimistic concurrency control or version numbering embedded within the database schema. For example, the posts table might include a version counter that increments with each update. A serverless function can verify version consistency before committing an update, ensuring that conflicting changes do not overwrite one another.

Maintaining a clean separation between the presentation layer and the data management layer is critical. The CMS's API endpoints, which interface with the Supabase backend, are designed to be RESTful and logically segmented. Each endpoint caters to functionalities such as retrieving a specific category of posts, searching for content based on keywords, or fetching the history of a particular post. Such structuring simplifies client integration and improves maintainability. Documentation of these endpoints, coupled with clear versioning, assists developers in extending the system and troubleshooting issues effectively.

Given the sensitivity of content management systems, performance optimization and security go hand in hand. Database queries are optimized using proper indexing strategies on frequently queried columns such as author_id, status, and created_at. Additionally, caching mechanisms can be employed to reduce the load on the primary database, especially when serving static content or popular posts. Supabase's scalability features, combined with serverless functions that scale automatically with demand, ensure that the system remains responsive under high traffic conditions.

Integration with third-party tools further expands the capabilities of the CMS. Analytics tools can be integrated to track user engagement metrics, such as page views, average time on page, and content bounce rates. Similarly, SEO tools can be coupled with the CMS to provide content recommendations and keyword optimizations automatically. These integrations are typically achieved through webhooks that send real-time data to the external service or via periodic data exports that analyze usage patterns.

From a development perspective, a modular approach is adopted where components such as authentication, content editing, media management, and auditing are developed independently and then composed into the final CMS product. This strategy not only speeds up development but also simplifies future enhancements and maintenance. Developers can focus on refining individual modules without the risk of introducing regressions into unrelated parts of the system.

Error handling mechanisms are implemented throughout the CMS to ensure robust operation under unforeseen conditions. Both client applications and serverless functions include error logging and notification mechanisms that alert administrators to issues. For example, if a scheduled publication fails due to a network error or version conflict, the system can automatically retry or notify the responsible team to take corrective action. Code snippets managing error states are integrated with careful rollback strategies to maintain data consistency.

```
async function savePost(post) {
    try {
        const { data, error } = await supabase
            .from('posts')
            .upsert(post, { returning: 'representation' });
        if (error) throw error;
```

```
        console.log('Post saved successfully:', data);
    } catch (err) {
        console.error('Error saving post:', err.message);
        // Provide feedback to the user and initiate corrective
    procedures
    }
}
```

The comprehensive integration of Supabase into a CMS environment demonstrates how modern backend services can streamline data management and user interaction. The case study illustrates that by leveraging PostgreSQL's rich feature set, real-time functionalities, and serverless architecture, developers can build systems that are both flexible and highly performant. The modular design allows content creators to focus on content quality, while the underlying technology efficiently handles data processing, security, and scalability.

Each component, from the granular control afforded by row-level policies to the dynamic user interfaces powered by real-time subscriptions, coalesces into a system that addresses the multifaceted requirements of contemporary digital publishing. This architectural strategy not only meets immediate content management needs but also establishes a foundation for future enhancements and deeper integrations with ancillary systems, ensuring the CMS remains adaptable in a rapidly evolving technological landscape.

10.5. Implementing an Event-Driven Application

Event-driven architectures are designed to respond to changes in system state by propagating notifications that trigger subsequent actions. Using Supabase as the backbone of an event-driven application offers a robust environment for real-time event handling and rapid data processing. The approach benefits from PostgreSQL's powerful features, integrated with Supabase's real-time subscriptions, serverless functions, and webhooks. This section presents an in-depth study of how Supabase can be leveraged to build an event-driven application, discusses design choices and best practices, and provides coding examples to illustrate the implementation.

The foundation of an event-driven application lies in its ability to capture, process, and act upon events with minimal latency. In a typical setup, various components act as event producers—these can be user actions, sensor data feeds, or system state changes. These events are then published to a central system that coordinates processing through event consumers. Supabase integrates this capability by combining PostgreSQL's triggers and the LISTEN/NOTIFY features with modern real-time APIs. This allows the application to immediately react to data changes, such as inventory updates, sensor readings, or user interactions.

A common approach to implementing event handling with Supabase is to use database triggers to detect changes in key tables. When a change occurs, a trigger function can invoke the PostgreSQL NOTIFY command, which in turn alerts the application. For instance, in a logistics application that tracks shipment statuses, each update to the shipments table can generate a real-time notification to trigger downstream processing, such as status updates to user dashboards or integration with external tracking systems.

```
CREATE OR REPLACE FUNCTION notify_shipment_update() RETURNS TRIGGER
    AS $$
DECLARE
  payload JSON;
BEGIN
  payload = json_build_object(
    'shipment_id', NEW.id,
    'status', NEW.status,
    'updated_at', NEW.updated_at
  );
  PERFORM pg_notify('shipment_events', payload::text);
  RETURN NEW;
END;
$$ LANGUAGE plpgsql;
```

413

```
CREATE TRIGGER shipment_update_trigger
AFTER UPDATE ON shipments
FOR EACH ROW
EXECUTE FUNCTION notify_shipment_update();
```

In this example, the trigger function `notify_shipment_update` constructs a JSON payload containing the shipment identifier, new status, and timestamp of the modification. The `pg_notify` command communicates this event over a channel named `shipment_events`. This mechanism ensures that any subscribed client or service can immediately begin processing the event data without polling the database.

Real-time client subscriptions are essential to capture events generated through such triggers. Supabase's client libraries provide simple mechanisms for subscribing to channels and handling asynchronous messages. Consider an application dashboard that displays real-time updates on shipment statuses. The JavaScript code below uses the Supabase client to listen to events on the specified channel and update the user interface accordingly:

```
import { createClient } from '@supabase/supabase-js';

const supabaseUrl = 'https://your-project.supabase.co';
const supabaseKey = 'public-anon-key';
const supabase = createClient(supabaseUrl, supabaseKey);

supabase
  .channel('public:shipment_events')
  .on('postgres_changes', { event: 'UPDATE', schema: 'public', table:
      'shipments' }, payload => {
    const eventData = JSON.parse(payload.new);
    console.log('Shipment update event received:', eventData);
    updateShipmentDashboard(eventData);
  })
  .subscribe();

function updateShipmentDashboard(eventData) {
  // Update UI components based on the event data.
  console.log(`Shipment ${eventData.shipment_id} is now ${eventData.
      status}`);
}
```

In this scenario, the Supabase client subscribes to changes on the shipments table using a dedicated channel. When an update event occurs, the client processes the payload and triggers a function to update the dashboard. This real-time event propagation minimizes delay between a state change and the required response, ensuring that the system remains reactive and responsive.

Beyond simple notifications, event-driven architectures often decouple event producers from event consumers by incorporating middleware or serverless functions that process events asynchronously. Supabase's support for serverless functions allows developers to write code that reacts to notifications, processes the data, and even enqueues additional tasks. For example, consider a scenario where shipment updates are used to trigger an email notification to customers. A serverless function can be designed to listen for events, verify the data, and then interface with an external email service.

The pseudo-code below outlines how a serverless function might process an event and send notifications:

```
def process_shipment_event(event):
    import json
    payload = json.loads(event.data)
    shipment_id = payload.get('shipment_id')
    status = payload.get('status')

    if status == 'Delivered':
        send_delivery_notification(shipment_id)

def send_delivery_notification(shipment_id):
    # Connect to an email service and send a notification to the
    customer.
    print(f"Notification: Shipment {shipment_id} has been delivered
    .")
```

In this code, the serverless function extracts the shipment identifier and status from the event payload. Upon detecting a status change to "Delivered", it initiates the process to notify customers. This modular approach ensures that each event is handled by specialized functions,

415

reducing system complexity and increasing maintainability.

Event-driven applications also benefit from the integration of logging mechanisms and error handling strategies. Since events often trigger multiple asynchronous processes, it is essential to incorporate robust error capture and retry logic. Supabase's logging facilities and hooks allow developers to record event processing outcomes, track failures, and implement automated recovery mechanisms. For instance, if a webhook call fails, the system can be configured to log the error and retry the operation at a later time, ensuring data consistency and system reliability.

An example of error handling in an event processing function in JavaScript might appear as follows:

```
async function processEvent(eventData) {
  try {
    // Process the event (e.g., update dashboards, notify customers)
    await updateDatabase(eventData);
    console.log('Event processed successfully:', eventData);
  } catch (error) {
    console.error('Error processing event:', error);
    // Retry logic or enqueue for later processing can be implemented
      here
  }
}

async function updateDatabase(eventData) {
  // Simulate a database update operation
  return new Promise((resolve, reject) => {
    if (eventData.shipment_id) {
      resolve();
    } else {
      reject(new Error('Invalid event data'));
    }
  });
}
```

In this example, the function processEvent encapsulates the event processing logic with appropriate error handling. If an error occurs during the database update, the error is caught, logged, and opportunities for retry are identified. This pattern ensures that transient issues do not interrupt the event-driven workflow.

Scalability is a central consideration in event-driven systems. By decoupling the system into individual processing units, each responsible for a specific event, the overall architecture remains modular and highly scalable. Supabase's serverless functions scale automatically based on demand, ensuring that the application can handle bursts of events during peak times. Moreover, by leveraging PostgreSQL's built-in scalability features, such as partitioning and indexing, the system can efficiently manage high volumes of event data without degradation in performance.

Decoupling the event handling from the primary application logic also allows developers to extend the system with additional event types without major restructuring. For instance, an application initially designed for shipment notifications might later integrate events related to inventory management, customer interactions, or even IoT sensor data. Supabase's flexible event channels and real-time subscriptions provide the necessary framework to support these enhancements. Each event type can be monitored, processed, and archived independently, allowing the underlying system to evolve in response to changing business requirements.

One important design decision in implementing an event-driven application is whether to use synchronous or asynchronous processing. In many use cases, immediate processing with synchronous notifications is essential to maintain system responsiveness. In contrast, asynchronous processing—as demonstrated by serverless functions—can handle tasks that are less time-sensitive but require significant computation or third-party integration. Supabase supports both models by offering real-time APIs for immediate notifications and serverless functions for deferred tasks.

For example, consider an application that processes events from a sensor network. Immediate alerts on abnormal readings require synchronous notifications to the monitoring dashboard. At the same time, a batch processing function can asynchronously analyze historical sensor data to identify trends and anomalies. This dual approach maximizes both responsiveness and deep analytical capability, enabling a broader range of use cases within the same architecture.

Comprehensive testing and monitoring are crucial when implementing an event-driven system. Developers should employ unit tests for individual processing functions and integrate end-to-end testing to verify that the entire pipeline—from event generation to processing and acknowledgment—operates correctly. Tools that simulate high event throughput can validate the system's resilience and identify bottlenecks before they affect production workloads.

Implementing an event-driven application using Supabase requires careful design of database triggers, real-time subscriptions, serverless functions, and robust error handling mechanisms. The use of PostgreSQL's NOTIFY mechanism, coupled with Supabase's client libraries, enables the application to deliver rapid, scalable responses to events as they occur. Through modular design and decoupled processing units, the architecture accommodates high throughput, supports asynchronous processing, and maintains system integrity under load. The strategies and code examples presented in this study illustrate how Supabase can streamline the creation of modern, event-driven applications that respond to real-time events with precision and efficiency.

10.6. Supabase for Educational Platforms

Modern educational platforms require a blend of dynamic content management, real-time interactions, and secure user management. Supabase provides the essential tools to build such platforms by integrating PostgreSQL's robust relational data model, real-time subscriptions, authentication, and serverless functions. The use of Supabase supports the construction of a platform where educators can publish courses, students can interact through live sessions, and administrators can track progress and performance.

The foundational database schema for an educational platform typically encompasses several key tables including users, courses, lessons, assignments, and enrollments. The users table stores profiles for students, teachers, and administrators. The courses table holds meta-information such as course title, description, and availability. The lessons and assignments tables facilitate content delivery and assessment, respectively. Finally, the enrollments table maps students to their respective courses, enabling personalized progress tracking and course recommendations.

A typical SQL schema for the courses and lessons tables might appear as follows:

```
CREATE TABLE courses (
    id SERIAL PRIMARY KEY,
    title TEXT NOT NULL,
    description TEXT,
    created_at TIMESTAMPTZ DEFAULT NOW()
);

CREATE TABLE lessons (
    id SERIAL PRIMARY KEY,
    course_id INTEGER REFERENCES courses(id) ON DELETE CASCADE,
    title TEXT NOT NULL,
    content TEXT,
    video_url TEXT,
    order_index INTEGER,
    created_at TIMESTAMPTZ DEFAULT NOW()
);
```

Real-time interaction is critical for modern learning environments. For instance, live classes and interactive quizzes can be implemented by leveraging Supabase's real-time subscriptions. Educators can update lesson content or post interactive questions, while students receive instantaneous updates. A typical client-side code example using Supabase's JavaScript library to subscribe to lesson updates is given below:

```
import { createClient } from '@supabase/supabase-js';

const supabaseUrl = 'https://your-project.supabase.co';
const supabaseKey = 'public-anon-key';
const supabase = createClient(supabaseUrl, supabaseKey);

const lessonSubscription = supabase
  .from('lessons')
  .on('UPDATE', payload => {
    const updatedLesson = payload.new;
    console.log('Lesson updated:', updatedLesson);
    // Update lesson content in the student interface
  })
  .subscribe();
```

Authentication in the educational context must accommodate multiple roles, such as students, teachers, and administrators. Supabase simplifies this with built-in authentication and offers support for third-party providers. To ensure that each user accesses only their permitted area, row-level security (RLS) policies should be established. For example, a policy that restricts access to course content based on enrollment is essential. Consider the following SQL snippet that enforces such a policy on the lessons table:

```
ALTER TABLE lessons ENABLE ROW LEVEL SECURITY;

CREATE POLICY student_lesson_access ON lessons
FOR SELECT
USING (
    EXISTS (
        SELECT 1 FROM enrollments
        WHERE enrollments.course_id = lessons.course_id
          AND enrollments.user_id = auth.uid()::INTEGER
    )
);
```

Effective management of educational content often involves

automated workflows for course publication, assignment deadlines, and notifications. Supabase's serverless functions can be used to handle scheduled tasks such as sending reminders before assignment due dates or publishing newly added lessons. For example, a serverless function might be triggered to send email notifications to students enrolled in a course when a new lesson is available.

A pseudo-code implementation for sending notifications might be structured as follows:

```
def send_course_notification(course_id):
    # Fetch enrolled students
    enrolled_students = fetch_enrollments(course_id)
    lesson = get_latest_lesson(course_id)
    for student in enrolled_students:
        message = f"New lesson available: {lesson.title}"
        send_email(student.email, "New Lesson Alert", message)

def fetch_enrollments(course_id):
    # Query Supabase for students enrolled in the course
    pass

def get_latest_lesson(course_id):
    # Query Supabase for the latest lesson in the course
    pass

def send_email(recipient, subject, message):
    # Integrate with an external email service provider
    pass
```

Educational platforms benefit significantly from the seamless integration of multimedia content. Supabase's storage solutions allow for efficient handling of video lectures, interactive media, and document uploads. For instance, teachers can upload lecture videos, which are then referenced in the lessons table. This method keeps the load on the main database minimal while providing fast access to rich media content.

A simple upload mechanism might involve a client-side implementation using Supabase's storage API:

```
async function uploadLectureVideo(file, courseId, lessonId) {
  const { data, error } = await supabase.storage
```

```
    .from('lecture-videos')
    .upload(`${courseId}/${lessonId}/${file.name}`, file);
  if (error) {
    console.error('Upload failed:', error);
    return;
  }
  console.log('Upload successful:', data);
  // Optionally update the lesson record with the video URL
}
```

User interaction within educational platforms extends to features such as discussion forums, peer reviews, and live question-and-answer sessions. Real-time chat and discussion boards can be implemented using similar techniques as outlined in the chat application section, enabling students and educators to collaborate effectively. Integration of these social features encourages a community-based approach to learning, where students can help each other and share insights.

In addition to content delivery, tracking student progress and performance is a key aspect of modern educational platforms. Supabase's analytics capabilities allow for the collection and analysis of user interaction data. For example, a `progress_tracking` table can log various metrics such as lesson completion, quiz scores, and time spent on each lesson. SQL triggers and serverless functions can be employed to update these metrics in real time:

```
CREATE TABLE progress_tracking (
    id SERIAL PRIMARY KEY,
    user_id INTEGER REFERENCES users(id),
    course_id INTEGER REFERENCES courses(id),
    lesson_id INTEGER REFERENCES lessons(id),
    progress_percentage INTEGER,
    updated_at TIMESTAMPTZ DEFAULT NOW()
);

CREATE OR REPLACE FUNCTION log_progress_update() RETURNS TRIGGER AS
    $$
BEGIN
    INSERT INTO progress_tracking (user_id, course_id, lesson_id,
    progress_percentage)
    VALUES (NEW.user_id, NEW.course_id, NEW.lesson_id, NEW.progress);
    RETURN NEW;
```

```
END;
$$ LANGUAGE plpgsql;

CREATE TRIGGER trigger_progress_update
AFTER INSERT ON lesson_completions
FOR EACH ROW
EXECUTE FUNCTION log_progress_update();
```

The modular nature of the educational platform also means that new functionalities can be added with minimal disruption. Whether it is incorporating advanced analytics, integrating external content providers, or adding gamification elements, Supabase's flexible architecture allows for straightforward expansion. Each additional component—be it further course categorization, personalized recommendations, or social learning modules—can be integrated through either serverless functions or direct database operations.

Security remains a primary concern, particularly in an educational environment where sensitive student information is handled. Supabase's comprehensive security framework, including role-based access control and RLS, ensures that data privacy is maintained across the platform. Encryption of data both in transit and at rest, coupled with secure authentication protocols, creates a safe learning environment that complies with regulatory requirements.

A complete educational platform built on Supabase is dynamic, scalable, and secure. Educators benefit from streamlined content management and real-time notification systems, while students enjoy an interactive learning environment that is responsive and tailored to their individual progress. The integration of multimedia content, live updates, and comprehensive analytics contributes to a holistic learning experience that is accessible and effective.

The use of Supabase allows developers to focus on enhancing user experience and pedagogical effectiveness rather than managing underlying infrastructure. By building on the capabilities already established in previous sections—such as real-time subscriptions, secure authentication, serverless functions, and efficient data management—the educational platform becomes a flexible and powerful tool for modern learning. The strategic integration of these elements demonstrates that contemporary educational systems can be both highly interactive and robust, meeting the evolving demands of digital education and supporting lifelong learning in a rapidly changing world.

10.7. Lessons Learned and Best Practices

An extensive exploration of multiple case studies using Supabase reveals a range of critical lessons and best practices that can guide developers in building robust, scalable backend solutions. A recurring theme across e-commerce platforms, real-time chat applications, content management systems, event-driven applications, and educational platforms is the necessity of a solid architectural foundation. Establishing a well-designed database schema is the cornerstone of any scalable system. For example, defining clear relationships between tables, employing proper normalization, and ensuring the use of constraints such as foreign keys and check constraints are practices that prevent data anomalies and promote system integrity. A common pitfall observed was the underestimation of future scalability needs. Developers who plan their schema with extensibility in mind experience fewer challenges as new features and data volumes increase.

Another critical insight centers on the use of real-time subscriptions. In case studies such as real-time chat applications and event-driven systems, leveraging Supabase's real-time capabilities allowed for immediate propagation of changes. However, the key to effective real-time integration lies in efficient client-side subscription management. Developers should minimize the number of active subscriptions and implement strategies to unsubscribe appropriately when components unmount. This prevents resource overuse and network congestion. The following JavaScript snippet illustrates a pattern for managing subscriptions and ensuring cleanup:

```javascript
import { createClient } from '@supabase/supabase-js';

const supabaseUrl = 'https://your-project.supabase.co';
const supabaseKey = 'public-anon-key';
const supabase = createClient(supabaseUrl, supabaseKey);

let subscription = supabase
  .from('messages')
  .on('INSERT', payload => {
    console.log('New message:', payload.new);
  })
  .subscribe();

// Later, when the component unmounts:
supabase.removeSubscription(subscription);
```

Authentication and secure access control are also vital concerns. Various projects benefited from Supabase's built-in authentication mechanisms and row-level security (RLS) policies. Implementing RLS correctly ensures data privacy and proper segregation of user data based on roles. However, a common oversight is the misconfiguration of these policies, which can lead to unauthorized access or overly restrictive data views. Rigorous testing and code reviews of RLS policies are essential. Consider the RLS example from a content management system, which grants editing rights only to the content author and administrators:

```sql
ALTER TABLE posts ENABLE ROW LEVEL SECURITY;

CREATE POLICY edit_post_policy ON posts
FOR UPDATE
USING (
    auth.uid()::INTEGER = author_id OR
    EXISTS (
        SELECT 1 FROM user_roles
        WHERE user_roles.user_id = auth.uid()::INTEGER
          AND user_roles.role = 'admin'
    )
);
```

Optimizing serverless functions and triggers is another key learning area. These components handle critical tasks such as automating inventory updates, logging content changes, or triggering notifications. An important lesson is to implement robust error handling and logging mechanisms in these functions. The ability to trace errors back to their source is invaluable in maintaining system reliability. A pseudo-code example of error handling in a serverless function can be seen in the following snippet:

```
def process_event(event):
    try:
        # Process the event data
        update_database(event)
        notify_services(event)
    except Exception as e:
        log_error(f"Error processing event {event['id']}: {str(e)}")
        # Optionally implement retry logic or additional error
    handling
```

Performance optimization emerges as a recurring best practice. Efficient indexing strategies within PostgreSQL can dramatically reduce query times, particularly when handling high-frequency operations in real-time systems. As the case studies demonstrated, even minor inefficiencies in query design can lead to significant delays under load. Developing a habit of performing query optimization and regular database profiling is advisable. Additionally, developers should consider employing caching strategies where appropriate. Caching frequently accessed or computationally expensive data can offload much of the traffic from primary databases and improve overall system responsiveness.

Modularity in design allows for incremental improvements and easier debugging. In several cases, projects that adopted a microservices or modular architecture experienced fewer integration issues. Each component—whether it is handling user authentication, content delivery, or event processing—should have a clearly defined interface and be independently testable. This division not only enhances maintainability but also allows for parallel development, especially when new features or integrations are required.

Testing and continuous integration are integral to mitigating risks associated with rapid development cycles. Case studies revealed that applications employing thorough unit tests, integration tests, and end-to-end tests exhibited greater resilience when subjected to production-scale events. Utilizing testing frameworks and automated deployment pipelines ensures that modifications in one area do not inadvertently break functionalities elsewhere. For instance, testing the integrity of a trigger function or a new RLS policy in a staging environment before applying changes to production can preempt potential data integrity issues.

The integration of external services, such as payment gateways, content delivery networks, and analytics platforms, also emerged as a domain that requires particular attention. When building systems like e-commerce platforms or educational portals, the seamless integration of these services is critical to providing a comprehensive user experience. Developers should prioritize secure API interactions, ensure proper rate limiting, and implement fallback mechanisms. In numerous case studies, the failure to adequately manage third-party dependencies resulted in system outages or degraded performance during peak usage times.

Another lesson learned concerns the importance of clear and comprehensive documentation. As systems evolve and become more complex, internal documentation—including API references, database schema diagrams, and detailed function descriptions—serves as an invaluable resource. Well-documented systems lower the barrier for new team members and improve the overall development lifecycle by reducing the reliance on tribal knowledge. Maintaining documentation in parallel with code changes is a best practice that prevents ambiguities and facilitates smoother handoffs during development cycles.

Monitoring and analytics are essential components of successful production systems. Integrating real-time monitoring allows developers to spot issues before they escalate. In several case studies, developers set up dashboards to monitor key performance indicators such as query response times, error rates, and system load metrics. Incorporating alerts and automated responses into the monitoring system ensures that urgent issues are addressed promptly, minimizing downtime and maintaining user trust.

A further best practice involves iterative development and user feedback loops. Early adopters of systems built with Supabase reported that continuously gathering user feedback, especially in educational and e-commerce contexts, led to rapid iterative improvements. Developers are encouraged to leverage A/B testing, beta releases, and detailed analytics reports to refine features and optimize user interfaces.

Finally, scalability must be considered as a fundamental design goal from the outset. Whether it is scaling serverless functions, managing large volumes of real-time events, or handling increasing numbers of users in educational platforms, Supabase provides tools that support horizontal and vertical scalability. A common pitfall is assuming that a system designed for a small user base will seamlessly scale without architectural modifications. Periodic load testing and careful capacity planning are necessary to ensure that the backend infrastructure can grow with the application's user base and data volume.

The collective experience from various Supabase implementations underscores the importance of strong foundational architecture, efficient real-time management, and security at every layer. Best practices such as rigorous testing, modular design, thorough documentation, and proactive monitoring not only improve the overall system quality but also enhance developer productivity and user satisfaction. By learning from these case studies, developers can avoid common pitfalls—such as overcomplicating the schema design, misconfiguring RLS policies, or neglecting performance optimizations—and build systems that are both resilient and scalable. The adoption of these lessons ultimately contributes to a more predictable and manageable development process, paving the way for the successful deployment of sophisticated applications across various industries.

www.ingramcontent.com/pod-product-compliance
Lightning Source LLC
LaVergne TN
LVHW052057060326
832903LV00061B/2916